Lords of Misrule

Also by Antony Taylor

DOWN WITH THE CROWN: British Anti-Monarchism and Debates About Royalty since 1790

Lords of Misrule

Hostility to Aristocracy in Late Nineteenth- and Early Twentieth-Century Britain

Antony Taylor

First published 2004 by
PALGRAVE MACMILLAN
Houndmills, Basingstoke, Hampshire RG21 6XS and
175 Fifth Avenue, New York, N.Y. 10010
Companies and representatives throughout the world

PALGRAVE MACMILLAN is the global academic imprint of the Palgrave
Macmillan division of St. Martin's Press, LLC and of Palgrave Macmillan Ltd.
Macmillan® is a registered trademark in the United States, United Kingdom
and other countries. Palgrave is a registered trademark in the European
Union and other countries.

ISBN 1–4039–3221–2 hardback

This book is printed on paper suitable for recycling and made from fully
managed and sustained forest sources.

A catalogue record for this book is available from the British Library.

Library of Congress Cataloging-in-Publication Data
Taylor, Antony.
    "Lords of Misrule" : hostility to aristocracy in late nineteenth and early
    twentieth century Britain / by Antony Taylor.
        p.   cm.
    Includes bibliographical references and index.
    ISBN 1–4039–3221–2 (cloth)
    1. Aristocracy (Political science)—Great Britain—History.   2. Power
    (Social sciences)—History.   3. Politics, Practical—Great Britain—
    History.   4. Great Britain—Politics and government.   I. Title.
    HT653.G7T39 2004
    305.5′2′0941—dc22
                                                          2004053949

10   9   8   7   6   5   4   3   2   1
13 12 11 10 09 08 07 06 05 04

Printed and bound in Great Britain by
Antony Rowe Ltd, Chippenham and Eastbourne

To Marsha,
For all I owe her

Contents

List of Plates

Acknowledgements

This is a book that did not really begin life as a book at all. A passing interest in Henry George led to a number of conference papers, and an eventual realisation that the issue of anti-aristocracy provided a subject in its own right. Since then I have accrued debts and obligations almost on a daily basis. Thanks first of all, to those who have read parts of the volume. John Baxendale, Michael Bush, Peter Cain, and David Nash all read the chapter on George, and improved it immeasurably with their comments. Many insights have been gleaned in particular from John and Peter over the photocopier, truly the last available space for old style, informal exchange of information and views in the modern university system. Michael Bush has contributed enormously from his inexhaustible fund of references and unique book collection. Thanks too for the commentaries of Matthew Cragoe, Malcolm Chase, and Detlev Mares, none of whom will probably be aware of how much they have unwittingly contributed to this volume over the years. Parts of this book have provided the raw material for conference papers, and my thanks go in particular to my ex-supervisor Iori Prothero, who always uses these occasions to supply additional thoughts and reflections. This book would not look the way it does were it not for the marvellous illustrations supplied by Chetham's Library in Manchester. Thanks go to Fergus Wilde for reproducing them, and for making Chetham's, as it should be, a place of informal scholarship and fun. Thanks too for his friendship over the years. I would also like to thank Nick Weaver for insights into the political economy of Henry George that could only come from a thorough grounding in economics. My thanks go to him for his companionship on the 'Manchester Circuit'. Work on the book could not have been completed without a sabbatical from Sheffield Hallam University in 2003 and without the help of the Robert Schalkenbach Foundation, who generously provided a travel grant that enabled me to consult the Henry George papers in New York. In addition, my thanks to Hannan, Liat and Sharon for pointing out to me that the summer really is not for working at all. Finally, this book is not to be confused with *Lord of Misrule*, a biography of Christopher Lee.

The publishers wish to state that they have made every effort to contact the copyright holders, but if any have been overlooked the publishers will be pleased to make the necessary arrangement at the first opportunity.

Abbreviations

BUF	British Union of Fascists
CPGB	Communist Party of Great Britain
ILP	Independent Labour Party
LCC	London County Council
MCRL	Manchester Central Reference Library
NYPL	New York Public Library
SDF	Social Democratic Federation

Introduction

The Right Hon. Sir William Alexander Louis Stephen Douglas-Hamilton, twelfth Duke of Hamilton and ninth Duke of Brandon, Marquis of Douglas and Clydesdale, Earl of Angus, Arran, Lanark and Selkirk, and Lord Hamilton, Avon, Polmont, Machanshire, Innerdale, Abernethy, Jedburgh Forest, Dare, and Shotclough, Baron of Dutton in the County of Chester, Duke of Chatelherault, Hereditary Keeper of Holyrood House, Premier Peer, and Knight Marischal of Scotland is dead. He carried the weary burden of his titles for fifty years, and then quietly laid them down by the shores of the blue Mediterranean.[1]

Aristocracy remains at the heart of British society. The view that the English 'love a lord' is in a long tradition. Writing in 1881, the visiting American scholar Richard Grant White wrote: 'In the history of England, one fact is remarkable in regard to its social aspect; there has never been that hatred of the nobles by the common people which has so often been manifested in other countries, and which in other countries has been the cause of so much political disturbance.'[2] Such views found their justification in the mid-Victorian state's benign view of itself as the guarantor of English liberties, and the exporter of the 'love of liberty' to the empire, and more benighted states. Central to this vision is the work of historians who see the British state as experiencing a tranquil, and relatively untroubled transition to popular democratic rule. In contrast to her near European neighbours, Britain was (and is) extolled for her exceptionalism, manifested in the values of restraint, a non-partisan sense of history, and a pragmatic politics rooted in a conception of the possible. For Jonathan Clark, Britain remains an *Ancien Regime* state in all but name, politically resilient and resistant to the ferment on the

1

Continent in the aftermath of the French Revolution.[3] In the grand narrative of the nineteenth century, aristocracy provided a social solvent, symbolising the English verities of continuity, stability, and selfless dedication to public service. In counties like Lancashire, where the great families were extinct or had declined, their passing was mourned, and the great manor houses became objects of pilgrimage, reverence, and local historical memory preserved intact by curators of antiquarian interest.[4]

Even the fiercest critics of aristocracy were indulgent of its foibles. The progressives, J.L. and Barbara Hammond, relating the history of the dispossession of the English peasantry, exonerated the gentry class of the charge of 'decadence' and were moved to list the virtuous aspects of British aristocratic rule. Noting landed society's involvement in local government, their rejection of the 'role of loungers and courtiers' at court, their role in warding off a French invasion in the Napoleonic Wars, and the strength of the Whig tradition, they saw the aristocracy as the custodians of classical ideas of political liberty, and as the architects of broader Liberal values:

> Foreign policy, the treatment of Ireland, of India, of slaves, are beyond the scope of this book, but in glancing at a class whose treatment of the English poor has been the subject of our study, it is only just to record that in other regions of thought and conduct they bequeathed a great inheritance of moral and liberal ideas: a passion for justice between peoples, a sense for national freedom, a great body of principles by which to check, refine and discipline the gross appetites of national ambition.[5]

On occasion, aristocratic 'die-hard' defenders of hereditary privilege were accorded a grudging respect for their bearing, candour, and platform presence. The obituary of the Tory reactionary, Lord Willoughby de Broke recorded of his last public appearance that 'the wavers of the Red Flag gave him cheers when he left the hall' and 'working men obviously imbued with advanced socialist or communist ideas actually listened without scoffing to his defence of heredity'.[6]

Central to such viewpoints was an acceptance of the aristocratic legacy in government, which was prized for its pragmatism and its acceptance of the necessity for change. For historians of the constitution, the role of aristocracy was pivotal in dictating the trajectory of nineteenth-century politics, and in expunging the narrow, sectional interests of unrepentant 'die-hard' elements. A traditional view of nineteenth-century politics sees aristocracy reconciled to the current of reformism by the 1840s, and its acceptance within the political system as dependant on the marginalisation of 'Refuseniks' within landed society. Norman Gash depicts the debates around the early and late nineteenth-century reform bills as setting the tone for a realist aristocratic outlook, in which the aristocratic Tory rump was saved from extinction and from themselves, by Peel's rapprochement with reform opinion.[7] Peel saw a potential weakening of the authority of the state and of landed society in Tory attempts to resist or stifle the impetus towards reform. According to Gash, his final years in office were devoted to the exclusion of irreconcilable Tory landed opinion, implacably opposed to the repeal of the Corn Laws, from his government. For critics of reform, the 1832, 1867, and 1884 Reform Acts were an assault on the citadel of privilege, that might have been successfully opposed by a more intractable and united landed interest organised around core landed values on the model of the Prussian *Junker* class. Instead, the hallmark of the British aristocracy was its willingness to give ground. During the Reform Bill crises of 1832 and 1884, the Upper Chamber recognised the threat to their position, and embraced a moderate reform outlook as the best defence against more outspoken radical opinion. In 1867 and 1884 the sweeping away of the old 'pocket' and 'closed' boroughs by the creation of new, regularised mass constituencies where landed influence and control became increasingly diluted, led to a diminution in aristocratic influences over electors. Both the 1832 and 1884 Reform Acts excised the worst excesses of the unreformed system, whilst enabling a defence of the purified constitution to be mounted by aristocratically attuned Conservatives. Here, the balance and harmony of the reformed parliament favoured a persistence of aristocracy who yielded sufficient power and position to ensure their continuation within a mixed and balanced constitution, whilst maintaining their status and position within the executive and the dignified part of the constitution. Thereafter, the image of the benign, moderate, and reform-minded aristocrat exercising a strong sense of *noblesse oblige*, yet learning to bend with the political wind, became a cliché in accounts of nineteenth-century politics.[8]

Following an apparent acceptance of the nineteenth-century view of aristocracy as great conciliators, the social history of landed society was entirely disregarded. Until relatively recently it was a subject that was both neglected and under-researched. The role of the great aristocratic dynasties was simply acknowledged, rather than analysed. In the 1960s a welter of studies of working-class and middle-class culture had consigned aristocracy to the margins. In contrast to the eighteenth century, where the context of connection, placemen, and patrician values was understood, in the nineteenth century the aristocracy was presumed to have declined in importance, and ultimately to have disappeared.[9] During these years, F.M.L. Thompson's study of the great landowning dynasties with its plea for further micro-level studies of the county aristocracy stood alone.[10] This neglect was grounded in the work of nineteenth-century Liberal historians like J.R. Green, who in his landmark 1874 *Short History of the British Isles* made his subject the victory of the common man: 'Not "English kings" or "English Conquest" but "the English people" were the matter of his writings' he declared.[11] In recent years, however, there has been a marked increase in interest in the role and position of the great titled families of the UK. This interest has been fuelled by reaction against an over-emphasis on those lower down the social scale, at the expense of the culture-formers and society leaders who shaped the social and political milieu of nineteenth-century society.

Not until the 1990s did the aristocracy find a cultural chronicler comparable with E.P. Thompson's epic study of the working class, or Lawrence Stone's analysis of the ascending middle orders. Through the researches of David Cannadine there has emerged a much fuller appreciation of political networks, aristocracy's role within party politics, and of the changed legal and cultural context of the aristocracy on the eve and in the aftermath of the Great War.[12] In line with a reappraisal of continental aristocracy, the British aristocracy was found to have a greater longevity and a more resistant and flexible social position than usually supposed.[13] Cannadine's books have fostered a plethora of new research that demonstrates a renewed interest in the activities and continuing political influence of aristocracy. The recent historiography of Victorian Britain has returned aristocracy to the heart of the economy, government, and cultural activity of Victorian towns. The years of relative neglect created a growth industry in studies of the aristocracy attuned to patterns of landownership, aristocracy's changed political role, and the 'society' connections that preserved their influence intact. It encompassed such divergent issues as their role as patrons, urban land-owners, as court bohemians, and analysed their position both at the height of their power, and in the period of waning political influence. During these years the stories of individual society families were recovered, and excavated for meaning about the broader dynamics of political change from the 1860s to the 1920s. In recent work, David Cannadine, Peter Mandler, and others have explored the function of aristocratic connection, the culture of the stately home, and the political landscape that enabled Britain's aristocratic families to retain their position at the apex of the social hierarchy.[14] Such work has restored something of the glamour and vibrancy of aristocratic salon culture which was apparent to contemporaries, but has been neglected altogether by the historians of formal high politics.

Scrutiny of landownership has also provided an avenue by which to explore aristocratic society and its social influences. Aristocracy, and the gradations of landed proprietors who make up the 'squirearchy', are defined by their relationship to the land. In the 1880s the social investigator John Bateman impishly coined the name 'acreocracy' to describe the hierarchy of land-owning in the shires. In places, the great land-owning dynasts were depicted, like the Derbys of Lancashire, as 'little kings' who controlled county government, sat as JPs, and were at the apex of a network of county families with long-standing ancestral links.[15] As late as the 1930s the Conservative MP and *bon viveur* Chips Channon could remark: 'It is the aristocracy which still rules England although nobody seems to believe it.'[16] Some of the large Scottish families exerted near feudal control over their tenantry in extensive areas of the Highlands and on the Borders of Scotland. The former Owenite reformer, Dr John Watts commented at a meeting in the Town Hall in Manchester in 1876: 'Sir George Campbell, who ought to know, said that there was no prince in India who was at all equal to the Duke of Argyll in Great Britain.'[17] Traditionally the decline of aristocratic networks in the nineteenth century is charted by analysis of its diminished importance on the land. From a situation of rural affluence in which they exercised near total control over the county government of the shires, they moved to a position of relative unimportance in the inter-war years. For most historians the agricultural depression of the 1870s was a watershed. After the collapse in the prices of arable yield in particular, depression set in, and land-owning became un-economic. Most successful families engaged in a diffusion of property-owning to buttress their declining fortunes.[18] For most scholars, this process marks the decline of the landed aristocracy proper. Analysis of the phenomenon suggests a move away from the aristocracy's traditional obligations on the land, to a new preoccupation with the realisation of the profits of the City investments and urban financial yield through ground rent and property speculation.[19]

In recent historiography, the centrality of aristocracy has been confirmed by a broader cultural reading of its impact and importance for nineteenth-century society. In the work of Martin Weiner and others, the failings of aristocracy have been held up as a warning, and an inspiration to the socially mobile. Historians like F.M.L. Thompson and Martin Weiner have constructed a societal vision around the model of a porous aristocracy that absorbed an *arriviste*, mobile, upper middle class into landed society. In this reading, aristocracy was prized for its leisured and cultivated manners, as opposed to the rough untutored ways of the self-made man. Weiner's work in particular created a social interpretation of the changes within British society that derived from the traditional role of aristocracy.[20] According to his interpretation, aristocracy took the lion's share of the blame for the decline of Britain's manufacturing base. He views industry and enterprise as retarded by the migration of businessmen into the ranks of the landed gentry, where disdain for the unglamorous nature of manufacturing and contempt for the rough, unmannered attributes of business, encouraged a migration of capital into unproductive landownership and conspicuous leisured consumption. Here aristocracy was criticised for its backward-looking impotence that served to hinder attempts to diversify, or refine the economic wealth emerging from the Industrial Revolution. Weiner's thesis was adopted by those who highlighted the endemic problems occurring within British industry and manufacture in the 1980s, and became conflated with broader debates about the lack of emphasis placed on technical education in schools and universities. It provided a stereotypical view of aristocracy, that linked the work of Clark on Britain as an *Ancien Regime* state, with concerns about a lack of competitiveness within British manufacturing, and notions of 'Englishness' as a sentimental outlook that impeded social and political progress.

Recent historiographical debates have also emphasized the importance of aristocracy for the cult of 'Englishness' and emerging national identity from the middle years of the nineteenth century.[21] As David Cannadine has pointed out, aristocracy not only provided society's cultural-opinion formers, it also safeguarded its position within the political establishment, and in its Celtic and English variants acted as a truly national institution, refracting the different identities of the United Kingdom and of Ireland.[22] Oswald Mosley wrote about his bloodline: 'The Irish blood came through my father's mother, who was the daughter of Sir Thomas White, sometime Mayor of Cork. Thus I can claim to be British as well as English, and through Saxon and European blood, also European; the island freeze-up is really quite a recent invention.'[23] Moreover, aristocracy shaped the topography of the fields and estates that became emblematic of England. In the field of public history, aristocracy and Englishness are inextricably linked. Stately homes, lovingly contoured gardens, and enclosed pastures conveyed the vision of a timeless hierarchy of order and harmony.[24] As Robert Colls has noted, aristocracy, whilst fading in terms of power and position, set the standard for a form of refined, cultivated, and aloof, 'Englishness' that aped and preserved intact some of the manners and values of aristocracy after it had disintegrated as a closed caste.[25] David Cannadine too has written about a 'Gothicisation' not only of England, but also of the empire, where the values of aristocracy were transplanted into a broader imperial domain.[26] In White Settler dominions like Canada, Australia and New Zealand, the aristocracy stamped their imprint on the surroundings. In such colonies the landscape was interpreted through a veil of English pastoralism as the habitat of a rural elite, defined by Anglicanism, a system of imperial honours, baronial architecture, and hunting. Here aristocratic incomers sought to replicate the English class system. Elsewhere in India they detected the trace elements of a feudalism similar in nature to the English structured hierarchy on the land, and much admired by those who saw Indian society as a mirror image of the values aristocratic governors and imperial bureaucrats sought to encourage in the imperial domains.[27]

Following the emergence of the Weiner thesis in the 1980s the study of aristocracy has reached an impasse. Since the early 1990s, most studies of the aristocratic state have concentrated on the economic and social circumstances of the patrician class. Nevertheless, dating the phenomenon of aristocratic decline remains problematic. Much of this new research is presented in biographical form. Charting the changing fortunes of aristocracy is complicated by a dependence on individual histories, and an over-emphasis on flamboyant case studies which necessarily dominate the biographical form. In addition, its timing and chronology remains vague, conveying a sense of uncertainty about the later changes in aristocracy in the twentieth century, where there is less available work on the nature of social mobility, and the evolving political role of aristocracy. Some of this material privileges heritage and nostalgia over a structural analysis of the role of aristocracy itself. Most histories have followed David Cannadine's view that aristocracy is best understood from the top down. Books like his *The Decline and Fall of the British Aristocracy* simply take on trust the views that aristocrats articulated about themselves. More recent treatments of land-holding have taken a regional focus, or confined their assessment of the political implications of landownership to the internal debates within the political parties.[28] Again aristocracy's fate is explored as part of the machinations and intrigues of high politics, rather than as a legitimate phenomenon in its own right. Other recent works are too indulgent of aristocracy's foibles and examine only their surface veneer, and opulent style, whilst ignoring the politics of country-house ownership.[29] In short, no recent books have attempted to bring together aristocracy, politics, and popular culture in a way that conceptualises the nineteenth-century view of aristocracy as a cultural force that expressed the tensions between the powerful and the powerless. In the nineteenth century, despite their depleted position, the aristocracy still held enormous sway and influence, and persisted as enormously powerful opinion-formers into the post-1945 period.

This is a book that takes a different view of the British aristocracy. In part it constitutes an exercise in reclamation. In addition it provides a scrutiny of the intellectual roots of anti-aristocratic ideas. It surveys the historiography of anti-aristocratic sentiment, analyses its centrality to the radical platform, and summarises the main intellectual currents of opposition to aristocracy. Viewing the notion of aristocracy in historical terms, it seeks to re-appraise contemporary arguments against privilege. Drawing together themes from intellectual history, popular politics and the historiography of British reformism, it considers the arguments against aristocracy, and scrutinises the occasions when the dislike of hereditary rule became the cornerstone of radical rhetoric. Despite the importance of this subject it has barely been explored in any systematic way. This book makes no claims for anti-aristocratic sentiment as a majoritarian movement within British political thought. Many of those who instinctively opposed the immorality, affluence, and indolence of aristocratic rulers in the nineteenth century are commonly regarded as outsiders inhabiting the fringes of politics. Nevertheless, it does explore terrain common to radicalism, Liberalism, and Labourism. Against the opulent backdrop of the royal state and a strong popular loyalism, those who oppose aristocracy have been forced to shout loudly about the misdeeds of tainted rulers. What opponents of aristocracy lacked in ideological weight they traditionally made up for in pungent prose. This is a 'raucous' tradition within popular politics that expresses the frustrations of those excluded from the glittering social world of nobility, and seemingly alienated by its excesses. Through an analysis of the political and literary opponents of aristocracy this book demonstrates the existence of a 'people's canon' that until now has barely been explored, and recalls anti-aristocratic spleen from some important sources.[30]

Historians of aristocracy have tended to overlook the critics of nobility. Despite this neglect, it is apparent that the history of aristocracy is one that was largely uncovered by its opponents. There is a lengthy historiography here that charts the evolution of British parliamentary institutions in attempts to usurp and supplant the influence of aristocracy. In its origins, the radical critique of aristocracy dates back to the seventeenth and eighteenth centuries. It draws in particular on the role of thinkers like Tom Paine, Adam Smith and James Harrington who popularised criticisms of aristocratic influence.[31] Such notions locate the origins of anti-aristocratic belief in key historical events claimed by radicals as part of a reform pedigree, amongst them the English Civil War and the Glorious Revolution of 1688. Grounded in the events of 1688, 1832, 1867, and 1884, this structural analysis of British constitutional development analyses the role of reformers who arrayed themselves against entrenched aristocratic interests within the British state. These familiar resting places of British history form part of a narrative of liberty and reform that succeeded in curbing the politics of faction, patronage, and vested interests that grew out of aristocratic concerns. They constitute a radical meridian, that heralded the mass enfranchisement of the British electorate, marked a rejection of attempts to manage and retard the political nation by the forces of privilege, and demonstrate the changing social and cultural balance between land and industry, town and countryside. Here, the decline of aristocracy unloosed the fetters of the political system. Campaigning in the aristocratic and clerically-dominated minister town of Beverley in Yorkshire in 1868, Anthony Trollope discovered that voters were interested in only two things, the secret ballot and temperance.[32] The Ballot Act of 1872, and the Corrupt and Illegal Practices Act of 1883 sounded the death knell for a system that for centuries had been mired in 'Old Corruption'. After 1884, the small corrupt 'pocket' and 'closed' boroughs that had been havens of aristocratic influence were consigned to the past. In the great urban centres the current of municipal reform was, in part, inspired by the idea of purging the old aristocratic ground-rent proprietors from the municipal heartland. Parliamentary reform then, purified the system of politics, expelled aristocratic influences, and professionalized political parties. Alongside the loss of rural property came a diminished military role following the Cardwell reforms of the 1870s, and the ebbing of aristocratic power and position in the shires in the wake of the County Councils Bill of 1888. Historians of party forms have analysed the late nineteenth and early twentieth centuries in very similar terms. The changing complexion of Toryism from a movement of landed proprietors, to a movement of business and urban working men, and of Liberalism from a party of land and trade to an orphaned agitation of adventurers and urban 'faddists' with few links to the land, is again seen as proof of a decline in aristocracy, and of an accommodation with increasingly urban-centred concerns. Again, the dynamic of politics is explicable in terms of a decline in the interests and privilege of this narrow sectionalised landed elite.

The Wiener thesis provides an overwhelmingly negative view of the attributes of aristocracy and coincided with a political agenda that sought to expunge 'Old Etonians' and other public school values from the corridors of power. It was adopted, and was in part inspired, by Thatcherite political agendas that sought a 'classless Britain'. Its popularity provided the perverse paradox of a populist reassessment of aristocracy rooted in a broader project to regenerate society along non-elite lines in which the impetus to a meritocratic Britain drew on populist and 'New Right' analyses of the failings of British industry and commerce. It was accompanied by a renewed interest in all things middle class as an antidote to the apparent dominance of the aristocratic salon. The aristocracy, judged alongside the vigour and vitality of the Georgian and Victorian middle class, was found wanting, and in its failure symbolised the worst of Britain. The virtues of thrift, industry and financial rectitude symbolised the middle orders, whereas extravagance, wilful debt, and insolvency were defects of the hereditary aristocracy (see Appendix 1). There is surely much merit in the historical view that the middle class was defined, and in part created, by opposition to the aristocracy, and re-constituted its public character and social ethos defiantly in opposition to its failings.[33]

Far less attention, however, has been devoted to plebeian readings of the aristocracy. Most studies of aristocracy are rooted in the verdicts of their peers, rather than in the opinions of those from below. The most vivid and arresting nineteenth-century images of the aristocracy derive from the underground ballad literature, street songs, and anti-hereditary principle street-literature. In such work aristocrats were depicted as 'moral transgressors'. This book uncovers a demi-world of anti-aristocratic sentiment that, whilst acknowledged by historians, has never really been explored in any detail. Expressed through hostility to institutions like the House of Lords, and the social phenomenon of landownership, opposition to aristocracy suffused the pages of radical reform journals, and featured strongly in the culture of the popular platform.[34] Such material circulated widely within the reform constituency. In the eyes of most reformers, landed society came to symbolise unrestrained, non-accountable, aristocratic dominance. Many reformers came to reform through exposure to this prevailing anti-aristocratic ethos. The radical and apostate freethinker Joseph Barker recalled:

> I had suffered grievously in my early days. I had been subjected to all the hardships and miseries of extreme poverty. And all these sufferings I believed to have been caused by the corn and provision

laws, enacted and maintained by the selfishness of the aristocracy. I regarded the aristocracy, therefore, and all who took their part, as my personal enemies; as men who had robbed me of my daily bread, and all but sent me to an untimely grave. I regarded them as the greatest of criminals, the enemies of the human race. I considered them answerable for the horrors of the first great French Revolution, and for the miseries of the Irish Famine. I gave them credit for nothing good.[35]

Building on plebeian readings of the aristocracy, this book pays close attention to the concerns of the critics of the aristocratic state. It defines hostility to the aristocracy in the broadest terms throughout, and takes a long view of radicalism that locates some of the trace elements of the anti-aristocratic posture in the legacy of eighteenth century debates about the purity of the constitution. Moreover, it analyses the rhetoric of anti-aristocracy in relation to the context of the time, and is attuned to the deficiencies in the personal conduct of the nation's titled rulers that were ruthlessly exploited in the radical press.

Examination of aristocracy has been unaccountably absent from the literature on the continuities in popular politics between the hiatus of the post-Chartist years and the emergence of independent labour in the decade before the Great War.[36] The issue of mobilising a platform of political opposition to aristocracy was central to the effectiveness of those political groupings that hoped to establish a national image and reclaim the country from titled and immoral aristocrats and their underlings. Aristocrats were a special interest group comprising political transgressors who subverted the will of the people in government. This book seeks to bring together recent scholarship on aristocracy, and the new interpretations of popular reformism available since the emergence of 'continuity' studies in the early 1990s. Informed by an awareness of the nature of popular politics after 1848, the relationship between plebeian and middle-class radicalism in bringing about the 1867 Reform Act, and the course that relationship took within the expanded political nation, this study refines the relationship between Liberalism and underground radicalism, and discusses ways in which the course of reform was influenced by hostility to aristocracy following the 1867 and 1884 Reform Acts. This book covers all aspects of the anti-aristocratic political platform. It probes the rhetorical spectrum, and demonstrates the ways in which politicians adapted both their methods of organisation, and their platform presence to the exceptional circumstances of combating unaccountable hierarchy, and non-elected wealth within the executive. Ranging across Whiggery, popular radicalism, reformism, and Liberalism, it brings together the worlds of high politics and the new methods of party mobilisation introduced in the aftermath of the Reform Acts of 1832 and 1867. Examining the interactions between radicals and Liberals, it seeks to establish the rhythms of the anti-aristocratic agenda, and demonstrate the unique dimension revealed by a reappraisal of the centrality of an anti-aristocratic approach to nineteenth-century politics.

Throughout the nineteenth and early twentieth centuries, anti-aristocratic ideas provided a congruence between radicalism and the Liberal Party. They were present in all strata of reformism, and bridged the divisions within progressive politics. Moreover, the subject of hostility to aristocracy extends the continuity debate into the 1890–1914 period which is usually overlooked in radical continuity discussion. As Jon Lawrence has suggested 'Old Corruption' arguments still had considerable mileage as late as the 1880s, and may be linked to the platform of Fabian Socialism.[37] The anti-aristocratic variant of radicalism also remained very marked in popular Liberalism. It reverberated in the work of John Stuart Mill, Richard Cobden, John Bright, and David Lloyd George who all had impeccable anti-aristocratic pedigrees.[38] John Stuart Mill's father, James Mill, was a self-taught small tradesman who disliked aristocracy which he castigated as a narrow caste responsible for the dispossession of the people. Later in life, Mill acknowledged the considerable debt he held to his father for his ideas about the economy and land-holding.[39] There is a common thread of anti-aristocratic sentiment linking both Liberals and radicals in the work of Tom Paine who exalted the role of small workshop proprietors as a counterweight to the great unaccountable landowners in government and society. A primitive producerist ethos was also apparent in the views of those radicals who sought a restitution of land plundered from the people by 'the great territorial power' of the aristocracy.[40] Many of the sternest critics of aristocracy, like G.W.M. Reynolds, were failed or struggling small businessmen, who felt themselves to be the victims of the unrestrained economic and political power of the aristocracy. The debate on free trade crystallised many of these sentiments. Joseph Chamberlain, an early influence on a whole generation of radicals, attacked the land-owning class as unproductive *rentiers* who manipulated state and economy in their own interests. Even after his conversion to Toryism he still saw his tariff reform campaign as a way of defending the rights of the small producer against the monopolistic landed interests who lived in lavish style off their unearned rent. Many of a later generation of radicals were

Paine's spiritual children in this regard. On the compass of radicalism, Keir Hardie was in essence an old-style land reformer, influenced by Chamberlain, Bradlaughite secularism, and the pothouse level of opposition to aristocracy vented by G.W.M. Reynolds. Hardie remarked, echoing the views of Chamberlain: 'The landlord, *qua* landlord, performs no function in the economy of industry or of food production. He is a rent receiver; that and nothing more. Were the landlord to be abolished, the soil and the people who till it would still remain, and the disappearance of the landowner would pass almost unnoticed.'[41] For him the aristocracy was simply an encumbrance on the backs of the people. For most reformers, abolishing or curbing aristocracy was pivotal to their view of a reformed society. The absence of aristocracy held out the prospect of a social order built around equality and a primitive communitarianism. Breaking up the great estates therefore provided a short-cut to a more harmonious social order.[42] The former Chartist and land nationaliser, Alfred A. Walton, wrote:

> We may at least admire their genealogical descent...thus far that when the great territorial system becomes broken up, as it one day will be, that some memento should be kept of their past greatness. It would certainly be worthwhile for the edification of future generations, that a model specimen or two of the great Mammoth landlord of the nineteenth century should be preserved in the British Museum or modeled in colossal proportions properly typifying the extent of their domains, and classed with the antediluvian models at the Crystal Palace.[43]

In short, this subject shows the overlap between Liberalism and radicalism on this issue, as well as delineating the boundaries of a popular radical constituency that expressed itself vociferously both inside, and outside, the structure of the Liberal Party.[44]

In addition, this book situates criticism of aristocracy within a broader debate about the composition of Victorian and Edwardian society. The timeframe extends from the late nineteenth century to the inter-war years, and examines key moments when criticism of aristocracy became paramount. Locating the origins of the anti-aristocratic critique in the seventeenth and eighteenth centuries, it merges analysis of the economic power of the aristocracy with scrutiny of their cultural role in town-life, their monopoly of the land, and their prominence on the hunting field. There is a continuity of dissent and reform here linked by hostility to aristocracy. Anti-aristocratic sentiment paved the way for a radical critique of privileged society grounded in aristocracy's traditional legislative and political role. This book stands as a corrective to accepted visions of a harmonious social order in which the misdeeds of the great territorial rulers were simply accepted or discounted as 'eccentricities' or 'foibles'.

In what follows, the traditional aspects of aristocratic deviance are subject to searching scrutiny. It contrast to the overwhelming majority of case studies of the English landowning class, this book takes as its starting point the moral, political, and social failings of the aristocracy. Hostility to aristocracy tends to be dismissed either as social envy, or as a failure to appreciate the virtues of a selfless and dedicated social group.[45] Here they are reclaimed as a serious component of popular politics. The undercurrents of radical hostility to aristocracy in the nineteenth century crystallised around the House of Lords issue, land-ownership, the immoral reputation of the aristocracy, and hunting. All these could be construed as serious failings that undermined the aristocracy's right to rule. This book considers in turn each of the cases made against aristocratic culture by reformers. Following the contemporary narrative of hostility towards the great landed families conveyed through the reform press and the pamphleteering campaigns of the late nineteenth century, it assesses the rhetoric of anti-aristocracy in detail. These arguments may be sub-divided into four major cases: the moral case against aristocracy, which sought to subvert their role as moral agents of the state and as 'patrician paragons', the economic case that revealed their detrimental impact on land-holding, the emotional case deriving from their lust for sport, and the legislative case that depicted them as a narrow neo-feudal elite. For its critics, these characteristics of nobility in turn fed the self-destructive urges within aristocracy. Many contemporaries saw them as harbouring avaricious tendencies that through their obsession with increased wealth and position lead to a coupling with the forces of an emergent plutocracy, hastening their own destruction. Articulated fiercely and profanely for many decades, these aspects of popular politics may be regarded as the basis of an anti-aristocratic platform. Taking up the notion of 'debt and debauchery' such antagonism posed the prospect of an imminent dissolution of aristocracy, and the creation of a society purified of inherited wealth and hereditary titles. From analysis of the coruscating and swingeing rhetoric of dislike for aristocracy, emerges a politics moulded around a platform of plebeian decency, artisanal moral self-improvement, popular egalitarianism, and primitive communitarianism. This book then is an exercise in the reclamation of failure. It argues that visions of a corrupted and depraved aristocracy demonstrate the tensions in the changing political and social function of aristocratic society. Analysis of the moral case against aristocracy demonstrates that radical journalists undermined the virtues of the aristocratic state by revealing it as profligate, dissipated, and self-destructive.

The themes outlined here are constants that recur within the spectrum of opposition to aristocracy. In recent years, hostility to bloodsports, the expulsion of the hereditary peers from the House of Lords, public access struggles, and the conflict between the Scottish Assembly and landowners over crofters' rights, have highlighted the persistence of aristocratic power in Great Britain. This book demonstrates that such criticisms are in a long tradition. Radicals played artfully on the dubious ancestry and inherited predisposition to immorality of the great families of the land, which they depicted as the outgrowth of a traditional neo-feudal aristocracy, depriving the people of their true rights and reducing them to the status of exiles in their own land. This book opens up new avenues for the study of aristocracy by revealing the perspectives of the opponents, rather than supporters of aristocracy. It demonstrates the connections between the land debate, criticisms of aristocratic immorality, animal welfare politics and concerns about the legislative role of the House of Lords in the late nineteenth and early twentieth century. The book concludes with a consideration of changing patterns of hostility to aristocracy in the years preceding and following the watershed decade for aristocratic fortunes in the 1930s. Through a re-examination of the narrative of anti-aristocratic sentiment in late nineteenth- and early twentieth-century Britain, it is hoped that the radical preoccupation with aristocracy will be both illuminated, and explained. Far from providing a backward-looking hostility to the fading forces of feudalism, anti-aristocratic sentiment constituted a measured and rational response to the continuing power and significance of the territorial nobility. Sometimes represented as a mere distraction, anti-aristocratic sentiment may be reclaimed as a central plank in the reform platform. It stood at the heart of radicalism, helping define the shifting alliances between radicals, Liberals, and socialists, and providing a rational and attainable goal for greater equality within society, as well as opening up the possibility for the redistribution of land-holding, and at its wilder fringes, wealth itself. For most reformers the surprise was not that aristocracy had endured for so long, but rather that the British people had proved so tolerant and compliant in their acceptance of the manifold injustices that accompanied aristocratic rule. Richard Cobden was astonished 'that the people at large are so tacit in their submission to the perpetuation of the feudal system in this country as it affects the property in land'.[46] It is the purpose of this book to explain the outlook and attitude of those reformers who proved far less tolerant and submissive in their attitudes to aristocracy.

1
Aristocratic Debauchery and Working-Class Virtue: The Case of Colonel Valentine Baker

> If there be one thing more ominous than another in opening a book of the peerage, it is the queer look of the armorial escutcheons by which the aristocratic families are distinguished... Are they meant to be emblems of the nature of aristocracy – of the origin, history and merits of these people?...Then surely the sooner the whole body of them were swept out of civilized society the better...What are the crests of these arms? Lascivious goats, rampant lions, fiery dragons, and griffins gone crazed; bulls' heads, block-heads, arms with uplifted daggers, beasts with daggers, and vultures tearing up helpless birds...They are the most singular assemblage of all that is fierce, savage, rampageous, villainous, lurking, treacherous, bloodthirsty, cruel, and bestial in bestial natures.[1]

Traditionally, aristocracy stands at the pinnacle of the social hierarchy. In the nineteenth century its influence was all-pervasive. Arbiters of taste and refinement, espousing an idealised conception of gentility, aristocrats set the standard in the arts, theatre, and fashion. At their height, they were central to the salon cultures of politics and elite society, and took a leading role in the military, in bureaucracy, and in the nation's diplomatic legations. The links between monarchy, courtly circles, and the great territorial families of the land cemented aristocracy's status. The boundaries between monarchy and the aristocracy were porous. Aristocrats were prominent in the entourages of monarchs, attending the royal family as equerries, ladies of the bedchamber, and as royal companions. Throughout the nineteenth century they were instrumental in establishing and refining courtly protocol. The royal family, in turn, moved in the great aristocratic circles of the realm, mingling on an equal footing with the aristocracy at race meets, on the hunting field, and at society weekends in the shires. Individual families sought preferment by such means, benefiting from favours, honourific titles, and places at court. Royal favour, wealth, power, and influence characterised the closed social world of the British aristocracy in the latter part of the nineteenth century. Even the lower rungs of the gentry occupied exalted positions in municipal and local government. Aristocracy, then, functioned both as a tool of social advancement and as a stabilising factor in the closed social world of nineteenth-century Britain. The aristocracy's pivotal role meant that, for contemporaries, the great titled families set their stamp on society in Victorian and Edwardian Britain, colouring it with their enthusiasms, follies, and foibles.

For many critics the landed elite compromised, quite as much as it augmented, genteel society. Under the influence of Thomas Paine, radicals saw the key to power and influence as residing in formal structures of landownership. Drawing on ancestral memories of the 'Norman Yoke' radicals conflated the cultural context of monarchy and aristocracy, projecting regal power as a usurpation of the throne by a delinquent dynasty, supported by a venal church and a closed aristocratic order. In the years between the early 1860s and the Great War this view of aristocracy remained unmodified. Radicals projected debt and debauchery, frequently associated with the younger sons of aristocratic families, onto the aristocratic circle of Albert Edward, the Prince of Wales. Images of a royalty degraded by its contact with an indolent and predatory aristocracy lingered into the later twentieth century. In 1930, G.K. Chesterton wrote of the British monarchy that 'it had been profoundly modified by aristocratic traditions, both of liberty, and of license'.[2] Albert Edward and his circle were seen as amoral voluptuaries who expressed some of the worst aspects of the degraded character of aristocracy. At the Prince of Wales's residence at Marlborough House the excesses of the titled and privileged provided ammunition against the royal family and the aristocratic interests that clustered around the throne. Queen Victoria herself was concerned by the frequent misdemeanours associated with the name of the heir to the throne and his aristocratic circle. In her private correspondence she cautioned against the influence of the prominent aristocratic families at court, and highlighted: 'the immense danger and evil of the wretched frivolity and levity of the views and lives of the higher classes'.[3]

I

The frequent chastisement of the wrongdoings of aristocracy in the radical press has been noted by historians, but rarely been explored in any detail. This has problematised the narrative of anti-aristocratic sentiment itself and contributed substantially to the view that the radical press and its proprietors are somehow marginal to more pressing issues of social concern. Behind a historiography that has struggled with the contemporary and historical significance of aristocracy is the ghost of the idea that the concern of the radical press with a decadent nobility and a corrupt court indicates the underdeveloped nature of British socialism and the inability of radicals to interpret the dynamics of the nineteenth-century urban economy. Despite the best efforts of recent scholarship in this field, the phenomenon of newspapers like *Reynolds's News* is still seen as fundamentally inexplicable, as backward-looking and as saturated with nostalgia for an imagined pre-industrial past. Often it is simply conflated with the hopeless romanticism of Ruskin and the impracticability of the ideas of Edward Carpenter and others on the fringes of the early Labour Party.[4]

Taking up the notion of 'debt and debauchery' this chapter pursues the moral case against aristocracy. It takes as its theme the notorious Victorian sexual assault case of Colonel Valentine Baker. It demonstrates that traditional views of a depraved and dissolute aristocracy lingered into the high Victorian period. Rather than fading from public view, the great families of the land retained a strong public presence. Their prominence at court, close association with the monarchy, and continuing role within government and financial circles made aristocratic power emblematic of *Ancien Regime* decay. Ernest Jones represented the upper reaches of the titled classes as a protective carapace for the monarchy: 'Dukes, marquises, earls, viscounts, barons, baronets, knights, esquires, right honourables, and honourables are placed between it and the masses as buffers on a railway carriage, to break the force of contact with the power next to it.'[5] In addition for radicals, the Baker case exemplified the corruptibility of aristocratic connection and the durability of entrenched modes of behaviour that were characteristic of landed families. Rather than diminishing with the contraction of landed wealth, families like the Bakers raised the prospect of a new urban elite, powered by wise investments, experienced in the art of colonial administration, and rooted in the social milieu of the metropolis. For reformers, the Baker case demonstrated that whatever else had changed, the low corrupt morals of aristocracy remained. The behaviour, boorishness, and lack of manners of many of the great noble dynasties left a feeling that the courtly clan of aristocratic retainers refused to moderate their behaviour, or in the case of royal German relatives from Hanover, refused to 'indigenise' altogether. In this sense the affair surrounding Colonel Valentine Baker was central to radical perceptions of aristocracy. Radical views of a low debauched aristocracy pivoted on the case, and received fresh impetus from this exposure of low morals in high places.

The Baker family embodied many of the correct military and social values of Victorian England. The family could trace its ancestry back to an extinct Tudor baronetcy with a romantically ruined seat at Sissinghurst Castle near Cranbrook in Kent. Val's grandfather had diversified the family wealth into estates in Jamaica and Ceylon where the Bakers became a wealthy dynasty of planters.[6] Valentine Baker enlisted in the Twelfth Lancers, and saw action in the 'Kaffir War' in the Cape Colony in 1852, and later in the Crimea. In the 1860s he rose steadily to become the commanding officer of the Twelfth Lancers, and by cultivating its Colonel-in-Chief, the Prince of Wales, graduated to the Marlborough House set. In time he became the prince's equerry and a close personal confidante. His brother was the colourful Samuel Baker, who served in Egypt and helped map the headwaters of the Nile. By the mid-1870s Valentine Baker was an assistant quartermaster general, posted at Aldershot. With a family home in Gloucestershire, close friends at court, and a distinguished military career behind him, he was the epitome of the mid-Victorian gentleman.[7]

Moreover Baker typified the mobile and porous nature of the Victorian aristocracy. The Bakers from their background of new money in the Indies, via service in Ceylon, were illustrative of the diversified patterns of wealth that characterised the aristocracy in Victorian society. Whereas traditional aristocracy was perceived as timeless and unchanging, the rise of the Bakers showed that it was increasingly undermined by aspirational entrants to titled status, who brought with them rejuvenating infusions of finance capital. The radical press drew on popular anger and resentment against an aristocracy that was seen as remote, wealthy and privileged, and fanned it still further with a regular diet of titillation, and disclosures about their finances. *Reynolds's Newspaper* set out to reveal the true sources of their wealth and position, the social circles they moved in, and the conduits whereby they gained access to titled status and position. This was the 'pestilential atmosphere' of aristocracy that has 'infected and rendered diseased the classes next to it'.[8] For many reformers, Britain had fallen prey to a rapacious new class encased in the faded apparel of the old aristocracy. As radicals frequently demonstrated, an emerging plutocracy supported by wealth raised from the city and the international money markets was buttressed by new expensive sports and recreational pastimes that inflated the currency of titles and landed wealth. Radicals increasingly targeted these parasitic financial interests and *nouveau riche* elements who clustered around the throne and the person of the Prince of Wales, whilst aping the degraded morals of the traditional peerage.

The hammer of aristocracy was the radical newspaper *Reynolds's News*. The paper was an openly republican journal traditionally critical of the queen and the heir to the throne. In the 1860s it claimed to have instigated the campaign around the issue of Victoria's seclusion after Prince Albert's death. *Reynolds's News* occupies a significant position in the history of the monarchy and attempts to reform it. In this period the paper captured the public mood towards an introverted and discredited court at the nadir of Victoria's popularity. It remains the only overtly republican British newspaper to have achieved a mass circulation both at the time and subsequently. The republicanism of G.W.M. Reynolds locates the politics of his newspaper outside the mainstream of Liberal support and within the ambit of an older style of radicalism in which the failings of a corrupt court and executive were privileged over an adherence to Gladstonian state reformism. The real key to understanding the appeal of Reynolds's writings is the minute attention he paid to the origins of aristocratic connection and position. Throughout his work he artfully played on the dubious ancestry of the nation's social and cultural elite which he represented as the outgrowth of a traditional territorial aristocracy depriving the people of their true rights and reducing them to internal exiles in their own land. As Reynolds himself announced at one of his regular soirees for his employees in 1875, his self-appointed task was 'to show up royalty and aristocracy in their true light'.[9] He recalled of his formative years that: 'Monarchical and aristocratic institutions, with their exclusive privileges became to my mind the objects of hatred, abhorrence and disgust, and thus it was that as a very young man I began to write *The Mysteries of London*.'[10]

Reynolds is sometimes seen as an enigmatic and marginal figure. Despite the phenomenal success of his newspaper, *Reynolds's News*, he remains difficult to position within the context of mid-nineteenth-century popular politics.[11] His interventions opened up the debate about the monarchy in the 1860s and kept the image of debauched dukes and immoral aristocrats before the public gaze. Moreover, the paper's attacks on aristocracy were part of a sustained campaign to undermine the future prospects of aristocracy that were widely supported by radicals and even by those traditional aristocrats who despised the court. Reynolds himself died in 1879 leaving little documentary or family material behind him. In addition many of his contributions to the paper were unsigned. What is, however, important about *Reynolds's Newspaper* is that this house style, created by Reynolds, was continued by his brother Edward for many years and adopted in the 1890s by William Thompson, his successor as editor. In what follows I deal in general terms with the content of the newspaper and the model of anti-aristocratic discourse it established. *Reynolds's* was above all a winning formula, embraced by Reynolds's successors, precisely because it worked, and indicative of a robust element in popular politics that sought to penetrate the 'phantasmagoric chaos of ranks and grades' that cocooned and obscured the misdeeds of Britain's traditional titled rulers.[12]

II

On 17 June 1875 the well-connected Colonel Baker took a train from Liphook in Hampshire to Waterloo. He shared his carriage with a young woman called Rebecca Dickinson. During the journey she was seen hanging from the running-board of the train apparently trying to escape from her fellow passenger inside. She later claimed that Baker had 'insulted' her, a euphemism for attempted rape. Baker denied the accusation, saying she had misinterpreted a harmless remark, but his clothing was in disarray, and he repeated the words 'I shouldn't have done it.'

The case rapidly became a benchmark of sexual impropriety in public places. During a slack news period it was an overnight sensation. Press and public opinion was convulsed by the apparent attempt to 'ravish' Miss Dickinson. Concern about crime on the railways following Britain's first railway murder in 1864 gave the case a particular public interest. The killing of Thomas Briggs by the German immigrant Franz Muller whilst traveling between Bow and Hackney Wick set the scene for a moral panic about crime that highlighted the inaccessibility and vulnerability of passengers in isolated railway compartments. Following the attack *The Times* wrote: 'A railway carriage is a place where we are cut off for a time from all chance of assistance, and this feeling of helplessness in case of emergency has been a bugbear to many travelers, male as well as female. Without the means of communicating with the guard we are almost at the mercy of fire, collisions and fellow passengers. This last danger is to most minds by far the most intolerable of the three.'[13] The Baker case exacerbated these fears about railway travel, generating immense popular interest. The trial took place on August Bank Holiday, 1875 at Croyden in the full glare of the media spotlight. *The Times* wrote: 'Since the day Colonel Baker was brought before the magistrates, a large part of the public have taken more interest in his case than in any political event of the day.'[14] Bank holiday trains were crowded with mobs of voyeurs making their way to the court; during the afternoon a number of spectators tried to force their way in. At times the noise made by the large crowd outside drowned out the proceedings altogether.[15] In this display the public were expressing revulsion at Baker's actions, and reaffirming their right to pass judgement on the accused lost with the suspension of public executions in 1868.[16] Baker maintained his innocence, but could not really offer any convincing explanation for why Miss Dickinson should choose to endanger her life by clambering from a moving train travelling at forty miles an hour. Mr Justice Brett who heard the case had a reputation for severity. Refusing to countenance an adjournment, Baker was cleared of 'assault with intention to ravish' but found guilty of indecent and common assault.[17] Brett pronounced a sentence of one year's imprisonment, a fine of five hundred pounds, and payment of costs on Baker. Despite representations to the Queen she was unwilling to intervene on his behalf, and he was cashiered and dismissed from his position with the quartermaster's department.

Baker's family saw the verdict as unduly harsh, and in part driven by an inflamed public opinion. There was little corroboratory testimony for either party's version of events, and Baker had a previously unblemished military record and an untarnished public reputation. Nevertheless, the jury of small tradesmen and artisans made their disapproval of Valentine Baker's conduct apparent from the outset. The Baker family closed ranks around 'Val', insisting that he was wrongly maligned on the basis of unreliable testimony, and that there had been no impropriety on the train. Subsequent biographers of the Baker family continue to insist that a misguided sense of gallantry led Baker to restrain his barrister from too vigorous a cross-examination of Miss Dickinson that would have exposed the flaws in her story. At the time of his death in 1887, his obituarists steadfastly maintained that his service in Egypt for the Khedive showed his honourable character, and his conduct at the battle of El Teb in 1884 had redeemed him from the 'lamentable blot' on his family name.[18]

Few contemporaries shared this view. Indeed most opinion was appalled by the leniency of the sentence, rather than its harshness. Amongst the radical community there was uproar at the circumstances surrounding the verdict. Radical journalists were outraged at an apparent gross perversion of justice. In the weeks following the trial the reform community campaigned against a punishment which seemed disproportionately lenient. John Stuart Mill's niece, Helen Taylor, believed the sentence to be such a flagrant maladministration of the judicial process that it demanded a popular campaign around this one cause. For radicals it communicated the simple message that wealth and power bought exemption from the consequences of immoral behaviour. Moreover, it indicated that aristocracy and the law colluded to preserve intact the public position of prominent families. Taylor noted that 'the judge not only spoke of the past services of the prisoner in eulogistic terms – by these very terms striving to enlist the sympathy of the public – but, in addition, remarked that the prisoner might yet be an ornament to society and in this hope he should spare him "the physical degradation which would probably be a torture to him"'.[19] Correspondence in the reform press made the point that indecent assault might reasonably be expected to carry a penalty of two years hard labour. For Baker such legal precedents were waived. Yet, as *The Bee-Hive* pointed out, 'if Colonel Baker had been a rider in a third class carriage, and if he had been a poor man, there is no reason to believe that any leniency of any kind would have been extended to him by the judge'.[20]

In addition, the Valentine Baker case revealed that a criminal who displayed breeding and refinement might reasonably expect to receive preferential treatment whatever his moral transgressions. Baker was housed in an opulent cell, had wine and food brought in from outside, and caroused with his friends throughout his imprisonment.[21] Years later George Jacob Holyoake contrasted the treatment Baker received to that of the Chartist leader Ernest Jones, from a similar social class, and imprisoned for two years solitary confinement after a conviction for incitement to riot in 1848: 'Jones was required to pick oakum. Being a gentleman, he refused to be degraded as a criminal. Politics was not a crime. In the case of Colonel Valentine Baker, the government had just respect for a gentleman; but not when the gentleman was the political advocate of the poor, though Jones was socially superior to Baker.'[22] In a similar vein *Reynolds's Newspaper* drew attention to the plight of two gas-stokers tried for sleeping on the job, and allowing an interruption in the gas supply to London's street lights. In this case Mr Justice Brett awarded a sentence of two years with hard labour. The paper concluded that 'there is only one law, but there are two modes of administering it'.[23] Radical opinion was incited by Brett's well-known antipathy to trade unions. For many reformers Valentine Baker's treatment contrasted with the conditions provided for trades unionists imprisoned under the

Combination Acts. The case remained a benchmark of the double standard in the administration of justice for many years. *Reynolds's Newspaper* returned to it obsessively, noting Valentine Baker's later rehabilitation by polite society and reception back into his old clubs in the 1880s.[24] As late as the 1890s, the radical press still saw their role as one of exposing the inconsistencies in a system that operated discriminatory practice in its treatment of felons. In 1893, *Justice* noted the preferential treatment shown to the Dowager Duchess of Sutherland, imprisoned for contempt of court, but allowed books, newspapers, friends, and half a pint of wine every day. It concluded that she was housed as a 'first class misdemeanant' and there was 'nothing to prevent her from furnishing [her cell] in a manner befitting her station'.[25]

Radicals used the Baker case to morally censure aristocratic wrongdoing. Seeking to understand the case in contemporary terms, this chapter offers a cultural reading of the event. It demonstrates that the case became emblematic of aristocratic debauchery, inspired by memories of the Regency, and inflamed by the relatively lenient sentence of one year's imprisonment passed on Baker by the Bench. The Baker case not only indicated a double standard in the administration of justice, it also revealed the persistence of underground traditions of hostility to aristocracy. The imaginative world of Victorian radicalism was populated by debauched aristocrats and professional rakes. The trial received extensive coverage in the radical press, particularly in *Reynolds's Newspaper*, which continued many of the traditions of popular hostility to aristocracy that were emblematic of radical news-sheets during the Chartist years. These visions of a corrupt and depraved aristocracy demonstrate the tensions in the changing political and social role of aristocracy. Radicals believed that aristocrats like Baker had moved from the broad acres to become grounded in the morally dissolute urban world of the season, the court, and high society, merging the worst aspects of rural and urban culture in the process. Radicals took a 'Sex and the City' view of this process, exploring the morally depraved demi-world of urban aristocracy, and exposing their fabulous wealth and numerous wrong-doings to public scrutiny. Reflecting on the Baker case the radical land reformer John de Morgan commented of aristocratic life:

To read the *exposé* of modern society in the columns of the aristocratic papers *The World* and *Vanity Fair* makes the blood run cold. Vice has become a profession. Under the cloak of business, men and women carry on the most shameful of practices. Money in large sums is lent to young, marriageable ladies, the interest being the sacrifice of their virtue. Married ladies worshipping the foul fiend called fashion get deeply in debt to milliners and others until they find themselves in the clutches of abandoned *roués*. Shame on the one hand, vice on the other . . . It is not safe for a young lady to travel unattended in a second or first class carriage even on our suburban lines.[26]

Radicalism presented the perverse paradox of a culture of anti-aristocracy that produced the most avid watchers of high society. Sensationalist radical journalists like G.W.M. Reynolds played artfully on the dubious ancestry and inherited predisposition to immorality of the great families of the land, which he represented as the outgrowth of a traditional neo-feudal aristocracy, depriving the people of their true rights, and reducing them to the status of exiles in their own land. The aristocracy represented by Valentine Baker was a feral and predatory one. Viewed in these terms the Baker case demonstrated the assertion of traditions of feudal 'droits de seigneur' over the insulted and violated women of the people.[27] *Reynolds's Newspaper* recalled other celebrated aristocratic sex scandals and commented: 'Our readers possibly will recall to mind the perfidious sentiment sworn to by the Hon. Major Yelverton – namely that he saw no serious offence in seducing a woman "provided she was not of gentle blood". We wonder if this view is still held in fashionable circles. We are half inclined to think that it is, and that the heads of society have a moral code of their own which is perfectly irreconcilable with the Decalogue.'[28] Radical journalists then used the case to undermine the 'patrician paragons' of the aristocracy by revealing them as profligate, dissipated, and self-destructive.

III

Radical outrage at the verdict in the Baker case was in a long tradition. Anna Clark has demonstrated that a 'politics of seduction' was a marked feature of radical rhetoric from the 1790s onwards.[29] Concerns traditionally revolved around the younger sons of aristocratic families, cut out of the family inheritance by the legal constraints of primogeniture, afflicted with the monstrous appetites of aristocracy, but running up unpayable debts, and forced to resort to opportune marriages. Critics derided a system 'which inverts the natural order of human life, accustoming them to ease and luxury in youth, but offering them no adequate provision either for an early settlement or an early retirement'.[30] Abandoned women, dallied with and then cast aside in a search for wealthy brides, were portrayed as the social wreckage of this phenomenon, and became part of a moral case against primogeniture explored in the radical press. One victim wrote: 'Wheresoever are the younger sons of your aristocracy, there behold idleness, luxury, helplessness, debt, prodigality, dissipation. What means of having it otherwise? What would you have where a system unites in one person the vices of the aristocracy and the vices of pauperism. I have known many cases which were just as mine – of girls who sacrificed themselves like me to those who could not, even if they would, offer them an honest and lasting affection.'[31] At a darker level it was believed young male aristocrats simply took, rather than asked for, their sexual pleasures, leading to the prevalence of images of sexual coercion that gathered around aristocracy. In his poem, 'The Two Races' written in the 1840s the Chartist leader Ernest Jones condemned aristocrats as 'lurers of the village maid'.[32] Lurid depictions of aristocratic libertinage occurred in plays and popular stories designed to highlight the betrayal of the poor by the rich. Rape became a metaphor, demonstrating the exploitation of the weak and passive by the wealthy and depraved. For William Cobbett, society's disintegration in the wake of the Industrial Revolution was revealed by the emergence of degraded patricians who turned their backs on their traditional paternalistic role, and instead exploited and defiled their social inferiors. Here the stories of wicked aristocrats and honest but naïve peasant girls ravished by their sly and untrustworthy seducers shaded into melodrama. The ruling class was 'morally bankrupt'. Absentee landlords, of little social or political worth, preyed on local women, producing bastard offspring sent to the foundling hospitals. In the late 1830s the Anti-Poor Law movement which preceded Chartism stigmatised the Bastardy Laws of the 1834 Poor Law Amendment Act as an aristocrat's charter, designed to conceal the unwanted children of their illicit and often enforced liaisons with lower-class farming women. As in the Baker case, a dichotomy was set up here. The poor underclass was portrayed as morally virtuous, if financially poor, whereas the wealthy were financially rich, but destitute of all morals. Whilst Miss Dickinson by no stretch of the imagination could be portrayed as a poor peasant girl, her plight, nevertheless, came to represent the ravished victims of aristocratic excess. This image of debauched and satiated nobles, and lascivious landowners was to remain a familiar and still potent symbol for much of the nineteenth century, and remained far from exhausted in the writings of the first generation of Labour leaders.[33] The Baker case, however, brought the world of Gothic misdemeanours out of ivy-clad abbeys and crumbling mansions into the modern world of comfortable passenger transport where women in enclosed railway carriages were still not safe from the lusts of aristocratic *roués*.

Moreover, the Baker case drew on the vision of high aristocratic families that moved in a subterranean demi-world populated by itinerants, thieves, and vagabonds. Keir Hardie remarked that if George V had been born in the ranks of the working class 'his most likely fate would have been that of a street-corner loafer'.[34] Criminality in personal and political behaviour was part of this world. Here his association with the indiscretions of the Marlborough House set compromised Baker. The classic trope of anti-aristocratic rhetoric was to stigmatise the nobility as pleasure-seeking tourists, moving through the subterranean underworld of Victorian England in search of new and exoticised pleasures. In many descriptions their destinies and social circumstances appear closely intertwined with the carnivalesque underworld of metropolitan low-life.[35] Aristocrats were often represented not as refined and mannered, but rather as crude and degraded in their everyday language as a result of these experiences. Lord Randolph Churchill was seen as appropriating 'the language of Billingsgate' and said to be very successful in 'gathering the stinking verbal offal of the very Saxon English'. Henry Hyndman talked of aristocratic language 'more English and less nice, when any fearless man begins to rake up the history of their "sacrifices" to patriotism'.[36] The radical press depicted 'slumming aristocrats' as part of a depraved working-class saturnalia; Charles Bradlaugh described Randolph Churchill and the Marlboroughs he was descended from as: 'the scum and dregs of the nation'.[37] Their outward display was not simply bluff behaviour and demeanour, it was the acquisition of the argot and style of the poor they rubbed shoulders with in the villainous drinking dens of Victorian cities. In this way the aristocratic world became a vulgar and debased one, coarsened by their oafish ruffianism and exposure to the customs of the slum-dwellers. *Reynolds's Newspaper* described the peers of the House of Lords as 'Old men who have spent their worthless lives in the stews of London and Paris, who have squandered the incomes derived from their wretched tenantries upon strumpets, singers and stud-groomers...Youths reeking from the brothels of St John's Wood...whose thoughts by day, and dreams by night, are centred on their horses and harlots'.[38] Temperance reformers in particular were attuned to this style of rhetoric. They depicted drunken aristocrats as poor examples to their social inferiors, and hopelessly compromised in their everyday lives by their exposure to drink on the aristocratic social circuit. In reports in the temperance press, the antics of Lord Randolph Churchill and his drinking companions brought dishonour on the Marlboroughs, and embarrassed his college at Oxford. During one celebrated 'drunken rampage' at Merton College, an inebriated

Churchill brawled drunkenly with a policeman. The *Alliance News* spoke of an 'aristocratic orgy' held 'almost within the shadow of his ancestral palace at Blenheim'.[39] Temperance Chartists were highly critical of the Beer Acts which sought to curb the culture of low-class drinking dens, but 'leaves the vile, profligate clubs of aristocracy open'.[40]

In keeping with the disdain for the legal system associated with aristocracy, reformers often portrayed aristocrats as glorified pick-pockets, dipping into the pockets of the people at will and extracting the economic surplus like a wallet: 'England is a paradise for those who can live upon the labour of others; or such as can put their hands into the pockets of their fellow men, and extract hundreds of thousands for their own use.'[41] Such images became a marked feature of the radical and land reform press. Noble landowners were 'common thieves', or little better than 'foot-pads'. On occasion they were portrayed as hereditary and inverted Robin Hoods: 'They glory in their descent from robbery...What their forefathers, real or pretended, did, was to take from the many and give to the few.'[42]

There is a survival from the image of carnival in the 'topsy-turvydom' of aristocratic immorality. The Baker case coincided with a series of high-profile public trials that questioned the moral integrity of the aristocracy. These trials were important in inciting populist hostility to the traditional titled elite and their supporters. In the early 1870s the celebrated Tichborne case stoked radical distrust of aristocratic untrustworthiness. The case was an incendiary one. A Wapping butcher, Arthur Orton, claimed to be the long-lost Sir Roger Tichborne, and heir to the Tichborne baronetcy and family estates. Despite overwhelming evidence to the contrary, there was strong popular support for his position, and allegations that the family sought to preserve their fortune for themselves. When he was convicted of perjury in 1874, it was popularly believed that his family and the judiciary had conspired to suppress his claim.[43] The Tichborne case represented the image of an aristocracy dragging its loutish manners into the public domain and exposing to public view the dysfunctional nature of one of England's oldest Catholic gentry families. In the Tichborne case radicals saw the aristocracy arraigned before the bar of history, and aristocratic integrity, rather than the claimant, on trial before the people.[44] Edward Kenealy, the claimant's lawyer and a Tichbornite MP for Stoke, saw the connection with the Baker trial and asked questions about the verdict in the House.[45] *Reynolds's Newspaper*, which was strongly supportive of the claimant, specialised in the exposure of aristocratic criminality. Swindling confidence tricksters, leaders of aristocratic street gangs, and gambling and dog-fighting dukes were the everyday fare of the paper. As in the Baker and Tichborne cases, *Reynolds's* excoriated the maladministration of justice involved in the conduct of the trials and the verdicts passed. Writing of the aristocratic con man and swindler Sir Sibbald Scott who had been apprehended by the police, but released without charge, it emphasised the relatively lenient sentences handed down to noble miscreants: 'Had he been a poor man, without rank and influential friends at his back, we think it quite possible that the youth, instead of breathing the air of freedom, might be exercising himself on the treadmill within the narrow limits of a prison.'[46] The Baker case elevated such commentary into a truism, widely accepted and discussed within the radical community.

The social elite exposed by the Baker case was primarily an urban one, rooted in the upper ranks of the military, the Marlborough House set, and the glittering whirl of the London season. For radicals it demonstrated the existence of a languid urban aristocracy addicted to pleasure. The themes of a corrupt court and a wily pleasure-obsessed heir played well in the regions where *Reynolds's Newspaper* had a substantial readership, and linked the nobility with a tradition of wrong-doing that emphasised the decadent and corrupting power of the capital. Such notions set up a contrast between the morally pure and Nonconformist-dominated regions, and the metropolis, where the innocent were lured into vice by the debauched retainers of the Prince of Wales. An American visitor to London, Daniel Joseph Kirwan wrote: 'The young lad has since surrounded himself with pimps, panders, parasites, and blackguards of the lowest kind. His name is a bye word of scorn in the British metropolis, and for a lady of rank or position to be seen three times in his neighbourhood, is certain dishonour to her and her relatives.'[47] Albert Edward's intimacy with Baker was mentioned several times during the trial. He was amongst the party selected to accompany the Prince on his 1875 tour of India that began soon after the trial ended. *The Weekly Dispatch* cautioned: 'If we are to know a man by the company he keeps [such] cases ought to be a warning to a certain distinguished personage to be more careful than he has hitherto been in the selection of his acquaintances.'[48] Such revelations also opened the way to a reconsideration of the territorial aristocracy in the light of their past misdeeds. The keynote here was the absentee nature of the urban *rentiers* who populated the houses of high society in London. The rootlessness and itinerancy of young, dissipated nobles in the capital created a link with the world of the low and dangerous indigent poor of London. Both the wealthy and the very poor were mobile and casualised, simply passing through London en route to somewhere else. *Reynolds's* described the young

Duke of Hamilton after his involvement in a brawl with the police as 'a young Scottish nobleman, possessing immense estates in Scotland, which he never visits, and whose time and fortune are spent on the race-courses of England and France, and apparently in the night-houses or the fashionable haunts of low dissipation of London'.[49] Similar condemnations of 'lordly absentees' appeared in *The Single Tax* which chastised the type of aristocrat 'who lifts his rent [through an arrogant factor] spends it in London or Monte Carlo, or other centres of aristocratic dissipation, and comes home for a month or two with a retinue of foreigners, English and other, to shoot the game'.[50] The strongest criticism came from Thomas Ainge Devyr who wrote of 'rampant land thieves' to whom London is 'the world'. He continued: 'The theatres, operas, public gardens, museums etc do not, I believe, form much attraction for the nobility. Their clubs, gaming halls, . . . "parliamentin" as Burns calls it etc, fill up most of their nights; days they have little or none – they are all dozed away in bed.'[51]

Sex was a constant in the depictions of a rootless aristocratic life devoted to self-indulgence and pleasure. Baker's lustful intentions were seen as characteristic of the class as a whole. In these representations the aristocracy was born out of the stews of immoral love-beds, the harlot's boudoir, and wrong-side-of-the-blanket liaisons with women of easy virtue. Throughout this period, radicals paid minute attention to the origins of aristocratic connection and position. Radicalism presented the perverse paradox of a culture of anti-aristocracy that produced the most avid watchers of high society. Recounting a series of sex scandals that included a noblewoman keeping a brothel and a peer living simultaneously with three sisters, Ernest Jones wrote of the aristocracy in the 1850s: 'Disgrace after disgrace imprints itself on the unblushing front of the ruling classes and still they smile with stolid insolence and self-complacency.'[52] Elsewhere he expounded on examples of an aristocratic white slave trade, abduction of a young girl by members of the officer corps of the marines, pederasty, and prostitution amongst the nobility, asking the rhetorical question: 'What are the vices of the uneducated working man compared to them? What is drunkenness or even a theft committed in the dire extremity of hunger by comparison.'[53] This was the semi-pornographic and voyeuristic view of aristocracy embodied in the suggestive language of William Benbow's *A Peep at the Peers* and present in Jack Mitford's imagery of looking behind the curtain of royalty to discover the true character of the court.[54] By emphasising the immoral and debauched origins of titles handed out to royal paramours and court mistresses in the sixteenth and seventeenth centuries, *Reynolds's* presented aristocratic titles as a corrupt and debased coinage: 'As it is with the origin of scores of great fortunes, so it is with rank. "Harlot" might be written broad over the roots of many a family tree in the aristocracy. Hamlet's reproach to his mother about the "rank sweat of an incestuous bed" might well take place of the family legend in dozens of families, the price of a woman's virtue and the issue of her bastard offspring.'[55] For reformers, the 'bogus' nature of the titles and sequestered estates handed out by dynasties like the Stuarts, and the corruptibility of those they adorned, not only undermined the nature of inherited privilege, it also revealed the brittle foundations of society itself, and cast light on the dubious claims to the throne of the House of Saxe Coburg Gotha, as well as the pedigree of the institutionalised aristocracy. The Stuart peerages bestowed by Charles II were especially notorious. Writing in 1884, *Reynolds's Newspaper* commented 'Such peerages as those enjoyed by the Dukes of Richmond, St. Albans and Grafton are of shameful origin. They were bestowed by a profligate monarch on his bastard offspring by different concubines.'[56] *Reynolds's* remarked: 'Other "great families" sprang from the filthy strumpets of Charles the Second' and called the sinecures, Civil List payments, and military ranks attached to their positions 'the wages of prostitution'.[57] Moreover, as the paper never tired of reminding its readers, when the first Hanoverian monarch George I arrived in the country, he was accompanied by 'a scanty amount of baggage and a couple of prostitutes'.[58]

Reynolds's obsession with immoral earls coincided with an upsurge of interest in the history of the Regency period. There was a strong Regency flavour to the Valentine Baker case. Baker mobilised a group of aristocratic supporters who like Regency rakes 'huzzaed' his public appearances. At the bail hearing in Guildford when his plea for bail was accepted he was cheered by fellow army officers who had packed the court. The paper remarked: 'These "sneaky poltroons" were actually received with a storm of cheers instead of a shower of rotten eggs, such as they deserved.'[59] The images apparent here were of Regency bucks and 'flash' dandies. In depictions of the Marlborough House set in which Baker moved there were unmistakeable echoes of the gilded pleasure-seekers who surrounded the throne of George IV: 'It has been publicly known for a long time that the intimate companions of the Prince of Wales have been dissolute young noblemen who took him, or accompanied him, "about town", visiting places of which he and his fast friends had much better been unacquainted.'[60] There is a strain of the Wilkesite style of political journalism in *Reynolds's* that attacked a system mired in patronage, sinecures, and other sexual and political manifestations of 'Old Corruption'.[61] As part of these exposures the careers of celebrated rogues and rakes were often exhumed. The obituary of the Earl of Lonsdale who died at the age of 85 in 1872 read:

> Lord Lonsdale's early life was one long round of profligacy. He was never so happy as when surrounded by French prostitutes and poodles. Whilst occupying the position of Post-Master General his distribution of patronage was a public scandal. The relations of his various mistresses were all placed in high situations, and some are still living in the enjoyment of large pensions at the public expense. Unfortunately the death of this disreputable, filthy old debauchee will not relieve the country of the burden he placed on it.[62]

Taking their cue from such revelations, in 1869 ballad sellers and street-hawkers on Ludgate Hill used the opportunity provided by the Prince of Wales's alleged involvement in the Mordaunt divorce case to sell lurid accounts of the Queen Caroline divorce scandal embossed with the *Fleurs de Lys* of the heir to the throne.[63] By such means a tangible link with the dissolute past of the Hanoverian Court and of George IV was perpetuated. It reminded the public of the court's inherited predisposition to debauchery, and of the tainted personal lives of the royal hangers-on. Edward himself was rumoured to read it to catch up on the scandal surrounding himself and his paramours. Whatever the truth of this story, the personal history of the Prince of Wales would look very different without *Reynolds's* coverage of his life and its exposure of the involvement of the Prince in the tangled affairs of the Mordaunt family. There is a case to be made for the Mordaunt divorce scandal and the memories it evoked having lastingly tarnished Albert Edward's reputation. The radical press linked all his misdemeanours together and, inferring no smoke without fire, suggested that if he was not guilty on this occasion, he certainly had been in the past and was likely to be so again. Nevertheless, there was more here than simply the revival of traditional Regency images of debauchery and their indiscriminate application to the court followers of the Prince of Wales. In such descriptions the young Prince of Wales appears as a re-incarnation of the youthful George IV. *Reynolds's Newspaper* depicted the heir to the throne as an amoral voluptuary, more intent on his sporting pastimes, shooting, and womanising than the affairs of state. The career of George IV provided a lasting template of royal misdemeanours and a warning for future heirs.[64] In a story by G.W.M. Reynolds, *The Mysteries of the Court of London* from 1850, George IV is haunted in his sleep by the spirits of the wrecked and wretched cast-offs of his previous indiscretions and affairs, amongst them Mrs Fitzherbert, who had married him in secret in the 1780s. Moreover, a baleful authorial voice interjects to promise that one day the excesses of the Prince will be exposed for all to see.[65] *Reynolds's* graduated from criticisms of royalty that merely treated the problem of monarchy as a history lesson, and instead used the memories of the past to probe the rituals, style, and significance of the aristocratic and royal state itself.

For many reformers the loose morals of the aristocratic dandies of the Marlborough House set were of an even more ancient lineage, pre-dating the Regency. Some radicals saw them as a physical inheritance from the tainted bloodstock of William the Conqueror and the 'vast spoilation' that eroded chivalric values.[66] Here the myth of the Norman Yoke took on a physical dimension. Normanism persisted in polluted blood that undermined pretensions to gentility, and stimulated aggressive and anti-social behaviour:

> Show the people that our old nobility is not noble, that its lands are stolen lands – stolen either by force or fraud, show people that the title deeds are rapine, murder, massacre, cheating or court harlotry, dissolve the halo of divinity that surrounds the hereditary title; let the people clearly understand that our present House of Lords is composed largely of the descendants of successful pirates and rogues; do these things and you shatter the romance that keeps the nation numb and spellbound while privilege picks its pocket.[67]

What I would argue for here is the relevance of Reynolds's journalism. Far from being populated simply by the escapist fantasies of utopian and romantic radicals, the pages of his newspaper teemed with essential truths about Victorian society and culture. The paper was popular and widely read, on the grounds that it revealed the social reality behind the manner in which the court, society, and even the monarchy operated. Whilst the glittering ascent of the great noble grandees of the nineteenth century lauded in works like *Society in London* written in 1885 by T.H. Escott, editor of the *Fortnightly Review*, papers like *Reynolds's Newspaper* simultaneously undermined them by depicting them as a degraded and rapacious caste, carrying on the traditions of the Norman freebooters. 'Blood will out' was the watchword of reformers. Seeking explanation for the lustful and deviant behaviour of the aristocracy, *Reynolds's Newspaper* subjected their pedigree to close scrutiny, tracing them back to the bloodthirsty Vikings, the ancestors of the Normans, and the piratical 'vultures' who accompanied the descent on England: 'The proud aristocracy of England are actually descended from the Danes! They are the legitimate issue of this bloody and barbarous people that nobody wishes to acknowledge as ancestors.'[68] The Bakers themselves were descended from pirates and privateers, who consolidated their land-holdings in the Caribbean by armed force and naked thuggery.[69] For other reformers the urbane cosmopolitanism of aristocracy was an illusion, masking the lusts of near-savages. At a meeting of the Land and Labour League on Clerkenwell Green the land reformer Patrick Hennessey drew comparisons between nobles and the Maoris of New Zealand recently defeated in the Maori Wars, and shot 'because they were savages and held vast quantities of land waste' on the model of the British aristocracy.[70] Elsewhere they were compared to the Zulu tribesmen of South Africa, with again reference to their degraded nature, and monopoly of land-holding, or to the notorious Russian boyar nobility. The rack-renting Rosses of Strathcarren in Scotland were memorably dubbed 'The Russians of Ross-shire'.[71]

The combination of lurid sexual intrigue, the rootless, peripatetic nature of the aristocratic *rentier* class, and the element of historical archaism and anachronism evident in images of aristocratic misrule led radicals to seek comparison between nobility and vampirism that reflected the prevalence of such tropes in popular literature. There was something of the vampire motif in the image of Valentine Baker leaning over the passive and prone body of Miss Dickinson. Recent work in literary criticism has highlighted the centrality of aristocracy to the construction of the vampire myth. For contemporaries it was a tempting comparison. The aristocracy literally sucked out the life essence of the poor and the passive to fund a life lived in indolence. The origins of the literary representation of vampirism is in the system of feudal relations between landowner and his tenantry. The vampiric feast provided a metaphor for a predatory exercise of power over the powerless. Again, women featured strongly as victims and objects of debased carnal lusts by rowdy aristocratic debauchers. Thomas Spence spoke of the 'the iron fangs of aristocracy';[72] Ernest Jones luridly described the depredations of Major Robertson of Greenyard, Glencalvie against his tenants and dubbed him 'a greedy old vampire in human shape who has been sucking their life-blood all his days'.[73] For *Reynolds's Newspaper*, Europe was dominated by a caste of 'royal, clerical and aristocratic leeches...all at one time busily sucking at the veins of the people and vampire-like, drawing their life-blood'.[74] As late as 1905, the radical Lancashire dialect poet 'Casey' replied to Lord Stanley's attack on the 'continual blood-sucking on the part of the public servants' by recounting the deeds of aristocratic 'bloodsuckers and blackmailers'.[75] Vampiric images of blood-sucking provided a more robust condemnation of aristocracy than the usual language of 'drones of the hive' familiar from the days of William Cobbett and continued by Joseph Chamberlain into the 1880s.[76] Lassitude, *ennui*, boredom and inertia typified the condition of the vampiric aristocrat once satiated after his nightly depredations. This condition contrasted with the industry and hardwork of the urban and rural poor, who provided replenishment and nutrition for his table.

The maladministration and mismanagement of the Crimean War by a clannish and titled officer class also lingered long in radical memory. It was recalled during the scenes of riotous brother officers demonstrating in support of Valentine Baker at his arraignment in Guildford.[77] Baker was on his way to dine with the Duke of Cambridge, the famously inept Commander-in-chief of the British Army in the Crimea, when he assaulted Miss Dickinson.[78] Moreover, two of the chief protagonists of the war, Lord Lucan and Sir Thomas Steele, attended the trial; Steele was prepared to testify as a character witnesses on his behalf. The Liberal/ radical *Weekly Dispatch* ridiculed Baker's own pretensions to Crimean hero status, deriding his military achievements as fraudulent in comparison to Miss Dickinson's courage in fending off her attacker. She 'fought far more bravely for her honour than Colonel Baker for the "Bubble Reputation" in the Crimean War'.[79] In addition the Baker case continued many of the debates set in train by the Crimea. In 1871 under the Cardwell reforms the purchase system for commissions had been abolished, but questions remained about the competence and efficiency of existing officers with pre-1871 rank.[80] The appearance of so many senior officers at the trial fostered the image of a narrow officer caste under siege. Baker's boisterous supporters symbolised the worst aspects of an officer corps that treated their position as an inherited fiefdom, rather than as a sacred trust. For some radicals the warlike spirit and aggression that had characterized the Norman Freebooters was now turned inwards and internalised in times of peace. For others, aristocracy was inadequate and impotent at the very task in which it was meant to excel: placing its swords at the service of the king. Olive Anderson has written that 'In 1855 the ultimate historic defence of aristocracy – its supreme value in time of war – received for the first time in England an outright denial.'[81] Degraded and softened by lives of dissolute pleasure, aristocratic officers had become hopeless sybarites, interested only in the satisfaction of the basest instincts. A debased and venal officer class made up of the idle younger sons of the aristocracy had long been an object of radical attack. In 1855 at the height of the Crimean War, the Chartist Ernest Jones campaigned in the interests of the other ranks against a representative type of officer which he described as:

A fellow who has never smelt powder in his life, because he is the honourable Mr Nincompoop, or Lord Augustus Cabbageheart, or the son of Scrapecorner the Usurer, buys his commission, purchases grade after grade in the service, and with his dirty money, which perhaps he filched as an army contractor out of cheating the soldiers, obtains the power of tyrannizing over a little host of gallant fellows, breaking their hearts by tyranny, and mutilating their bodies by torture.[82]

Moreover, they ruled the other ranks by fear and the discipline of the lash. Hostility to corporal punishment in the army was in a long tradition that portrayed aristocratic officers as worthless and unfeeling in their exercise of a neo-feudal discipline over the heirs of the Saxon peasantry.[83] Crucifixion imagery abounded in representations of spread-eagled soldiers receiving vicious punishment for relatively minor misdemeanours. One private, Frederick White, who died from a severe beating of 150 lashes for attacking a sergeant, became a martyr for the movement. His fate established the representative image of a plebeian Calvary suffered in military service.[84] Many of these images of sadistic and tyrannical officers lingered around the Baker case. For *The Weekly Dispatch* Baker's actions amounted to a declaration of war against the people by undisciplined officers, causing them to reply: 'If they dare to insult our wives and daughters they will be kept out of harm's way in the "stone jug" of the county gaol; and if they go very far, their fate will be the crank and the treadmill, which anyone who has ever visited a model prison can assure the honourable and gallant profession is no joke at all, but very hard labour indeed, too heavy to be borne by shoulders only accustomed to gilt epaulettes.'[85]

IV

The world inhabited by the Victorian aristocracy was increasingly an urban one. The correlation between the dangers facing women that lurked in this urban sphere, and the transgressive behaviour of a debased urban aristocracy mirrored the social and cultural evolution of the British aristocracy into a predominantly urban class. Seen in these terms, the aristocracy was an adaptable financial power that transported its portable capital into the urban *milieux* of Paris, London, and New York. Moreover, as Amy Srebnick has commented, the great non-industrial cities were increasingly symbolic of the erosion of social relationships, the atom-isation of society, and the proliferation of arbitrary victimhood.[86] This was the urban world in which the peripatetic territorial aristocracy was able to prey on the weak and the helpless. Radicals were acutely aware of the changes to industrial Britain that fostered the emergence of a metropolitan *rentier* class living off its rural and urban investments. As the radical press was keen to point out, the metropolitan aristocracy was an artificial creation, displaced from the countryside and profiting from the pre-industrial nature of London. During the season bracketed by the end of fox-hunting in March and the beginning of the great grouse-hunting meets in August it donned an elaborate social finery paid for out of the pockets of the working poor. London became inextric-ably associated in the popular mind with unaccountable aristocratic excess, showy opulence, and a rapacious uncontrolled landlordism. *The Single Tax* commented: 'Nearly everyone of the principal London landlords is now a peer. No other metropolis is to such an extent in aristocratic hands.'[87] Some joined hands with developers to rent out land, and claw back the 'unearned increment' for further investment. In 1909 Lloyd George included condemnation of aristocratic investors who had drained and developed the 'golden swamps' between the Lea and the Thames in his Limehouse speech against landownership.[88] George Bernard Shaw commented: 'Confiscation of capital, spoliation of house-holds, annihilation of incentive, everything that the most ignorant and credulous fundholder ever charged against the socialist, rages openly in London, which begins to ask itself whether it exists and toils only for the typical duke and his celebrated jockey and his famous racehorse.'[89] Living off their venture capital the great aristocracy kept up immense London town houses, staffed with armies of flunkeys, and created an infrastructure of leisure that existed to service their needs. Writers like William Thackeray and Douglas Jerrold were savagely satirical of the great metropolitan lords and their uniformed 'flunkeys', depicting a closed aristocratic world policed by magnificently attired factotums.[90] Thomas Ainge Devyr wrote: 'The immense population of 2 and 3 millions is supported by the unclean drippings from these fortunes, which in their collection beggar and starve the whole face of the country where these fortunes are produced. My Lord has his gaming house, his mistresses of every kind. So has my Lord's valet, and groom and foot-man on in humbler scale: but the whole is brought and kept together mainly by the land rents, and such portion of government plunder as is consumed in the metropolis.'[91] Visiting London for the first time the Chartist Robert Lowery depicted such unbridled aristocratic dominance as determining the character of the metropolis and converting it into a servile centre of fawning aristocratic acolytes and their corrupt hangers-on. He described it as a 'sink of corruption' where 'the wealth of the aristocracy was spent … and the artisan lived by their extravagance and, therefore, could hardly be expected to be so virtuous as the workmen in their own provincial towns'.[92] In addition, a concentration of aristocrats in the capital pushed up rents, led to a monopoly of civic amenities in areas of aristocratic dominance, and accentuated the social and cultural gulf separating East from West London. *Freedom* reported the impact of a literal 'gentrification' on the more opulent areas of London: 'Now park and park improvements should be, we would think, a blessing to the community; but unfortunately they turn out to be just the opposite. As usual, the richer classes monopolise for their dwellings all those thoroughfares near the park, which results in rise in rent all through the district, and metropolitan street improvements mean more houses pulled down, and consequently more crowding in the streets remaining.'[93] Where such aristocratic estates proliferated they were frequently gated to exclude, apparently vindicating 'the seigneurial rights to treat some of the populous districts of London as if they were private gardens'.[94] For many radicals the great aristocrats seemingly promoted urban growth and expansion at whim. Elsewhere, where urban expansion impinged on the great estates of the Home Counties, aristocratic dynasts stood accused of blocking the expansion of towns that closed down the possibilities for accompanying social and sanitary improvements in the rural districts.[95]

The prestigious social role of aristocracy in London was linked to their more visible presence in the finance and money markets of the empire. London was not only capital of the United Kingdom, it was also an imperial capital. Increasingly, empire provided an outlet for the energies and surplus funds of the great dynastic houses. Both Samuel Baker and Valentine Baker had colonial backgrounds in Ceylon. Following his disgrace, Valentine Baker returned to colonial service and commanded the army of the Khedive of Egypt. *Reynolds's Newspaper* sensed that the emerging cult of imperialism created the perfect conditions in which aristocracy might flourish. It is a reflection of the cosmopolitan instincts of Reynolds that he should have considered the overseas dimension to aristocracy and highlighted the role of displaced aristocratic administrators in this way. From the 1850s onwards *Reynolds's Newspaper* wrote frequently about the impact of imperial growth on the power elite in Britain. Anticipating many of the critics of imperialism in the 1890s, he drew attention to the titled bond-holders and colonial millionaires who profited from the wider imperial system and augmented their fortunes at home with the plunder of empire. Such images were an integral part of attacks on the aristocracy. These were the 'empire pirates' much despised in the Irish radical press.[96] Writing in 1856 'John Hampden' saw the role of aristocratic administrators as emblematic of 'how everything – crown, charter, church, House of Commons, crown lands, public charities, and even the vast extent of our own colonies, are engrossed and enjoyed by this mighty and all-grasping aristocracy'. For him their influence imperiled, rather than buttressed the imperial mission. He ascribed the loss of the American colonies in 1783 to 'the aristocracy of England, stupefied by luxury and overloaded with national plunder'.[97] Moreover, *Reynolds's Newspaper* interpreted the trappings of colonialism as an important aspect of the public face of the aristocratic elite. Colonial servants surrounding the queen, foreign princelings abasing themselves before the royal retinue, and the new currency of imperial titles added to the pomp and finery of state occasions. The paper attributed the broader cause of the expansion of empire in the 1870s to aristocratic machinations for the acquisition of new territories ripe for exploitation. It concluded in a verdict on Beacons-fieldism: 'And how many millions is to be drawn from us to pay for glory? The old aristocratic brain is at work in our midst. The crown seeks for a new lease in a blaze of military pomp, and in the exercise of prerogatives. The feudal hereditary aristocracy sees in an imperial system of government a means to perpetuate their power, and to reduce to slavery those who live by labour.'[98] For radicals, imperialism demeaned those who promoted it, as well as those who witnessed it. Too much imperial splendour pointed up the moral failings of royalty, courtiers, and the imperial system that sustained them, whilst presaging impending disaster when the Prince of Wales ascended to the throne.[99]

As part of the process of imperialism Reynolds was also a shrewd observer of attempts to transplant the British social hierarchy to the colonies. Distance and loyalism, it was believed, made colonists susceptible to the lure of rank. The white settler colonies in particular were perceived in the words of E. Carton Booth as 'Another England' where customs, the built environment, and local industry possessed 'a strong family likeness to the same things at home'.[100] Here a system of governors, the vice-regal representatives, and colonial honours created by service to the empire from the 1850s were interpreted in the pages of *Reynolds's News* as merely an attempt to replicate the English class system abroad.

As David Cannadine has pointed out, the theatrical aspect of empire is apparent in the glamour and opulence of imperial hierarchy that appealed to the atavistic feudal inclinations of transplanted colonial rulers.[101] In New South Wales, William Charles Wentworth, Chair of the 1853 Select Committee that drafted the New South Wales Constitution and staunch advocate of a colonial peerage, portrayed the dominions as a social and financial salvation to the landed aristocracy, steadily declining in influence and power in the Mother Country.[102] Throughout the Australian colonies the radical press advised vigilance against the imported trappings of aristocracy, suggesting settlers 'will awaken presently to find that they have slumbered too long; to find the good old English gentleman over them; the good old English squire over them, the good old English lord over them, the good old English aristocracy rolling around them in cushioned carriages, scarcely deigning to rest their eyes on the "common people" who toil, starve and rot for them'.[103] Images of this nature were suffused with ancestral memories of the British aristocracy and of the 'remittance men' transported to the colonies by their families alongside convicts and poor settlers. Ged Martin has pointed out that the landowning elite of the Australian colonies lagged behind the 'mother country' in a 'Merrie Australia', in which memories of an unreformed political system, and social customs such as duelling that had long died out at 'Home', were preserved. Even the term 'squattocracy', much used about the large Australian landowners, carried echoes of the rural British past.[104] Colonial radicals also high-lighted the peripatetic nature of the regimes created by gubernatorial rule. Professional salaried governorships provided an international tour of duty for colonial administrators who performed circuits of service in the Crown colonies. Most criticism, however, centred on the freelance aristocratic bureaucrats sent to the more prosperous self-governing colonies. Once in post they were difficult to remove, and were often accused of venality, fortune-hunting, and asset-stripping in the empire. Drawing on images of an itinerant and vagabond poor, John Bright famously christened the empire 'a gigantic system of outdoor relief for the aristocracy' that serviced the needs of the rapacious travelling entourages of displaced domestic dynasts.[105] The colonial press echoed the hostility to imported and pretentious aristocrats found in the domestic press in Britain. *The People's Advocate*, an Eastern Australian Chartist journal in exile, wrote: 'Australia is still to be a milch cow, like the colonies generally, for aristocratic sucklings, and the hangers-on of the ministry.'[106] As in Britain, roistering colonial aristocrats received as much negative exposure as their county cousins at home. Individual malefactors were singled out for execration in the pages of the radical and Labourist press, and their conduct was judged on the grounds of morality, and social and political propriety. At the time of the appointment of Lord Hampden as Governor General of New South Wales in 1897, John Norton's paper *The Truth* recalled of his predecessor Sir Charles Fitzroy:

> One of the numerous bastards of the bastard house of Grafton . . . was even a more libidinous, lecherous, drunken beast than his foul-mouthed, rotten-carcassed father. He came to us from the Nigger plantations of the West Indies, bringing with him his wife of that other house of royal bastards the Duke of Richmond. He was at once a fool, a fraud, and a fornicator. He was denounced by Dr. Lang as the worthy exponent of all the vices of his infamous ancestor, the Duke of Grafton, pilloried by Junius. When drunk, he managed to kill his wife, by upsetting a coach, which he would insist upon driving. He and his sons debauched all the girls they dared to tamper with, the sons sharing the conquests of the father, and *vice versa*.[107]

For Norton, the name of Hampden and the aristocratic vice surrounding the role of the governors mocked the traditions of English liberties symbolised by John Hampden's role in the English Civil War and aspired to by many Australian reformers. Unsurprisingly, *Reynolds's Newspaper* played well to a colonial audience. The paper's hostility to 'titled rogues and ruffians' travelled effectively to areas administered by appointed governors and ageing court favourites. Correspondence in its letter columns demonstrates that the paper had a considerable following in Australia, New Zealand, and the Cape colonies. In Australia it inspired at least one direct imitator: *The Truth*, 'the Australia *Reynolds's*', edited by the emigrant British radical John Norton, which tried to match its hostility to monarchy and the colonial office during a similar period of royal unpopularity in Australia. In his description of Queen Victoria as 'flabby, fat and flatulent' there remains something of the robust style of *Reynolds's News* absorbed during his boyhood in Bristol.[108] The radical Australian nationalist and aspiring French Bonapartist, J.F. Archibald, who put his own unique Jacobin-derived stamp on *The Bulletin* newspaper, has also been credited with finding inspiration in the paper.[109] The raucous and radical culture that grew up around *The Bulletin* fuelled the radical nationalism of the 1880s in Australia that, by limiting governor's salaries and curtailing the vice-regal representatives and royal honours connected with the Colonial Office, sought a step-by-step approach to an Australian republic.[110]

Those who have written about the anti-aristocratic politics of G.W.M. Reynolds have tended to see in him the survival of an older and more traditional style of politics, less concerned with the changes in industrial society and more interested in stasis within the Victorian state. Radicals were, however, more closely attuned to the rhythms of a changing aristocracy than is often realised. Consideration of the recent historiography of Victorian Britain returns aristocracy to the heart of the economy, government, and cultural activity of Victorian towns. What emerges from a close scrutiny of G.W.M. Reynolds's journalism is a subtle and sophisticated understanding of the distribution of power within Victorian government. Mediated through the journalism of this radical newspaper the state appeared as monarchical, patronage-ridden, and still driven by the demands of landed society. Unsurprisingly supporters of Henry George regarded Reynolds as a 'John the Baptist' for the Georgeite land campaign at the end of the nineteenth century. After all, why bother with a monarchy that was losing its power to influence the executive, or with an aristocracy that was giving way to an upwardly-mobile urban bourgeoisie, unless the picture of nineteenth-century culture is actually rather more nuanced and complicated than the traditional readings suggest. In this sense, Reynolds's depiction of Victorian culture might be seen as more accurately reflective of the revisionist approach of a new set of late twentieth-century historians who maintain the continuities, rather than disjuncture, between 'Victorianism' and the nineteenth century's Regency forebears. In short nineteenth-century culture as portrayed by *Reynolds's* is now more recognisable to a generation reared on the notion of continuity with the eighteenth century, and who have learnt to challenge the canon of 'great men' and the authenticity of defining and 'watershed' moments.[111] Reynolds's personal experience of radicalism informed most of his musings on the politics of mid-Victorian Britain. As a young man he had been a disciple of Bronterre O'Brien and maintained an interest in the land in the pages of *Reynolds's Newspaper* where some residual O'Brienism lingered. Reynolds's emphasis on landed wealth above all displays a concern for the social basis of power and prosperity that provided the superstructure of the royal state. More recent analysis of landed society in the nineteenth century has emphasised the continuing importance of landed wealth within the Victorian elite. As David Cannadine in particular has demonstrated, the key to power and influence continued to derive from the formal structures of land-holding. Such territorial power was augmented by wealth acquired from the ownership of land in the large towns. Families such as the Mosleys, the Devonshires and the Dukes of Norfolk accumulated vast sums from their ownership of land in the new industrial centres which they rented out or sold to new urban entrepreneurs. Here Reynolds's criticism of the landed interest, and of the original land confiscations at the time of the Norman Conquest from which such wealth derived, echoed the ideas of Paine, Ricardo, and others who maintained that all other sectors of the economy were squeezed to provide revenue for landowners. The same point was made by Reynolds's contemporary Henry George (like Reynolds a fierce republican) who two years after Reynolds's death toured Britain to promote a message of hostility to the existing injustices of landownership already familiar to the readers of *Reynolds's News*. When George lectured on the theme of the 'Robbers of the Poor' or was greeted with banners marked 'God Gave the Land to the People' he was making substantially the same point made by Reynolds over many years from the late 1840s onwards.[112] These links between Georgeism and Reynolds's crusading style of journalism deserve a more extended treatment. Versions of George's classic *Progress and Poverty* first appeared in 1879 in the year Reynolds died.

Reynolds's Newspaper provided a critical corrective to the cult of aristocracy in the nineteenth century. The fact that it was the favoured reading of the Prince of Wales, an object of its attacks, suggests it was frequently consulted as much for its titillation-value as for its politics. None the less *Reynolds's* provided a civic education for many of its readers who were ill-disposed to the exactions of monarchy, privilege, and aristocracy on the public purse. It shaped the attitudes of early Labour leaders, heightened awareness of unaccoutable privilege, and campaigned for greater public scrutiny of the private and public lives of the aristocracy. It should not be judged for its failure to bring about the British republic. Rather, *Reynolds's News* stood at the heart of a penumbra of unrespectable belief that remained defiantly outside the existing political consensus and paradoxically shaped many of the agendas that prompted the royal family to reform itself from the middle years of the nineteenth century.

2

'The Apostle of Plunder': The Influence of Henry George in England Reconsidered

> Go to any workman's meeting, be it convoked by Tories or Whigs, by Radicals or Socialists, and listen to the speakers. Let them speak about what they like. They may be supported by the audience or not, but let them, however incidentally, touch on the land question and attack the great landowners, and immediately a storm of applause will break out in the audience. Go to a meeting of Londoners and denounce there the owners of the soil of the metropolis; go to the miners and denounce the mining royalties – and you are sure of finding one who supports you, however mixed the audience.[1]

> The rain is falling which moistens and fertilises the whole face of the country. The air is free to all, and the light is direct from heaven; the aristocracy cannot bottle up the sunlight and the air. In this open air it is fitting for us to demand an equally broad share of liberty which, to the Englishman, is in the air he breathes; without it, he dies.[2]

Contemplating his pessimistic view of the future in *Brave New World*, Aldous Huxley speculated that there might be a sane path for man's future development that he had overlooked. 'In this community', he wrote, 'economics would be decentralist and Henry-Georgian, politics Kropotkinesque and co-operative.'[3] Huxley's pairing of the American economist Henry George and Kropotkin recalls the celebrity status of George in the years between 1880 and 1930. Now almost forgotten, or dismissed as methodologically and conceptually unsound, George occupies an uncertain position in the history of radicalism. Despite bridging the worlds of economic thought and political activism, and offering British radicals their most inspirational text since Thomas Paine, there has been no major study of his life since the mid-1950s. Even after Steven B. Cord's attempted rehabilitation of Georgeite economics in 1965, he is still usually dismissed as a 'crank' or the 'dreamer' of Cord's title.[4] For historians of British radicalism his emphasis on land reform symbolises the under-developed nature of British socialism. This follows the view of some of his contemporaries. Walter Besant wrote: 'The book he wrote was one of those which precede Revolution, but do not preach Revolution.'[5] For the generation who built the Labour Party his ideas were compromised by his apparent connection with Liberalism. For historians of ideas, he is quite simply a fossil, expressing outmoded palliatives to the new economic problems posed by industrialisation during the nineteenth century. Marx and his followers dismissed him as someone who fundamentally misunderstood the relationship between capital and labour.[6] Georgeism therefore represents a puzzle. At one level popular in the closing decades of the nineteenth century, but apparently much less significant in hindsight and diminishing as the twentieth century progressed, by the 1930s it had become a byword for eccentricity, associated with the declining years of Liberalism and with Single Tax fundamentalism.

Yet for contemporaries George was the 'philosopher king' of the nineteenth century. His major work *Progress and Poverty* was selling 400,000 copies annually by the end of 1884 and has been continuously in print since its publication in 1880.[7] Amongst his readers were Queen Victoria, urged to consult the book by Dr Randall Davidson, future Primate of England, and Tolstoy, who dreamt about him.[8] Moreover George's tours of Great Britain in 1881, 1882, 1884, and 1889 were sell-out affairs that galvanised a new generation of political radicals.[9] George Bernard Shaw testified to the power of his oratory after attending one of his meetings,[10] and reformers as assorted as Keir Hardie, Philip Snowden, and Robert Blatchford were Georgeites first, and representatives of Labour second. In Britain much of the early hostility to 'socialism' was precipitated by the spasm of opposition to his visit, and grew out of the misidentification of socialist doctrine with his land reform ideas. This chapter seeks to reconcile these conflicting images of George by placing his Single Tax notions in context, by questioning prevailing assumptions about George and his relationship with Liberalism, and by recapturing a radical milieu that distrusted government, exalted the Jeffersonian idea of the small proprietor, and campaigned for the abdication of the great landowners. In so doing it raises questions about the role of George in relation to recent continuity debates within radicalism, and examines the relationship between Georgeism, Liberalism, and a newly emergent Labourism during a period of incipient Liberal decline.

Progress and Poverty begins with a vision of hopes blighted. Concentrating on the technological and commercial achievements of the nineteenth century, it emphasises 'the persistence of poverty, amid advancing wealth' and questions the benefits of a system that by depressing overall wage levels increased the disparities of wealth between rich and poor in overcrowded cities. Contemporaries commented on the apocalyptic tone of the book. In its opening pages George prophesied social breakdown, and the collapse of civil society as outcasts gathered outside the citadels of the nineteenth century's cultural achievements: 'Upon streets lighted with gas and patrolled by uniformed policemen, beggars wait for the passer-by, and in the shadow of college, and library, and museum are gathering the more hideous Huns and fiercer Vandals of whom Macauley prophesied.'[11] George's solution to such social problems was a straightforward one. Drawing on the Ricardian doctrine that all wealth derives from land, George saw the antidote to poverty in a transformation of land tenure. Land, he suggested, should be available to all. He proposed a single tax on the site value of land replacing all other taxation and forcing proprietors to put it to its full use, or to sell it on to those who were willing to improve it. This he hoped would lead to a lifting of the tax burden on the poor, the restoration of small peasant proprietorship, and result in the systematised break-up of the great aristocratic estates in the British Isles.[12] Behind his ideas were the vestiges of Cobdenite thinking on the land.[13] The intellectual roots of Georgeism lay in Cobden and J.S. Mill's distinction between productive and unproductive wealth. For classical political economists in the nineteenth century economic surplus seemed to be drained off by unproductive landowners. If landowners were forced to be more productive by a single tax on land values, and the poor could be re-settled on the land, the glut on the labour market in cities might be reduced, and the value of wages increased. It thus acted as a possible redress for the problems of both town and countryside. Moreover, a single land tax would lead to the abolition of income tax and indirect taxation, creating the 'Free Breakfast Table' of long radical lineage.[14] For Cobdenites attracted by George's ideas the Single Tax would finally destroy the last great unjust monopoly, that on land. Mirroring the injustices of that monopoly, Georgeism was unforgiving of landowners, and postulated a non-compensatory system for those unable to meet the demands of the Single Tax. It was this feature of his plans that led to George's nick-name: 'The Apostle of Plunder'.

Georgeism emerged in answer to the land revelations and disclosures of the limited distribution of small rural proprietorship made in the 1870s. In 1872 Lord Derby commissioned a land survey to counter radical arguments about aristocratic dominance of the shires. Reformers from John Bright onwards levelled the accusation that the land mass of the British Isles was concentrated in the hands of a narrow elite. The figure of 30,000 was traditionally used and became notorious as an index of narrow oligarchic rule. Bright famously declared that 'fewer than 150 men own half the land of England'.[15] The 'New Domesday' Survey provided ammunition for the researches of John Bateman, who demonstrated that this was a considerable understatement. Confirming the narrowness, rather than the wide diffusion of land-holding in the United Kingdom and Ireland, the survey revealed that a much smaller proportion of the population, barely 7000, controlled some four-fifths of the land acreage of the United Kingdom. Bateman's disclosures added weight to the anti-aristocratic platform. The Survey became the bible of radical land reformers, much quoted and revered as a revelation of injustice. Bateman reported that the work was frequently consulted in London clubs: 'The copy of the work at the "Ultratorium" was reduced to rags and tatters within a fortnight of its arrival – a lesson which was not wasted on the library committee of my own club, who caused the book to be so bound as to defy anything short of a twelve-year-old schoolboy.'[16] Armed with Bateman's disclosures, by the early 1880s radicals were able to declaim with confidence against aristocratic monopoly of the land. The Georgeite MP for Salford, Arthur Arnold, arrived 'at the astonishing result that the representative owners of four-fifths of the soil of the United Kingdom could be placed within the compass of a single voice in one of the great public halls of the country. The landlords of more than 52,000,000 of acres might meet together in the Free Trade Hall of Manchester, and discuss the accuracy of these statements.'[17] Inspired by Bateman, Georgeites saw the movement as a purgative of the sectional interests of aristocracy that sullied government and manipulated the political system for its own ends. The Duke of Buccleuch, revealed by Bateman's survey as the largest landowner in Britain, became a byword for this unjust land monopoly, owning land 'over which he can ride thirty miles in a straight line'.[18]

George's strongest impact, however, was in the towns. Georgeite land policies are often misinterpreted as a solution to the problems of arable farming. In fact they were designed primarily to tackle issues of urban, rather than rural, living. From the 1880s high unemployment and fears about the 'degeneration' of urban man inspired by Boothite revelations about the condition of the poor in the East End of London fostered a moral panic about the fabric of urban life. Contemporaries believed that the crisis on the land diminished the potential of the fitter rural population to replenish tainted urban stock.[19] For many reformers the phenomenon of aristocratic ownership of prime sites in towns and cities provided a barrier to the development of municipal ownership, and prohibitively increased urban rent. Georgeites often claimed that there were incentives in urban areas for proprietors to subsist off ground rents and leave building land stagnant and undeveloped.[20] Moreover, titled landlords inflicted inflated rents on the shopocracy which was in turn passed on to the consumer in the form of higher food prices. Jane Cobden-Unwin noted relative indifference to Georgeism in the countryside, but suggested: 'In the towns it is different. The municipalities, conscious of their great opportunities for effective social work and at their wit's end for means to finance them, are generally eager for the power to rate vacant sites and undeveloped sites on their capital values.'[21] George's followers argued that the stabilisation of municipal finances would do much to alleviate poverty, and reduce endemic urban problems like crime. Urban Georgeism thus provided an antidote to aristocratically inspired emigration policies and Malthusian over-population doctrines in Britain's towns and cities.[22] The campaigns of urban Georgeites set the tone for the later land agendas of Liberalism. During the Liberal Land Campaign of 1909–1910, Lloyd George chose the great urban centres of Limehouse and Newcastle for set-piece speeches highlighting the urban implications of land-holding.[23]

Georgeism is difficult to locate within late nineteenth-century politics. As a doctrine it was always inchoate. Georgeite scholars have identified at least three different strains of Georgeism.[24] Whilst drawing particularly on Cobdenite free trade ideas, Georgeism clearly had ramifications for all those concerned with the re-distribution of rural proprietorship, either to individual farmers or to the state. In the late nineteenth century it expressed a desire for the pastoral redemption of the British race. Beyond Georgeism proper was a penumbra of fringe organisations advocating communal living, small allotment schemes, town planning, land nationalisation, and the sequestration of crown lands. During this period most movements rooted in self-sufficiency showed a tinge of Georgeism.[25] Charles Gide in *Political Economy*, the definitive economic textbook of the day, saw little difference in practice between the two systems of 'Single Tax' and Land Nationalisation (or more properly compulsory state purchase of unused and waste land).[26] Those who have discerned in the tensions between the Georgeite English and Scottish Land

Restoration Leagues, and the Land Nationalisation Society a fracture line between Liberalism and socialism, have made an unconvincing case. The membership of the three organisations overlapped, and *Land and Labour*, the journal of the Land Nationalisation Society acknowledged that: 'The two methods...are not antagonistic, but at the most alternatives... for the forcing open of the land to use which one method proposes to do directly, is exactly what the other proposes to do indirectly, and the practically revisable rent is only the Single Tax under another name.'[27] Theorists of the two approaches to land reform appreciated the similarities, noting that they constituted a break with the pure Cobdenite aim of reform of entail and primogeniture, and sought kindred remedies to low wages and pauperism. The land nationaliser A.R. Wallace was a great admirer of George's work, even recommending it to his colleague Charles Darwin.[28] The influential role of Helen Taylor, John Stuart Mill's step daughter, in introducing George to British radical circles also brought him into contact with the ideas of the later, collectivist Mill on land, still expounded by Taylor at land reform meetings in the 1890s.[29] A movement that encompasses an economic critique, elements of sect, with characteristics of a mass political agitation is not easily compressed within traditional explanatory categories like parties or movements. This may account for the recent paucity of historical analysis of the organisation. The Single Tax is best understood as a cipher, a catch-all banner unfurled against aristocracy that epitomised the injustices, imbalances and historical wrongdoing of Britain's 'territorial magnates'. It occurs within the programmes of both Liberalism and Labourism during these years, and constitutes the last major attempt to resolve the nineteenth-century land question.

For historians the popular support for Georgeite ideas remains problematic. There has been a tendency to dismiss Georgeism as a 'fad' or even as a sect, connected with land millenarianism and end-of-century angst. This reading views Georgeism as nostalgic and anti-modern, describing the movement as populated with rural fantasists and 'back to the land' fundamentalists.[30] Less contentious is Georgeism's connection with progressive taxation measures. In the hands of the Liberals, Georgeite ideas are often seen as part of a broader debate about the economic implications of state intervention. Here George is bracketed with L.T. Hobhouse, J.A. Hobson, and Charles Masterman as part of a grouping within the New Liberalism that sought a limited redistribution of wealth by reducing indirect taxation, exploring social welfare reform, and squeezing the unearned increment of land for the good of the community.[31] This view stands in fundamental opposition to a more traditional reading of George that locates his ideas within the ambit of a declining and fragmented Liberalism. In this reading the structural weaknesses within the Liberal Party are stressed, and Georgeism is portrayed as a vehicle for a backward-looking Cobdenism, mired in the past, and dependent on traditional Liberal slogans that rallied the faithful, but increasingly failed to connect with the electors at a time when the New Liberalism was moving towards a more social democratic consensus. This places Georgeism within a broader debate about Liberal decline, in which his ideas are portrayed as emblematic of a revived Cobdenism, blocking reform, preventing the exploration of non-traditional Liberal strategies, and failing to stem the haemorrhage of urban electors deserting Liberalism for the Labour Party.[32] Fabian radicals like Cecil Chesterton saw Georgeism as a conscious distraction amongst Liberals, concentrating radical energies on the 'land robber' and distracting attention away from the more deadly 'capitalist robber': 'It is the capitalist, not the landlord who is the most active and dangerous enemy of the labourer, and the talk about "the land monopoly" is merely a clever if somewhat transparent dodge to the part of [the Liberals] to divert public indignation from himself to his sleeping partner in exploitation.'[33] Cobden's daughter, Jane Cobden-Unwin, made substantially the same point, remarking: 'not a few people probably regard the abolition of private property in land as the most effective barrier *against* socialism'.[34] Finally the Georgeite presence within Labourism has also been explored. Where Georgeism surfaced in the early Labour Party, it is sometimes argued, it fulfilled the role of a half-way house between radical Liberalism and something more. The analogy here is with a revolving door. Many early Labour reformers once exposed to Georgeite ideas, absorbed them, rejected them, and then moved on to a more socialist future in the Independent Labour Party (ILP).[35] This is at the core of George Bernard Shaw's view of George as 'stopped on the threshold of socialism'.[36] Georgeism emerges from this analysis as shifting and insubstantial. For David Matless land reform was a forgotten avenue of Labour advancement, rejected in the 1920s as Labour increasingly recast itself as the party of the urban masses and became amnesiac about its erstwhile zeal for land reform. By the 1930s it had almost entirely abandoned rural issues to the Tories and vacated the rural constituency.[37]

To account for the popularity of Henry Georgeism is to enter the world of late nineteenth-century autodidact culture. George himself symbolised the best features of autodidacticism.[38] An entirely self-educated scholar who had served at sea in merchant ships, travelled America as a hobo, and visited Melbourne during the Gold Rush, he portrayed himself as a seer whose unconventional route to knowledge had equipped him with a privileged insight into the inner workings of society. The secrets of Georgeism could only be revealed through a similar programme of study, contemplation, and instruction.[39] The size and length of *Progress and Poverty* contributed to this process. The inaccessibility and sometimes tortuous prose of the book were part of its mystique as a document with a revelatory impact. The fact that George was an unofficial economist, working outside the academy whose ideas were often held up to ridicule by the conventional thinkers of the day and who was heckled off the stage at the Oxford Union, only increased his image as an honest man who spoke an unacknowledged truth.[40] Critics of *Progress and Poverty* tended to be dismissive of its status as debating club fodder; writing at the height of Henry George fever, E.G. Fitzgibbon sneered at its cult status amongst 'asses' bridge juvenile debating society orators'.[41] For ardent Georgeites, however, *Progress and Poverty* provided an exercise in the retrieval of the people's history. Land reformers hoped to correct a situation in which landlordism thrived on ignorance of titles, duties, landlord responsibility, and the fake pedigrees of usurping families. In the Georgeite introduction to the land reform writings of William Ogilvie, D.C. Macdonald wrote that 'in order to perpetuate landlord serfdom it is necessary to keep our mothers systematically ignorant of their children's birthright'.[42] In its analysis of land confiscations, evictions, tithe exactions, and villages scattered by rapacious landowners, *Progress and Poverty* catalogued the atrocities of a suffering yeomanry, and rekindled a burning sense of injustice at the process of its destruction (see Appendix 2). For Georgeites this was a re-education necessary to sustain the movement, recruit followers, and pave the way for a purified social order following the imposition of the Single Tax. Georgeite newspaper like *The Single Tax* and a vast array of land reform pamphlets therefore fulfilled a basically educational and instructive role. To enhance this process Georgeism catered for all levels of understanding. In the 1890s specialist puzzle books were prepared for children featuring shape games in which landlordism was depicted as a rat, and its nemesis appeared in the form of a cat, gradually revealed, that symbolised the power and adaptability of the Single Tax. This was the meaning behind the enigmatic banner carried by the children of the Single Tax MP, Josiah Wedgwood, at land reform demonstrations: 'Have you seen the cat?'[43] In addition, Georgeite ideas were marketed in the form of popular board games. In the 1900s, the Maryland Quaker, Lizzie Magie, patented a game called 'The Landlord's Game' as an educational tool that highlighted the inequities of landownership, and in later incarnations became the basis for Monopoly. There was occasionally an element of conspiracy theory evident in such material, in which a true understanding of the secret forces manipulating the economy shed light on the problems of the past and of the future.

At the heart of the appeal of Georgeism was the continuing popularity of the American democratic ideal. Admiration for American democratic liberties had a long pedigree within British radicalism. For British reformers Georgeism was in a direct line of inheritance from Jeffersonian democracy.[44] Viewed in these terms, Georgeism was simply a continuation of an older style of radical culture that looked to America for inspiration in the purification of democratic institutions. America offered up the vision of a meritocracy that lacked a resident aristocracy, had no state church, and provided a utopia for the small proprietor. Ernest Jones wrote of the contrast between British soldiers rewarded for their service with 'a wretched medal' whereas American veterans received a stake in society with 'a happy cottage'.[45] Recently, however, there has been a marked tendency to see such sentiments as emblematic of an earlier phase of radicalism, still important in the 1840s, but of much less significance following the end of the American Civil War, and the increasing recognition of America's shallow materialism, coupled with the exposure of corrupt Tammany Hall politicians.[46] Anti-Georgeites frequently accused him of plotting to import a similar flawed American style of politics into Britain.[47] To suggest an end to previous radical visions of an idealised 'Yankeedom' is perhaps to understate the enduring appeal of American meritocratic values. Much of the popularity of George in Britain was rooted in the frontier inheritance he apparently symbolised. Newspaper reports of George's visit in 1884 portray him inaccurately as a Davy Crockett figure, hardened in the wilderness, and offering the same cheap land proposals that had fuelled the land rushes on the frontier under the Homestead Acts.[48] There is evidence that he may have artfully conspired in this image of himself as a 'plain, straight-thinking American' in the mould of Lincoln or of General Grant.[49] For many British radicals George represented the common transatlantic inheritance of liberty rooted in John Locke, memories of 1688, and the achievements of the American Revolution. Georgeite hagiography made much of the proximity of his birthplace in Philadelphia to the historic State House 'of revolutionary fame' where the Declaration of Independence was signed.[50] For the Scottish Georgeite D.C. Macdonald, George was 'a child of 1776 in spirit and in truth'.[51] A common store of recent political experience underpinned such notions. For many reformers the American and British traditions of liberty were cemented by British radical support for the North during the American Civil War and in campaigns against the slave trade.[52] Some Georgeites used the image of slavery recalled by this common culture as a shorthand to describe the position of the landless labourers of England, and portrayed the landlord's claim for compensation in the same terms as the slave owner's, as an unjust and immoral demand. George himself saw the fight against unjust landlordism as a continuation of the struggle to end slavery in the United States: 'The struggle for relative human rights had not triumphed at Appomattox, as enthusiastic patriots of the period like myself had confidently believed.'[53] Former anti-slavery campaigners who remained popular in Britain, were enlisted in his campaign, notably William Lloyd Garrison's son Frank Lloyd Garrison, and songs, poems, and stories by prominent American writers expressive of American liberties remained at the core of the Georgeite phenomenon and of radical culture more generally.[54] The New England poet Henry Longfellow was often cited, as were other voices representative of a transplanted Puritanism. John Greenleaf Whittier, who George quoted at the beginning of *Progress and Poverty* and who had featured in the Chartist newspaper the *Northern Star*, was perennially popular, as were James Russell Lowell and Walt Whitman, the former an abolitionist, the later a Union soldier in the Civil War.[55] In later years hymns by Whittier and Lowell were frequently sung at Labour Party meetings.[56] In his journalism William Clarke highlighted the compatibility of New England crusading puritanism and the Scots Lowland Covenanting tradition in the Borders where such writers were widely read, and the Scottish Land Restoration League found the bulk of its supporters.[57]

Moreover, Georgeism posed as the purgative of American democracy. For many land reformers the true pressures that polluted the arcadia of the 'Republic of the West' were those imposed by corrupt landowners in Great Britain. Writing in the mid-1870s, Charles Bradlaugh blamed the long arm of landlordism for the excesses of Tammany Hall. The depredations of the Irish gangs that ran New York were laid squarely at the door of aristocratic misrule in Ireland, where the clearing of the land had bred a race of dispossessed migrants, non-conversant with the habit of democracy. The tools of Tammany were ignorant itinerant Irish workmen, thrown off their smallholdings by the scourge of Irish landlordism: 'These men, to escape death by starvation, left their own shores absolute paupers; and the country of their adoption has had to pay some of the penalties attending the early practice of full political rights by a mass of men not yet educated to the consciousness of their duty.'[58] Similarly for Bradlaugh, the prevalence of slavery in the American

South was a legacy of 'the English monarch to the new republic'. For most radicals, the slave owners of the American South were an aberrant fragment of aristocracy that sought to emulate the gracious landed living of English forbears. Aristocracy thus served as a medium to retard the progress of American democratic values. Radicals stressed the degree to which dynastic aristocratic government in England had supported the slave-holding South, 'and permitted, without protest, the building in, and issue from, its ports of war, vessels to be used against its ally the North'.[59] Some gloated at the irony of the collapse of numerous aristocratic fortunes, undercut by cheap grain imported from the US in the 1870s. It was depicted as revenge for the pressures leading to migration and for aristocracy's hostility to the Federal cause: 'They stole the land, oppressed and degraded the poor in a multitude of ways, depopulated their estates, and forced many millions of the hard workers to emigrate. They never suspected that the emigrants would return and invade the land from which they were driven, and destroy the ruthless power that once expelled them...Not with warships and implements of destruction do they come, but with corn!'[60] The return of Georgeism was thus a gift from the infant republic. It provided restitution for the religious and political persecution of 'the Pilgrim Fathers', who featured regularly in Georgeist rhetoric.[61] At the same time for many radicals it was also a harbinger of a more intimate Atlanticism during an era of increasing harmony between the Anglo-Saxon powers over matters of race and empire.

There was a strong revivalist quality to Georgeite meetings noted by both his admirers and detractors alike. For his enemies they were like 'Negro camp meetings', for his friends they had a luminous quality perhaps more fitting to the pulpit.[62] This tied in strongly with George's own concept of *Progress and Poverty* as a social gospel presented in religious terms and revealed to him through divine intervention.[63] Philip Snowden who saw George speak in Aberdeen in the 1880s wrote that his demeanour was of a preacher: 'In appearance he was of middle height, well built, had a full brown beard, and would have passed for a Nonconformist minister.'[64] The radical MP Josiah Wedgwood wrote that after exposure to George's ideas 'I acquired the gift of tongues' and spoke of 'most elect, thrice-born Georgeites'.[65] Other observers recalled themselves transported by his words in a semi-mystical way. In his autobiography *From Crow-Scaring to Westminster* the agricultural labourers' leader George Edwards includes his discussion of George in an account of his devotional literature, and remembered nocturnal readings of his works: 'Many a time have I gone out at eleven o'clock at night and wiped my eyes with the dew of the grass in an endeavour to keep myself awake.'[66] In the Australian colonies Bruce Scates has recorded claims of miracle cures of ailments and illnesses following contact with *Progress and Poverty*.[67] In the early 1880s Georgeism drew on the legacy of the tour of the American evangelists Moody and Sankey. Taking Britain by storm in 1873–1875 and returning at the height of George-fever in 1883, they set the tone for a revivalist moral populism that sought to empower the people and undermine the religious monopoly of the existing Nonconformist sects. As John Coffey points out, in the aftermath of the 1867 struggle for reform they were seen as dangerous levellers eroding traditional religious and social hierarchies.[68] Henry George's strong Congregationalist beliefs and his upbringing as the son of a religious publisher coloured his platform presence in a similar way to Moody and Sankey. Writing in the 1950s, Heilbroner was inclined to see him simply as a popular millenarian.[69] Contemporaries were scarcely less frank about the religious undertones to Georgeism. William Morris described *Progress and Poverty* as a 'new gospel',[70] whilst Keir Hardie, who was probably converted by Moody and Sankey during their tour of Britain, renewed his faith at the feet of the master.[71] Throughout George's career religious appeals provided the cornerstone of platform Georgeism. Speaking in Glasgow in 1888 on the subject 'Thy Kingdom Come' he made this explicit, reworking the parable of the ungodly rich turning the poor man away from their table, and speaking of Christianity as 'a great movement of social reform...The Christian revelation was the doctrine of human equality...It struck at the very basis of the monstrous tyranny that then oppressed the civilised world; it struck at the fetters of the captives and the bonds of the slave.'[72] Foundation texts of the movement included psalm cxv.16: David's injunction that 'God hath given the earth to the children of man' and *The Book of Common Prayer* interpreted as counselling merciful treatment of defaulting tenants.[73] Elsewhere Georgeites referred to the moral leadership of the Old Testament prophets, God's distribution of the land to the tribes of Israel, and portrayed George as armed with the renewed moral authority of a returned law-giver. Years earlier Joseph Arch had referred to the emotive symbolism of the radical leader leading his people, 'the white slaves of England', like Moses, back to their lost rights.[74] As part of this rhetoric dispossessed clansmen in the Highlands were often portrayed as the Children of Israel driven from their native land into exile by a new Pharaohism: 'The clansmen have been deprived of their inheritance and, to an extent, only paralleled by the children of Israel, have been scattered and dispersed.'[75] Unsurprisingly then, Georgeites saw themselves as missionaries, taking their faith and the Georgeite message to 'the open road' which they wandered like mendicant friars, preaching the one true word to the people.[76] For their part, landowners were stigmatised as selfish, ungodly, and heedless of divine teachings. In 1895, *The Labour Annual* satirically announced the establishment of a 'Society for the Propagation of the Gospel amongst Landlords' to instruct them in their Christian duty.[77]

Georgeism legitimated the long-standing British radical campaign against the abuses of landowning. A movement which had been seen as purely visceral and instinctive was now provided with intellectual justification by *Progress and Poverty*. When George lectured on the theme of the 'Robbers of the Poor' or was greeted with banners marked 'God Gave the Land to the People' he was making substantially the same point articulated by a previous generation of radicals. A sustained campaign since the 1830s provided hard evidence of the restricted and privileged nature of Britain's ruling caste, a rapacious 'few' as opposed to the needy many whose doings were chronicled in radical *exposés* of perpetual pensioners and placemen.[78] Speaking at Manchester in 1850 the Chartist leader Ernest Jones harangued his audience: 'We have not tried to destroy, but to make the robber disgorge his plunder. The nation is the great landlord; the aristocracy were its tenantry, who won leases from its ignorance, perpetuated them by fraud, violated them by force, and now hold them by your apathy and disunion.'[79] In Georgeite rhetoric the claims of the territorial landowners to vast swathes of England and Scotland were punctured, and their pretensions to the moral leadership of the nation overthrown. The Norman Conquest was at the heart of this critique. For Georgeites the Conquest was a powerful and emotive symbol that began the process of the dispossession of the English yeomanry. Over centuries it created a territorial aristocracy who deprived the people of their true rights and reduced them to internal exile in the land of their birth. Examining this theme the popular historian Robert Heath wrote of an 'English Via Dolorosa' for the peasantry.[80] The land movement was suffused with the memory of the sixteenth-century peasant revolts that resisted this process in 'mansion-ridden country'.[81] Jack Cade and Wat Tyler were frequently invoked as predecessors of the land agitation and platform audiences reminded of those forced 'by the unanswerable arguments of musketry and the hangman's rope . . . to submit to the loss of common rights'.[82] Here words like 'robbery' and 'swag' had emotive connotations. Oliver Goldsmith's 'The Deserted Village' became the lament for those driven from the land, much cited in oratory and debate.[83] Most radicals saw the true literature of the British Isles as deriving from this sense of dispossession in which impassioned champions of the soil like Robert Burns and William Shakespeare expressed the people's pain and loss. Burns was the most celebrated casualty of landlordism, ruined by financial pressures, and seeking to free the Scottish peasantry from the 'mental-fetters' of a 'laird-ridden' Scotland.[84] For Georgeites, titles and land were part of the currency of 'Old Corruption'. Even moments of liberty like 1688 were sullied by the process of narrow aristocratic rule. The dream of liberty unfulfilled or compromised in the aftermath of the Glorious Revolution haunted land reformers, apparently providing the opportunity for a tiny, unrepresentative cadre to usurp the constitution and establish oligarchic rule under Lord North, Pitt the younger, or the Duke of Portland. Secularists and radicals shared this view, seeing oligarchy as suppressive of democratic politics and natural rights: 'For the last 163 years this landed aristocracy has been the real governing class, superseding the crown, and until 1832, entirely controlling the people.'[85] For most Georgeites the steady erosion of the landed yeomanry through enclosures and the destruction of the commons, begun in the past but gathering pace in the nineteenth century, represented an unholy alliance between the traditional folk-demon of the lawyer, and an ascendant landlordism. Eli Hallamshire, the working-man land reformer who coined the slogan 'Three Acres and a Cow' characterised this movement as a three-pronged assault on the rights of the people by 'the three great locusts [who] cause the blight of England', 'the perpetual pensioner, the lawyer [and] the Conservative MP'. Traditionally lawyers were compared to the plagues of Old Testament Egypt: 'like the reptile curse of pharaoh they enter every man's house, and come up into every man's kneading-trough and money-box'.[86] Land reformers were keen to reverse this dispossession and in so doing re-claimed the term 'plunder' frequently used against them in the land debates of the 1880s. For them the true plunderers were the landowners and aristocrats who had stolen the land from the people. The land nationaliser A.R. Wallace, saw the land campaign of the closing decade of the nineteenth century as a legitimate reclamation of an Englishman's birthright and condemned the role of the great landowners in breaking up the sacred ground of the English at monuments like the prehistoric henge at Avebury.[87] For George speaking in Bolton in 1884: 'He averred that he was no confiscator, but the reverse. He did not propose to break the sixth commandment, but to enforce it.'[88] At the Land Reform conference of 1880, reformers were told to wear the abuse heaped on them with pride: 'Land Law reformers should not be deterred by shouts of "spoilation" and "robbery" of "communist" and "socialist".'[89]

Georgeism was, above all, a movement of moral censure, expressive of the transgressive behaviour of Britain's noble families. Georgeites were experts at stripping away the allure and mystique of noble titles. They prided themselves on their refusal to succumb to the mythologies veiling aristocratic origins and claimed that they saw through the invented 'flummery' that girded the world of titles, the court, and ancestral inheritance. The real key to understanding the appeal of George and the rhetoric he inspired is the minute attention he paid to the origins of aristocratic connection and position in Britain. Georgeism carried on the tradition of Jack Wade's *Black Book*, and accounts of aristocratic libertinage by William Benbow who moved in a radical underworld of pornography and blackmail during the Regency that provided material for the critics of the aristocracy's self-indulgence.[90] Throughout his speeches George artfully played on the dubious ancestry of the great noble families. The aristocracy, which he represented as a class of gilded pleasure-seekers, is depicted through the prism of Georgeism as fundamentally fraudulent: 'The people who believe in blue blood and in the sacredness of long pedigrees may well feel ashamed as they read the annals of the peerage, and see how nearly every noble family either originated in vice or has thriven upon crime.'[91] In *Our Noble Families* Tom Johnston, a Georgeite and later strong ILPer, vilified the pretensions of the Scottish gentry, depicting them simply as a northern arm of Normanism, bolstered by blackmailers, cattle rustlers, and landgrabbers: 'Descended from border thieves, land pirates and freebooters, they still boast their pedigree. The blood of knaves and moonlighters has by process of snobbery become blue blood; lands raped from the weak and the unfortunate now support arrogance in luxury.'[92] In George's speeches the aristocracy moved in a world of mirrors in which titles could be disposed of, bought, upgraded, or traded in for better ones. Georgeites were obsessed with dubious honours, extinct peerages, illegitimate offspring, returned (presumed dead heirs) and debauched aristocrats. *Pace* George such slurs took on a new life, becoming a common feature of anti-aristocratic rhetoric from the 1880s onwards.[93] Georgeite exposures of the aristocracy set out to reveal the true sources of their wealth and status, the company they kept, and the conduits whereby they gained access to titles and position: 'Even parvenu peers, moreover, find it equally easy to forge pedigrees and to buy professional distinction. Only five noblemen are now allowed to sit in the Lords because their ancestors sat there in the thirteenth century.'[94] George also appreciated the importance of the large territorial landowners to the superstructure of the Victorian state and their centrality in defence, local government, and the social life of the countryside. Their settled 'timelessness' he saw in stark contrast to the casualties and victims of landlessness, low wages, and unemployment in the towns. This contrast was symbolised for Georgeites through the dichotomy of the aristocrat and the tramp. The tramp, who featured strongly in *Progress and Poverty* and loomed large in George's own experience, symbolised the rootlessnesss and desperation of the urban poor divorced from the land; the aristocrat was the titled thief who had deprived him of his livelihood. Robert Blatchford, for a long time a Georgeite, best expresses this tension in *Britain for the British*. Quoting from George he offered the following story:

> A nobleman stops a tramp who is crossing his park, and orders him off *his* land. The tramp asks him how came the land to be his? The noble replies that he inherited it from his father. 'How did he get it asks the tramp?' 'From his father' is the reply; and so the lord is driven back to the proud days of his origin – the Conquest. 'And how did your great, great, great, etc., grandfather get it?' asks the tramp. The nobleman draws himself up and replies, 'He fought for it and won it be'. 'Then,' says the unabashed vagrant, beginning to remove his coat, 'I will fight *you* for it'.[95]

The same image of dispossessed beggars recurs in the words of the famous 'Land Song' that was the anthem of Georgeism:

> The Land, the Land! 'Twas God who gave the Land!
> The Land! The Land! The ground on which we stand.
> Why should we be beggars with the ballot in our hand?
> God gave the land to the people!

The accusation most frequently levelled against George was that he was a plagiarist. Some described his notion of the Single Tax as entirely derivative. Contemporaries variously attributed the germ of his ideas to Thomas Spence, to the eighteenth century Scottish economist William Ogilvie, to the French physiocrats, to Herbert Spencer, or to the benevolent Scottish paternalist Patrick Edward Dove.[96] Georgeites defended him fiercely against these charges, arguing that 'he was always delighted to meet with authorities in England or Ireland in agreement with his views' and did much to encourage the re-printing of forgotten land reform tracts.[97] George himself was sensitive about these antecedents, and occasionally apologised for them in public. When Philip Snowden heard him speak he devoted much of the lecture to describing the

contents of a pamphlet he had discovered in Aberdeen University anticipating his arguments.[98] For many Georgeites the rediscovery of land
reform ideas by different generations demonstrated that they were in some
mystical way immutable and innate, and were therefore an expression
of a universal truth, implanted by god and expressed through 'social
saviours of our race!'[99] The situation is best summed up by the land
nationaliser Charles Wicksteed: 'He has perhaps said little that is
absolutely new, but what he has done is to bring light and truths
partially or wholly understood by others into one grand focus, which is
nothing short of a revelation to those who understand it.'[100]

The real relevance of the proto-Georgeism identified by his supporters
is that the ancestry of his ideas placed George's arguments in a long
and hallowed tradition within British radicalism.[101] George could claim
the authority of Paine, Thomas Spence, and more recently Joseph
Chamberlain.[102] Spence in particular was a 'John the Baptist' figure for
George. Memories of his residence in Newcastle and of Chartist land-
reformers like Bronterre O'Brien were revived on Tyneside at the time
of George's visit in February 1884.[103] Such recollections stirred the
memories of elderly Chartists, leading the *Newcastle Weekly Chronicle* to
put aside space for letters recalling the experience of previous land-
reform agitations.[104] These veterans frequently endorsed a Georgeite
perspective on the compensation of landowners. One example may
stand for many:

> Between 30 and 40 years ago I was a member of a phrenological
> society which held its meetings in a large room in a court in...the
> Groat Market, Newcastle. One night the land question incidentally
> cropped up. The late Mr. John Kane, who was a member, told the
> oft-told tale of how many of the great landowners got their land.
> Their ancestors came over with William the Conqueror, and that
> arch-robber divided the land of this country amongst them. I ventured
> to remark that would not justify us in taking the land from the
> present owners, as they had nothing to do with the robbery. Mr Kane,
> in his usual sarcastic way, replied: 'The receiver of stolen goods is as
> bad as the thief'.[105]

For many reformers the antecedence of Georgeite ideas was even older
and placed him in contact with the shade of the seventeenth century
Puritan tradition that inspired the Chartists and the reform campaigners
of 1866–1867. J.A. Hobson emphasised the continuing importance of
this tradition at the beginning of the twentieth century stressing its

'moral fervour' surviving into 'our times'.[106] It further manifested itself in the discussion journals of the period where George was portrayed with figures like Hampden and Oliver Cromwell as an embodiment of 'The Puritan Ideal'. The agricultural self-sufficiency journal *Seed-Time* devoted space to a discussion both of the continuing relevance of the Puritan movement and of Wiclif, the translator of the first vernacular Bible in English, as a possible intellectual ancestor of the author of *Progress and Poverty*.[107] Individual Georgeites were also inspired by the Puritan example. In Stafford, Josiah Wedgwood recalled the example of the robust defender of the 'Good Old Cause' Thomas Harrison, whilst the words of the unrepentant Cromwellian Richard Rumbold (architect of the Rye House Plot against Charles II) facing execution on the scaffold in 1684 were popular in land reform journals: 'I never could believe that providence had sent a few men into the world ready booted and spurred to ride, and millions ready saddled and bridled to be ridden.'[108] A revived land agitation in the 1880s led to the exhumation of those Commonwealthmen who had campaigned for a purified republic under Cromwell. James Harrington, author of *Oceana* and a favourite of the Chartists, was especially revered for his prediction that most land would inevitably end up in the pockets of the gentry, and for his maxim 'power always follows property'.[109]

Georgeism drew together the strands of existing radical experience and recrafted them for a late nineteenth-century audience. Traditional radical culture manifested itself strongly in the movement in a number of ways. Like other radical campaigns of this type the Georgeite agitation had its martyrs for the cause. Indeed, the Georgeite platform was constructed around the notion of suffering and exile amongst the dispossessed English peasantry. In his correspondence George appealed for more martyrs, along the lines of those imprisoned for furthering the cause of the Irish Land movement: 'There will be some risk of going to prison for a while, but this work requires men who are willing to face that.'[110] George, himself, was the movement's chief martyr, detained by the Royal Irish Constabulary as a suspected Fenian whilst evangelising in Ireland at the time of the Phoenix Park murders in 1882. This episode not only linked him with the Irish Land War and traditional radical images of a suffering Ireland, it also ensured advance publicity for his speech in the Memorial Hall in London.[111] For some reformers this was a distant echo of the gentleman leader, crucified at the hands of the state for the cause of the people. George pandered to this image, appearing in evening dress 'the only one on the platform to do so' at the St James's Hall meeting in January 1884.[112] Above all, George was a man who was portrayed as a self-sacrificing leader, wearing out his health in his campaign against the adamantine force of aristocracy and feudalism. In his correspondence he complained of nights without sleep, and of an unremitting schedule of speaking engagements.[113] The true essence of Georgeism resided in this appeal of David against Goliath. Far from being a 'gentleman leader', George was the antithesis of all things aristocratic, a plain, simple man, lacking the polish and urbane sophistication of Britain's landowning dynasties. George was the embodiment of the 'little man' tasking on powerful forces ranged against him, and seeking to bring down an unaccountable and unelected power. At Oxford University in 1884 admiring descriptions portrayed him 'confronting what promised to be a very hostile audience, he stood like a lion at bay and fairly cowed his opponents'.[114] As with a previous generation of radical leaders, self-sacrifice, dedication to the task in hand, and a total disregard for personal circumstances were a fundamental component of his platform presence. To the ageing Chartist George Julian Harney, he was reminiscent of the last Chartist leader, Ernest Jones. At the time of his death other obituarists lauded his zeal, self-sacrifice, and failure to make money from his writings.[115] During his tours of the United Kingdom an unremitting stream of fan mail expressed an open adulation for him. One zealot remarked that 'if I might speak for England, I would say that it is more deeply indebted to no living man than to you'.[116] Such sentiments validated the Georgeite platform and cemented the connection between leader and led.

Like radicals before them, Georgeite culture revolved around 'singing their rights'.[117] Its songs, poems and political symbolism were often rooted in an older radical milieu. The 'Land Song' is the most enduring example of Georgeite propaganda. Sung heartily at the close of public meetings, and even available in an early travelling phonograph version, the 'Land Song' came to express the hopes and aspirations of Georgeism. Indeed for many it was a substitute national anthem for the movement that looked forward to an England renewed. Josiah Wedgwood, who claimed authorship of the song, recalled that at a meeting chaired by his wife her words: '"We will now conclude with the usual song"' evoked the response '"God Save..."' and 'a burst of irreverent laughter.'[118] The 'Land Song' came to symbolise a pure, uncompromising strain of Georgeism. Georgeite dinners for the faithful at Josiah Wedgwood's house in Stoke usually concluded with it.[119] In 1920 it was sung lustily in parliament by dissident Liberal and Labour MPs protesting at the repeal by the Coalition of the Land Valuation Act of 1909 introduced by Lloyd George to value and tax the estates of the wealthy. Here it served as a public rebuke to his treachery.[120] The land movement also saw a rediscovery of, and visceral connection with, the style and poetic forms of Chartism. A follower of Birmingham's radical priest, the Rev George Dawson, found resonances of his sermons in the rhetoric of the movement, whilst Chartist land reformers like Ernest Jones and Bronterre O'Brien became the patron-saints of the agitation. The movement's legacy of songs and poetry was frequently invoked from the platform; verses by Gerald Massey, the Chartist poet, entitled 'The Earth for All' were quoted in land reform journals in the 1890s:

> Behold in bonds your Mother Earth,
>> The rich man's prostitute and slave!
> Your mother Earth that gave you birth,
>> You only own her for a grave!
> And will you die like slaves, and see
>> Your mother left a fettered thrall?
> Nay! Live like men and set her free
>> An heritage for all![121]

Elsewhere in land reform publications the land nationalisation resolution of the 1848 Chartist convention was recalled, while Chartist veterans were visible at meetings to welcome visits by the campaigning Red and Yellow Vans.[122] An even earlier style of radicalism was revived by a re-writing of William Hone and George Cruickshank's 'The Political House that Jack Built' of 1809 to read:

> This is the land that God gave,
>> This is the landlord that stole
> The land that God gave,
>> This is the farmer that pays
> The landlord that stole
>> The land that God gave...[123]

The true essence of Georgeism was to be found distilled in the old folk rhyme recited by generations of reformers

> Great is the crime in man or woman
>> Who steals the goose from off the common
> But who shall plead the man's excuse
>> Who steals the common from the goose.

Georgeites drew comfort from the fact that Richard Cobden, converted to the cause of parliamentary reform in the final year of his life, and dedicating his last public speech to the issue of the land in Rochdale in 1864, was heard to recite this verse on his deathbed.[124] For some in the Georgeite camp, this made him retrospectively a Georgeite.

Moreover, Georgeism provided a practical solution to the problems of restrictions on rights of public meeting in Victorian Britain. Georgeite agitators offered a powerful rationale for the occupation for public meetings and demonstrations of the undeveloped 'brown field' sites in towns and cities that were representative of the imbalances in land-ownership and property prices criticised in *Progress and Poverty*. Georgeite agitators like Matthew Gass in Glasgow colonised these sites, staking out a claim to the land in his regular orations at Glasgow Green.[125] Their re-occupation, however briefly, were symbolic victories against unjust patterns of landowning in Britain and the under-utilisation of the land in Britain's towns and cities. The land reform journals followed these struggles for public access to urban space closely, providing regular updates on their progress. Georgeite ideas were much in evidence in movements of mass trespass against urban landowners like Lord Sackville at Sevenoaks in Kent, who sought to impede access to his estate for the purposes of rational recreation and popular entertainment. Georgeite sympathisers described him as one 'who like so many of the so-called noblemen of England, appears unable to understand that the earth is the common inheritance of mankind'.[126] In addition Georgeites congregated in the disputed parks and green spaces that were the traditional meeting places of reformers.[127] During a speech at Newcastle, George congratulated reformers in the North-East for their preservation of Newcastle Town Moor for the people of Newcastle, and contrasted this success with the erosion of rights of access to the open ground in London:

> That moor belongs to the people, and is public property. That is one of the best and pleasantest things I have seen in England, that very moor...It is a relic of the old commoner rights of our ancestors. But look at the difference! Go down there to London, and you will see large squares surrounded by high railings in the most populous parts of the city. You will never see a human being inside them except a gardener, and yet, around them, within a stone's throw there are hundreds and thousands of little children playing in the gutters for want of a better place to play in.[128]

Finally Georgeite culture was characterised by a system of signifiers and oral and written codes that confirmed access to the inner ranks of the movement and an understanding of the Georgeite spiritual quest. These often had antecedents in traditional radical culture. *Progress and Poverty* included numerous examples of Georgeite ideas, couched in the form of parables, Socratic dialogues, and representative examples of Georgeism in practice. The most frequently quoted is his illustration of wages. To prove his point that wages were not drawn simply from capital, but were the product of labour in refutation of Adam Smith on this issue, he cited the example of 'an absolutely naked man, thrown on an island where no human being has before trod, [who] may gather birds' eggs or pick berries... there is no capital in the case'.[129] These images of castaways on islands recur in land reform parables. There is a suggestion of the 'noble savage' in George's lonely castaway. It is, however, less Rousseauist than it seems. An island partitioned on Georgeite principles of land-holding was a common way of explaining his ideas, and echoes the Spencean interest in Defoe's *Robinson Crusoe*. In 1782 Spence re-worked *Robinson Crusoe* into a vision of an idealised utopia colonised by friendly local tribes with a collective system of land-holding and no lawyers.[130] Such blueprints for the simple exposition of Georgeite argument created a shared dialogue and simplified George's main points for communication at public meetings and in the private conversions of new disciples. Other examples used varied from the troubled family ownership of a brickworks, through to a dialogue between an elderly, but trusting couple, John and Mary, about low wages that concludes with the moral:

> He who can tell why John does not get what he earns answers the riddle of the modern sphinx. The fact is that being dependent on others for employment because divorced from land, he never can, and never will, get what he earns, no matter how useful and how productive his labour may be.[131]

The nature of Georgeism has been distorted by an over-emphasis on the sect-like quality of the movement. One contemporary described George's supporters in terms reminiscent of ragged millenarian enthusiasts as 'poor and almost unknown, a knot of resolute English agitators [who] seized the opportunity arising from the interest excited by the fallacies of the Californian dreamer'.[132] Georgeism may best be seen not as millenarianism, Britain had experienced a spasm of such movements in the 1840s when industrialisation was novel and they lingered only on the fringes, but rather as of a piece with other contemporary attempts to locate the origin of modern property rights.[133] For European land campaigners like Charles Letourneau, Baron von Haxthausen, and George Ludwig Von Maurer, aristocratic usurpations undermined the relationship between land and Germanic tribal society, requiring a restitution that would reinvigorate the small proprietor and enable 'a recovery of the collective life of the *volk'*. Restored peasant commonwealths, it was believed, might ameliorate the worst excesses of *laissez-faire*.[134] Georgeism provided the British expression of such notions. It coincided with a cultural movement to reclaim the architectural form of the peasant cottage, rustic styles of dress, methods of husbandry, and cottage garden cultivation.[135] From the 1880s onwards reformers sought to supplant the retrogressive forces of squire and parson in the countryside and in local government. In revived peasant communities settlers and incomers inspired by notions of Tolstoyan anarchism, spade husbandry, and alternative living, sought to re-invigorate the withered husk of rustic life in an environment purged of landowners and the Church.[136] George therefore was central, rather than peripheral, to the popular radicalism of the last quarter of the nineteenth century. Often dismissed as fanciful, or lacking in substance, Georgeism captured the radical imagination during an important interlude between the collapse of radical reformism in the aftermath of the 1867 reform bill, and the emergence of organised labour.[137] George's view of the power of the territorial landowners now looks less eccentric than it once did. Recent reappraisals of Victorian culture stress the survival of the eighteenth-century aristocracy into an era of industrialisation and the degree to which they still derived their revenue from lucrative landholdings in the towns.[138] The Duke of Norfolk in Sheffield, the Mosley family in Manchester, and the Grosvenors in London all held family fortunes dependent all or in part on urban rent as detailed in *Progress and Poverty*. Viewed in these terms land reform made perfect sense. Georgeism was a popular creed, for example, amongst the pit-men of the Scottish coal-belt and the North-East of England where aristocratic control of local mineral wealth subjugated the hitherto independent collier to a new regime of wage slavery in the mines.[139] Indeed for many years the Scottish Labour Party remained firmly wedded to Georgeite beliefs. Many of the contradictions of Keir Hardie in particular are explained by his worship at the Georgeite shrine in an area of the Scottish Lowlands where the power of the major landowners proved an issue of continuing political pre-eminence into the 1920s.[140] Like Ramsay MacDonald or H.H. Champion he was a land reformer first, and an advocate of Labour second. In some ways Georgeism was an ur-belief, expressive of the point of view of producers as opposed to non-producers, and spreading across the political divide to suffuse Lib/Labbery during a period of progressivist ascendancy. Through Georgeism, reformers vented spleen against the feudal survivals within the British state and exposed the spiritual and intellectual destitution of an aristocratic life lived in idleness. For the Liberals it carried on Cobden's crusade against the territorial aristocracy; for early ILPers it stigmatised the 'pseudo-feudal offscourings' comprising financial speculators, self-made employers and armaments manufacturers making their way through the political establishment into the peerage.[141]

Georgeism was, however, ultimately an unsuccessful solvent for the New Liberalism. It divided quite as much as it united. Although it sought a common dialogue against privilege it frequently injected a profound note of discord into the Lib/Lab camp. The suspicion of landed wealth it expressed sowed alarm amongst the traditional Whig grandees and their fellow travellers. In 1884 when George debated in print with Gladstone's friend and former front bencher the Duke of Argyll he demonstrated the fragility of the relationship between the landed and non-landed wings of the Liberal Party.[142] Argyll, whose son the Marquis of Lorne had married Victoria's daughter, Princess Louise, in 1871, symbolised the great Scottish landowning establishment and the intractability of landlords in the face of land reform in Ireland: in 1881 he resigned from Gladstone's government over the Irish Land Act.[143] Georgeism therefore probed the gap between radicalism and Whiggery and exposed the fractures in the Liberal alliance. The Tories artfully played on this tension in order to reinforce their role as the defenders of landlordism and ground-rent proprietors in the capital.[144] There remained a whiff of treason about Georgeite sentiments. Single Tax proposals had implications for the integrity of Crown Lands and the royal estates.[145] In 1884 George's visit generated controversy regarding his republican sympathies after incautious remarks about pensioning off the queen, and references to the idle and dissolute character of the heir to the throne at a rally at St James's Hall. During a period when republicanism remained a sensitive issue, George seemed to be openly attacking the royal house when he declared at the meeting which was chaired by the noted republican Henry Labouchere: ' "He could speak of all our kings before George the Third, and looking at that list he said they were a lot of the worst scoundrels" . . . A reference to the Prince of Wales called forth a very mingled demonstration, but when it had subsided Mr George quietly remarked that his view was that it was not good for any man to be "elevated above his fellows so far".'[146] Subsequently he recanted, but George's frequent attacks against privilege and strong anti-Normanism meant that he never quite dispelled the feeling that his crusade against aristocratic landholding extended to all aspects of inherited wealth and authority within the political system. This was the 'great deal of wild talk' John Bright complained of at the time of George's tour in 1884.[147] Contemporaries versed in Georgeite ideas and classical republican precedents were aware that the ideal republican state was rooted in the land, whilst the Marquis of Lorne, Argyll's son, had already been the subject of vicious attacks for his inclusion in the Civil List during the republican campaign of 1870–1871.[148] Little wonder then that a sonnet dedicated to George by an admirer commented: 'Each glutted King and Priest who hears/Shall tremble, knowing that the hour is come.'[149] Such sentiments enhanced George's reputation amongst radicals, but laid him open to charges of extremism. Land militants traditionally inhabited the underworld of radicalism. In the countryside opponents of Georgeism portrayed the movement as a new *jacquerie* advocating land seizures, in which the Georgeite Yellow Vans imported the bacillus of revolution into the countryside. Georgeite orators were frequently attacked by vigilantes co-ordinated by local aristocrats.[150] On his 1884 tour George was denied access to public halls and meeting places by local notables, whilst in 1907, when the Tory MP Sir Alexander Acland Hood accused Georgeites of denouncing landowners as 'idlers, land-grabbers and despoilers of the poor', Campbell-Bannerman retorted: 'what obscure public house had he been spending his time in?'[151]

Georgeism has consistently been understudied and misrepresented. The assumption that it paved the way for socialism is Whig history. In reality the transition from radicalism to socialism was seldom achieved, problematising the position of the Labour Party in the 1920s and 1930s. Georgeism, consequently, remains difficult to integrate into the historiography of labour, and the structural history of the Labour Party. Nor can it successfully be portrayed as a ploy for short-term electoral gain by an embattled Liberalism, in which attacks on privilege distracted attention away from the industrial bosses, and forestalled a potential unravelling of urban Liberalism, precariously straddling the widening chasm between capital and labour. In his investigations into Georgeism, J.A. Hobson was in no doubt that Georgeites were integral, rather than peripheral to the popular politics of the 1890s:

In my lectures upon Political Economy, I have found in almost every centre a certain little knot of men of the lower-middle or upper working-class, men of grit and character, largely self-educated, keen citizens, mostly nonconformists in religion, to whom Land

Nationalisation, taxation of unearned increment, or other radical reforms of land tenure, are doctrines resting upon a plain moral sanction. These free-trading Radical dissenters regard common owner-ship of and access to the land as a 'natural right', essential to individual freedom.[152]

Moreover, hostility to aristocracy continued to feature strongly on Liberal platforms. For most Liberals, the image of aristocracy persisted as an embodiment of selfish economic and social interests. In the election of 1906, Joseph Chamberlain's Tariff Reform Campaign provided the opportunity for the revival of popular memories about the connections between aristocratic interests and protection. Aristocracy, it was alleged, by opposing free trade had augmented their wealth with the inflated profits of over-priced grain during the 'Hungry Forties'.[153] Georgeism was never simply a meaningless echo of older radical forms, or a mere reflexive habit of radical activism. The ideas it embodied continued to have a powerful resonance into the first quarter of the twentieth century. It has long been misrepresented as an expression of rustic pastoral nostalgia, yet the most relevant aspect of Georgeism was the key it provided to the problems of overcrowding, pauperism, and low wages in the towns. When in 1884 George spoke outside the Royal Exchange in London (metaphorically urging his audience to tear down the Temple of Mammon) he was articulating ideas that overwhelmingly found favour with discontented urban workers.[154] Here the American roots of Georgeism allowed him to translate the campaign against the triumvirate 'money power' of banks, railway companies, and monopoly capitalism, into a British domestic setting. Urban land redistributionists saw the earth as a people's resource, a 'National Inheritance' that might be sequestered and diverted into old-age pensions and unemployment benefit.[155] Furthermore, for many urban Georgeites, the Single Tax was a vehicle used to enhance, buttress, or implement municipal socialism, and programmes of urban renewal.[156]

Where Georgeism did express a surviving rustic tradition it was an enigmatic one, crossing the porous political boundaries between Liberalism and Labourism. In Scotland, where the great estate system was a source of particular contention, it contributed to the assertion of anti-landlord values and the crumbling of the traditional Liberal culture of the Lowlands. Here Liberals recoiled from it, seeing it as a reborn Jacobinism; Jane Cobden-Unwin spoke of the Scottish 'revolutionary spirit, of which we see little in England'.[157] J.S. Mill portrayed the abuses of landownership tackled by reformers as falling outside conventional

Liberal debates about property and requiring different more collectivist remedies.[158] Following Mill, Georgeism is suggestive of a constituency in part outside Liberalism and unsure of its relationship to the party. For land reform fundamentalists the Single Tax was a national crusade that superseded party boundaries and made traditional political divisions irrelevant. Speaking in Manchester in 1882, Joseph Arch referred to land reform as 'not a political question, but a grand national question which every man in the three kingdoms ought carefully to study'.[159] George himself expressed scepticism of conventional political parties, and derided politicians as 'a pharisaical priesthood'.[160] There were echoes of the American populism of the 1890s in his evangelising crusade against sterile machine politics and the narrow sectional interests they relied on.[161] Many confirmed Georgeites thus circled both the Liberal and Labour parties uneasily. The similarities Georgeite culture bears to both early socialist fraternal organisations and the self-help culture of Liberalism, demonstrates the congruences and overlaps existing in the crowded territory of late nineteenth century land reform politics.[162] J.A. Hobson represented the followers of George as 'typical English moralists' who held an identity in their own right that was non-party specific.[163]

The political inheritance of Georgeism also remains problematic. The inchoate character of Georgeism meant that it never became tethered to any one particular party, and defied institutionalisation within party programmes. Ian Packer has argued that despite the importance of the land issue to the Liberal Party, Lloyd George was an eclectic thinker, who incorporated only minor elements of the Georgeite platform into his budgets.[164] Some Georgeites, disappointed by the timidity of Lloyd George's Single Tax proposals in 1909, suggested that Liberalism had never been a suitable vehicle for the movement, causing considerable traffic by Georgeites in and out of the Liberal and Labour parties.[165] In the 1920s Georgeism still featured heavily in Labour Party policy documents, long after it is usually believed to have faded. Filtered through Fabianism it was a marked feature of the progressivism of the LCC. It was raised at the London party conference of 1923; as late as 1929 Lloyd George was still castigated by Labour supporters for his post-First World War repeal of the 1909 Land Duties.[166] Above all the popularity of Georgeism challenges the notion of a single monolithic Liberalism in the final years of the nineteenth century. Georgeite divisions over both the Boer War and the First World War also showed that there was little to unite Liberal Georgeites within the framework of the Liberal Party. Accordingly Georgeism exposes still further the fractured and partial nature of

Liberalism even during its meridian in the 1880s. Liberalism had a number of antecedents and destinations, and many Georgeites were both half-absorbed and half-excluded by the Liberal consensus. Nevertheless, Georgeism enabled some radicals to travel with the Liberals, who after all held the reins of power, whilst campaigning for something more outside the Liberal platform in conjunction with Labour.

There is more to Georgeism than just an elemental attachment to the land. Now that trade-union based Labourism has been reduced to the representation of the sectional interests of labour, and traditional class categorisations superseded, its emphasis on land-holding confirms the new historiography of the nineteenth century and gives it a fresh feeling in comparison to the traditional narratives of class and anti-employer sentiment usually ascribed to the early Labour Party. Its strong religious undertones and a campaigning style that included biblical-style parables, Socratic dialogues, Norman Yoke tropes, and a view that the land should be returned to the people of England who were exiled from it, marked it out as part of the common intellectual terrain of radicalism. Scraping away the Liberal accretions of Lloyd George's interpretation of the Single Tax, Georgeite economics retained a radical potential and a popularity that has been overlooked by historians working in this area. Far from being simply a half-way house for proto-Marxists, it posed a fundamental challenge to the landed aristocracy, and for many reformers expressed a radical potential emblematic of discontents outside, or barely addressed by, parliamentary Liberalism.

3
Hunting, Moral Outrage, and Radical Opposition to Animal Abuse in Nineteenth- and Early Twentieth-Century Britain

We are so steeped in the history of fox-hunting, so obsessed by its aristocratic associations, that it is almost sacrilege to catalogue fox-hunting among our national vices.[1]

The sporting set . . . some merely happy-go-lucky, some frankly dissolute, devoting their lives to hunting, racing, shooting and other forms of sport; utterly uneducated, wildly extravagant, reckless, thoughtless and vaguely apprehensive that certain movements are on foot which seem designed to deprive them of some of their fun. They are toadied and encouraged by a large band of followers who they love to patronise with easy familiarity. They find the lower orders with whom they associate ie. jockeys, bookies, keepers, ghillies, valets and grooms are in no way discontented with their lot. They are supposed to be a thoroughly British type, and they are immensely popular.[2]

> How many fell, the *Court Gazette*
> Better than I may say,
> Hares that escaped will live to tell
> Their children of that day!
>
> Long live the Game Laws, though with ills
> Some people say they're fraught,
> Long live the laws by which our Prince
> Enjoyed such glorious sport![3]

The connection between aristocracy and hunting is a long-established one. Historically, the ritual, display, and hierarchy of hunting shaped the character of landownership in Britain. For landed society it embodies the governing accord between royalty and aristocracy, symbolising the assumption of traditional gentry values by the monarch and the court. For 'Roundhead', a radical correspondent writing in *Reynolds's Newspaper*, hunting symbolised the 'Crown in league with the class landowner' and defined the forces arrayed in opposition to reformers.[4] Hunting also provides a representation of traditional baronial England, expressive of a 'deep' and impermeable Englishness. Huntsmen riding to hounds in the autumn light, and beaters flushing out the game on the mist-wreathed moors are often portrayed as emblematic of a nostalgic Englishness, rooted in sacred ties with the land and a timeless ancestral tradition. The recent debate in Britain about hunting gives some indication of the passions it can arouse and the social symbolism that surrounds the chase. Hunting then is about more than just sport or aristocratic leisure. A study of hunting and aristocracy's involvement in it raises issues about privilege and its collision with an expanding parliamentary democracy in the nineteenth century, the self-indulgence of nobles and kings, and the acquisition of the people's land to provide the requisite topography for the chase or the shoot.

The purpose of this chapter is to examine the historical construction of hunting and its links with aristocracy. What follows is a consideration of hunting, broadly defined, covering shooting, fox-hunting, and the full range of field-sports. The focus is on the roots of radical urban opposition to aristocratic involvement in hunting, and the narratives of privilege and animal abuse that became the scourge of patrons of the hunt from the closing years of the nineteenth century onwards. Following the demise of the Chartist mass-petitioning campaigns, urban radicals in the 1870s re-grouped around hostility to the great territorial landowners, aristocratic privilege, and hereditary legislators at court and in the House of Lords. A correspondent in the *Bee-Hive* newspaper summed up the position: 'The great necessity is to tackle great and patent evils – army expenditure, game laws, reform of [the] House of Lords. It's no use running a tilt against monarchy and the upper classes. Attack great and specific abuses.'[5] For critics of the established order the image of a barbarous and uncaring hunt was a distillation of the corruptions and privileges of aristocratic life that proved corrosive of the liberties of the 'freeborn Englishman'. A study of the politics of anti-hunting thus examines the strategies open to those who sought to contest the rituals and trappings of the aristocracy's public persona. By concentrating on the animal victims of a distant and remote aristocratic elite, radicals were able to highlight the violation of the natural world symbolised by arrogant and unfettered aristocratic rule.

Much of the historiography of animal defence has concentrated on anti-vivisection and the emergence of a campaign around a recognisable platform of animal rights. The impetus behind such studies has been to chart the course of opposition to a cold scientific rationalism and an uncaring scientific establishment. This sometimes had implications for aristocracy. In 1879 the House of Lords demonstrated its support for vivisection by voting down an anti-vivisection bill, a position that was seen as symptomatic of aristocracy's disdain for the natural world.[6] Much animal-abuse historiography, however, is dismissive of anti-hunting agendas, seeing them as a later twentieth-century addition to the popular anti-vivisection campaigns inspired by revelations about the painful dissection of an unnamed dog by a leading University College surgeon in 1907.[7] The cause of animal welfare has its own Whig History, in which opposition to hunting barely figures before the early 1960s when new public campaigns were informed by an awareness of the rights and wrongs of human relationships with the animal kingdom.[8] Much of the literature on animal welfare has concentrated exclusively on the philosophical origins of anti-abuse campaigning, but overlooked the mixed motives of those radical politicians who employed an anti-abuse rhetoric. Notions of rights for animals hardly existed in the nineteenth century, most popular responses to animals were (and still are) governed by sentiment alone. In the case of political radicalism, rights for animals were especially poorly developed. In 1875 *Reynolds's Newspaper* questioned the need for a Royal Commission on Vivisection of Animals when 'human slaughter' existed 'in the Black Country, in our coal pits, or amongst out agricultural labourers'.[9] Throughout the nineteenth century, militant working-class anglers defied the injunctions of the proletarian hero, Lord Byron, who was implacably opposed to the sport, and bitterly resisted encroachment by landowners on customary rights to fish in ponds and streams sanctioned under Magna Carta.[10] For most reformers animal abuse was far less important than the structures of power and authority that allowed privileged sections of society to escape the new laws curbing animal cruelty, whilst the lowly status of others made them subject to the full majesty of the law in the towns.[11] Radical opposition to hunting became enmeshed with the notion of lost rights. Radicals saw hunting courtiers as the spiritual heirs of the Normans. Anglo-Saxon society pre-dating the Norman Conquest of 1066 was a prelapsarian age for many radicals, in which sentimentalised and romanticised liberties were reduced to dust by an intolerant conqueror.[12] Until comparatively recently the radical and republican critique of hunting remained rooted in exhortations to strive for the restoration of lost ancestral rights to the land, impeded by princely huntsmen and debauched aristocrats. Such ideas found favour amongst urban radicals in the towns, but were less popular in the countryside, where the hunt gave the illusion of cementing a community of interests between landowner, tenant farmer, and labourer. They were also given a gloss of natural rights in the writings of the republican, Tom Paine, making the critique of hunting less about the rights of animals, than about Paine's *Rights of Man*.[13] It is the purpose of this article to reconnect opposition to hunting with older radical narratives of freedom from a corrupt aristocratic Normanism, which had as little regard for the lives of animals as for the lives of its subjects.

In its origins fox-hunting had a mixed social base. The mining terrier men of South Wales and the farmer and gentry hunts of the Scottish borders are in a direct line of descent from the beginnings of the sport as a plebeian and lowly pastime. In contrast to partridge and grouse-shooting, which was manufactured for a leisured elite, fox-hunting had a low social status during a period when stags kept for the more aristocratic stag hunts remained plentiful. In the seventeenth century fox-hunting in particular had a debased image; foxes were dug out of their earths and netted like badgers by farm servants and labourers. It was the decline of stag-hunting in the seventeenth and eighteenth centuries that brought fox-hunting into prominence as stags became rarer. Hunting, either by horse, or in shooting meets, came to typify a close relationship to the land and a proprietorship of traditional yeoman values.[14] For the Whig Venetian oligarchy of the 1740s it was illustrative of everything that was backward and unsophisticated about the squirearchy of the Country Party. In common with many other London urban politicians, John Wilkes professed a metropolitan disdain for fox-hunting. For him it symbolised the distance of the rural squire from power and position.[15] Country Party backwoodsmen embraced it for precisely this reason. It provided a gesture of opposition to urban cosmopolitanism. In hunting circles the fox is still known as 'Charlie', a reference to Charles James Fox, whose radical proclivities and sympathies with the French Revolution made him a traditional enemy of county Conservatism. The boorish, oafish image of fox-hunting clung to the sport for many years. As late as the 1860s the wearing of hunting pink by Lord George Bentinck and his followers was expressive of an unrepentant Toryism reluctant to concede ground to modernisers within the party.[16] At the time of Lloyd George's 1909 Liberal budget, the Duke of Beaufort told a meeting of his tenants that he would like to see Lloyd George and Churchill savaged 'in the middle of twenty couple of dog hounds'.[17] However, as hunting meshed with elite society in the countryside during the nineteenth century its less aristocratic followers steadily fell away. Subscriptions for the largest and most lavish hunts put them beyond the reach of all but the wealthiest, especially following the rural depression of the 1870s, which priced the smaller producers and rural proprietors out of the game.[18] At the same time shooting evolved from friendship groups of two or three hunters working closely with their ghillies, and involving local farmers, into a more formalised and ritualised structure bringing together county society, aspirational members of the 'fast set', and professional sportsmen. The invention of the percussion cartridge and fast, breech-loading shotguns introduced from France, enabled the emergence of a more industrial process of shooting.[19] In the *battue* military tactics and precision were used to flush out game birds, drive them across the guns, and bring down as many as possible. Some contemporaries saw this as a military action against nature, and decried the 'making [of] heroic war on pigeons and pheasants'.[20] Traditional huntsmen regretted the demise of the culture of sociability and companionship surrounding shooting and complained about the anonymity and formality of the large *battues*.[21]

As hunting became the preserve of a wealthy few, the tendency for sportsmen to seek titled and aristocratic patronage became more pronounced.[22] Throughout the nineteenth and early twentieth centuries the court had strong links with hunting. There is a lengthy history of noble and aristocratic involvement with equestrianism and equestrian sports. Harriet Ritvo emphasises that the selection process implicit in the division of the animal kingdom into thoroughbreds and vermin, breeding stock and victims, mirrored aristocracy's view of a social world grounded in heredity, inheritance, and the eternal verities of the bloodline. The managing of hunting packs, and the swapping and breeding of prize breeds emulated the obsession with improving bloodlines and consolidating dynastic links that were such a marked feature of aristocratic marriage arrangements.[23] Moreover at hunt-meets there was an outline of the hierarchical order in the rigid precedence of master, kennelmen, whipper-in, and earth-stopper. The ritual of the hunt was at the very least redolent of the 'flummery' and freemasonry that traditionally surrounded courtly and state ceremonial. From the 1870s invented traditions gave hunting a glamourous appeal and an apparent longevity that translated the pastime into an immemorial part of British custom, stamped with the imprint of princes. Noting with disapproval the blooding of royal children, Henry Salt commented: 'There is a double significance, it seems, in the expression "a prince of the blood".[24] Queen Victoria maintained antiquated and expensive household positions monopolised by the great aristocratic families including the Hereditary Grand Falconer and the Master of the Buckhounds. The cost of maintaining the Hereditary Grand Falconer alone was £1700 per annum in 1871.[25] Hunting metaphors also abounded in the scramble by traditional landed families for the profitable sinecures that grew out of court favouritism. The radical Henry Labouchere wrote: 'Whenever there is a change of administration they clamour for well-paid sinecures about the court like a pack of hungry hounds.'[26] Royal involvement in hunting completed the transformation of the sport into a 'society' pastime linked with antiquated ceremonial. Hunts like the Beaufort and the Quorn profited from their closeness to the great aristocratic dynasties and became places where court intrigue abounded.

Grouse-shooting also thrived against a background of court patronage. Despite its relatively recent advent as a sporting pastime it was inlaid with the veneer of aristocratic custom, creating a spurious air of antiquity. In 1871 Sir Charles Dilke ironically suggested that the court was in need of a 'Hereditary Grand Pigeon Shooter in Ordinary'.[27] Grouse-shooting was largely a society sport. It priced out all but the wealthiest, and for much of the late nineteenth and early twentieth century was a recreation that traditionally provided an *entrée* into society, possibilities for social advancement, and marriage opportunities. The American writer Richard Grant White recalled of a visit to England: '"Does he preserve" is a question that I have heard asked by one country gentleman about another with as much interest and seriousness as if the inquiry were about whether he had a seat in parliament. An engagement to shoot is paramount to all others; an invitation to shoot, like an invitation from the president at Washington, sets aside all others.'[28] The sport became so intimately associated with the closed circles of aristocratic shooting weekends that the great landed dynasties were dismissed acerbically by Carlyle as 'the partridge-breeders of a thousand years'.[29] These were the 'pheasant-fanatics' of long radical memory who became a byword for leisured living.[30] *Reynolds's Newspaper* grumbled: 'We find that a nation like England comprising, as it does, hundreds and thousands of the most intelligent and skilful working-men in the world, is to a great extent governed by a lot of fools, ignoramuses, gamblers, fox-hunters, cock-fighters and pigeon-shooters.'[31] The best shooting was in Norfolk, near Sandringham, where Albert Edward, the young Prince of Wales, became an acknowledged expert in the breeding and rearing of grouse and pheasants, attracting most of the 'Big Shots' of the day to his hunting weekends. This courtly hunting circle practised extravagant displays of shooting. Branded the 'pigeontry of Guelpho's knights', the shooting weekends they staged became the butt of jokes in the satirical and serio-comic press in the 1870s.[32] The years before 1914 were the highpoint of the sport, when the Edwardian 'cracks' like Lord Ripon and Rimington Wilson vied with one another for ever more Herculean game-bags.[33] The sheer weight of slaughtered animals amazed and appalled contemporaries. The radical MP, P.A. Taylor described one shoot in December 1868 that lasted five days, bringing down 8345 head of game, of which 4077 were hares and rabbits, the whole bag weighing 11 tons in all. Writing in 1945, C.E.M. Joad described 'one of these holocausts' on the Abbeystead Moors near Lancaster 'where as many as 2929 grouse were shot by eight guns in a single day'.[34] Refining, augmenting, and improving the experience of the shoot became an obsession for many landed proprietors, cementing the aristocracy's reputation for philistinism. By the 1920s new technology was developed to maximise kills and decrease the inconvenience of muddy fields and inclement weather for visiting dignitaries. The so-called 'caterpillar car' devised by Mr Keiller, Laird of Morven, and based on the design of tanks used in the First World War, became a common sight on the Scottish grouse moors in the inter-war years.[35]

In addition stag-hunting and the hunting of carted deer were still practised at the end of the nineteenth century. Stag-hunting was an expensive and labour-intensive pastime. Where it continued it was an extravagant affair, requiring large numbers of retainers and hounds: 'resembling, in these respects, and, indeed, in the mode of pursuing the game, the present customs on the continent'.[36] In Scotland enormous areas of land were given over to deer reserves where young deer were raised for shooting in the autumn. By the 1870s the extensive use of locals in the infrastructure of ghillies and game-wardens needed to police the reserves became one of the chief sources of employment in the Highlands.[37] The hunting of de-horned deer up to the point of exhaustion also remained an accepted part of the Hurlingham meets where the presence of royal and aristocratic patrons of the Royal Buckhounds gave apparent sanction to the very considerable cruelties involved.[38] In 1868 the Buckhounds pursued a deer through Wembley and Wormwood Scrubs before finishing it off in front of horrified passengers in the goods yard of Paddington Station.[39]

On the aristocratic estates masculine prowess was measured in terms of the number of animals killed and the competition involved in vying with, and defeating, rivals for large kills. This was 'the manly sport of shooting half-tame birds and quadrupeds' frequently derided by reformers.[40] The *National Reformer* jeered at its 'manly qualities': 'The Nimrod who rides to the hot corner on a hundred-guinea shooting cob, and slakes his thirst with [a] champagne cup, can hardly be thought to be cultivating an aptitude for hardship.'[41] For its devotees, however, hunting was a surrogate for war and martial glory. Linda Colley has pointed out that fox-hunting gives the impression of training for the battlefield.[42] The panoply of uniforms and suggestions of a parade present in 'riding to hounds' consolidated the great aristocracy's traditional links with martial preparations for warfare. For some critics 'blooding' into the fraternity of hunters implied an anointment, or tribal initiation into a closed warrior caste. The allegation that the pampered and indolent nature of aristocratic life effeminised the aristocracy was repudiated by the skill and stamina used to bring down large numbers of pheasants, to run foxes to ground, or to live under canvas. Hunting was an aristocratic re-affirmation of the upper nobility's masculinity. The physicality of hunting became part of its enduring appeal in aristocratic circles. Masculinity and aristocracy were closely intertwined in a rough camaraderie bound together by rituals of dining, drinking and physical exertion. Even the radical historians J.L. and Barbara Hammond agreed, seeing the persistence of country sports as explaining 'the physical vitality of the aristocracy'.[43] As the reverse side of such sentiments, opponents of hunting were characterised as 'old women of both sexes', 'hysterical' and 'namby-pamby' in their unjustified opposition to the pastime.[44] Hunting then came to symbolise the vigour, vitality, and ostentation of the nation's elite. It provided a prelude to all great social and political gatherings. Even the sitting of parliament and the rhythms of the London season were dictated by the vagaries of the sporting calendar. Henry Labouchere predicted in a satirical court diary in the radical journal *Truth* that at a shooting weekend in Westmoreland attended by Prince Albert Edward 'the slaughter of pheasants will be on a prodigious scale'.[45] Moreover, hunting metaphors abounded in wartime. During the Boer War it was seen as invaluable training for aristocratic officers serving at the front. The hunting journal *The Field* declared: 'from the very earliest times soldiering and sport have gone hand in hand' and quoted Alexander Somerville that hunting is 'the mimicry of war'.[46] The effectiveness of the Boer commandos in holding up the advance of the British army and matching the tactics used against them in South Africa was frequently attributed to an understanding of military strategy learnt on the hunting field.[47] Alternatively, defeat or the new forms of occidental imperialism emerging at the beginning of the twentieth century undermined the argument that manliness could be equated with chivalric prowess learnt through hunting rituals. Writing at the time of the defeat of Russia by the Japanese navy in the Russo-Japanese War of 1905, the radical journalist Maurice Adams wrote: 'the notion that blood-sports develop manliness and "made Britons the men they are today", and that if Englishmen cease to ride to hounds, to hunt the hare or otter, or shoot the pheasant and partridge, they would become effeminate, ought surely to have received its death-blow by the events of the Russo-Japanese War. When we hear of the rice-eating, gentle Japanese, who prefer taming gentle creatures by kindness to shooting or mangling them, performing prodigies of valour apparently quite beyond the capacity of the fiercer nations of the West, it is surely time to revise our conceptions of what true courage is and how it is nurtured.'[48]

From the 1880s onwards aristocracy sought to marginalise the opponents of bloodsports. Contemporaries depicted them as eccentrics or as ill-educated 'urbanites' who remained oblivious to the benefits conferred on the rural economy by sporting practises. Anthony Trollope, answering criticisms of the hunt as a coarse and brutal pastime, established the still existing parameters of the debate by depicting the anti-hunt fraternity as kill-joys, ignorant of countryside ways, heedless of the humane outcome of hunting for domestic livestock threatened by foxes, and preoccupied with this form of animal abuse over other more pressing urban cruelties.[49] In their memoirs huntsmen represented obstructionists as petty, mis-guided, or at worst, harmful to the countryside. Frequently opposition to hunting was dismissed out of hand, or treated with disdain. Siegfried Sassoon recalled: 'We were galloping full tilt along a road just outside a cosy village. An angry faced old parson was leaning over his garden gate, and as we clattered past he shook his fist at us and shouted "Brutes! Brutes!" in a loud unclerical voice. Excited and elated as I was I turned in the saddle and waved my whip derisively at him. Silly old buffer!'[50] Such accounts traded in the view of the opponents of hunting as a narrow, unrepresentative sect that commanded little support outside the ranks of 'faddists', political malcontents, and the intelligentsia. In hunting memoirs they were frequently described as 'cranks' or 'propagandists'.[51] Defenders of the sport highlighted the un-English or non-Christian basis of their beliefs: 'It is difficult to follow some of the reasoning...Someone writing to a Devonshire paper has discovered that one of the maxims of the Buddhist and Pythagorean canon says that no-one should kill or injure any innocent animal. It is asserted that they never touched fish, flesh nor fowl, wore no clothes made of skin or hair but lived as vegetarians and spun the material of their garments.'[52] This is to unfairly represent the history of opposition to hunting. Historians who have simply accepted the aristocracy's own view of the opponents of their favourite pastime, have missed the radical inflection within anti-hunting rhetoric that associated the huntsmen with the entrenched aristocratic interests that made hunting inimical to the rights of the 'freeborn Englishmen'. Far from being an aberrant viewpoint expressed by sentimentalists fixated on the shedding of animal blood, by the 1890s it was already in a long tradition with strong links to the broader radical platform. It is the purpose of this chapter to re-examine the nineteenth- and early twentieth-century campaigns against hunting, and to relocate them within an established current of hostility to land-lordism, and unbridled aristocratic interests.

Aristocratic involvement in what the humanitarian campaigner, Henry Salt, christened 'bloodsports' at the end of the nineteenth century was never without criticism. For some contemporary opinion it was the natural consequence of a life devoted entirely to luxury and excess. An editorial in the *Warwick and Warwickshire Advertiser* spoke of 'the pernicious example' of the great nobility in encouraging game preservation 'partly from ostentation, and partly to gratify a morbid taste for slaughter'.[53] Radicals saw the process of hunting and killing large numbers of animals as dysfunctional behaviour prompted by idleness and boredom. Revolted by the carnage, some of the earliest opponents of hunting were ex-members of society hunting retinues.[54] Prominent amongst them were women like Lady Florence Dixie, or the ex-mistress of the Prince of Wales, the Countess of Warwick, who were alienated by the masculine ethos of the sport. In Devonshire, a similar former hunter, Rosalie Chichester of Arlington Hall, was instrumental in highlighting the cruelties of stag-hunting on Exmoor. Her estate, which included an eight-mile wide fence to exclude the hunts, was one of Britain's earliest nature reserves.[55] Lady Florence Dixie and anti-hunting campaigners of the social stature of Angela Burdett Coutts became the darlings of rad-ical meetings at which denunciations of shooting were expressed.[56] Moreover, their writings were not just a defence of the cause of animals, rather they dripped revulsion at the emptiness and soullessness of a life devoted solely to the satisfaction of the basest human instincts.[57] This is the substance of comments about the deer reserves in Scotland in the radical *National Reformer*: 'This widespread loss, these desolated homes, these ruined lives, what mighty national benefit have these miseries brought for England? They all occur in order that a few rich men may occasionally, when other pleasures pall on the jaded palate, and *ennui* becomes insupportable, have the novel excitement of shooting at a stag.'[58] Anti-hunters pointed out that too often hunting showed the limitations of aristocracy's attainments, rather than its achievements. *Reynolds's News* reported that over-zealous marksmen on a shooting weekend in the West Country had missed their targets, but successfully shot down nearby telegraph wires.[59] Hunting accidents proliferated to the delight of radical journalists. *Lansbury's Labour Weekly* remarked 'These civilised gentry are never in any danger except from their own occasional ineptitude in handling a gun.'[60] For keepers and beaters, near-death experiences were an occupational hazard, leading *The Field* to debate the issue of compensation for blinded and disabled employees.[61] Such accidents, however, were seldom reported in the national press unless they involved prominent members of society. In 1864 the explorer John Hanning Speke, famous for charting the headwaters of the Nile, shot himself in a hunting accident at an estate near Bath.[62] In 1892 Queen Victoria's third son, the Duke of Connaught, accidentally shot his own brother-in-law, Prince Christian of Schleswig-Holstein, in the eye at a pheasant shoot. The episode was used by the socialist, Robert Blatchford to highlight the limitations of the landed elite even in activities in which it allegedly excelled, and caused him to question the competence of aristocratic princes who held senior rank in the army's High Command.[63]

A producerist ethos was evident in many of these attacks on hunting aristocrats from the 1880s onwards. Hunting provided a totemic emblem of 'waste' in land management. It led to the expulsion of tenants, contributed to a fall in home-grown produce, and created vast areas of non-cultivated land. Moreover, the uncultivated shooting estates were often equated with the phenomenon of 'absenteeism'. As agricultural rents fell, smaller landowners who owned more than one ancestral home, let out their shooting rights to syndicates of businessmen and middle-class entrepreneurs. In such cases the estates became a playground for the urban wealthy.[64] These 'joint-stock poulterers' received 'two rents for the same land, one from the farmers, and the second from shooters'.[65] The swathes of arable land given over to game in Britain at the turn of the twentieth century and the jealous husbanding of game birds and other quarry, encouraged opposition to hunting and shooting, which rapidly broadened into a wider campaign against landownership and lack of access to the countryside. The Anti-Game Law agitation attacked the aristocracy as vulpine and predatory, dismissing them and their retainers as 'this plague'.[66] Designed as a movement of small tenant proprietors it set out to persuade small farmers that they suffered at the hands of unbridled landlordism, convince them that the land was going to waste, and sought to enlist them in a campaign to boost rural yields by shackling the unfettered power of the great territorial magnates. Land, in their view, should be reserved for agrarian production. Tenant proprietors owed the big territorial magnates nothing.[67] As part of this outlook, a discourse of industry opposed to idleness, and thrift opposed to extravagance, emerged to counter the worst excesses of the hunting fraternity. Annie Besant declared that 'I deny the right of "the idle" to "clear out" the industrious. I deny the right of the wealth-consumers to evict the wealth-producers.'[68] For many radicals, hunting merely masqueraded as sport. In reality it underpinned an entire social system that produced nothing and provided murderous pastimes for idle hands. *The Humane Review* described a pheasant shoot in which birds were: 'mown down by lazy men who do not even load their own guns'.[69] Contemporaries highlighted the waste involved in the rearing and shooting of game: 'Every stag that is stalked, every pheasant that is mown down in the *battue*, and every hare or rabbit that is knocked down in covert-shooting has cost the country much more to produce than it is worth when butchered, and the game-preserver, far from being helpful to the community in this respect, is a positive encumbrance on it, as wasting labour in the production of what is not a food, but a luxury. Game is reared not for the benefit of the many, but at the cost of the many, to gratify the idle and cruel instincts of the few.'[70] For some, hunting was emblematic of a 'parasitic' aristocracy, that absorbed the labour, profits, and efforts of others. The emergence of notions of parasitology in medicine during the 1890s provided fresh evidence for those who sought to brand sporting earls as a deformation of the social system, and a drain on the economy.[71] Land reformers equated the 'rent-monopolisers' with blood-sucking ticks and declared that they had 'no hesitation in ridding ourselves of them in the summary fashion usual in dealing with parasites'.[72] For radicals, the sporting estates bore out the truth of the axiom that the hard labour of working men went to the upkeep of a pampered and idle class that could not even dress or bathe themselves. Ben Tillett remarked: 'The Lords would be lousy if they were not kept clean by the workers.'[73] Hunting then came to represent the wider failings of the aristocracy and evolved into a natural target for those seeking redress for aristocratic misrule in the countryside.

A further sub-text operated here. One of the strongest criticisms of the royal patronage of sporting events like that at Hurlingham, which attracted the great aristocratic families of the day, was that the games were symptomatic of an unnatural, German-inspired bloodlust. Pigeons were de-feathered and de-tailed, depriving them of the power of flight, and making them easier targets as they hopped along the ground.[74] This suggested an inherited instinct towards tyranny and cruelty. These notions undermined the royal family's pretensions to Englishness, revealing them as an alien and unnatural import. Henry Salt implied this strongly when he described the Hurlingham meets as 'Hunnish sports and fashions'.[75] Prince Albert was a noted enthusiast for the *battue*, cementing its association with 'Teutonism'.[76] The predilection for the mass shooting *battues* of the pheasant hunt was seen by many critics as 'a foreign horror, the shooter no longer an English gentleman, but a Parisian "gommeaux"' schooled in a European and tyrannical school of cruelty.[77] There is an echo of Paine's 'roving Norman banditti' here, in which power in England had not passed peacefully down through the generations, but instead had been usurped by ruffians, bandits, and their hangers-on.[78] Radicals depicted the court and its sinecurists as literal and figurative 'vandals', whose depredations defiled both countryside and constitution. For Paine aristocracy was an abuse, rooted in the accident of birth, unearned privilege, and the dubious or counterfeit pedigrees of royal bloodlines. Hunting was a constant reminder that regal power was held by a roguish foreign dynasty, supported by a corrupt church and an aristocratic mafia. The historian, E.A. Freeman, wrote:

> Nothing is plainer than that the love of hunting in its different forms has led to some of the worst acts, to some of the most unjust and oppressive legislation, to be found in all history. The accursed forestry laws of old times, surviving in a modified shape in our modern game laws, are the suitable monuments of an age of special devotion to the chase. It was the love of hunting which led directly to the worst deeds of our Norman kings, and, though no such results can happen now, yet the example is instructive. It shows the natural effect of the unrestrained indulgence of such pursuits on men who were but little under the restraint of law or opinion in other ways.[79]

These cruel feudal exactions by 'the ruthless Conqueror' were much lamented in the popular literature of the mid-Victorian period. P.A. Taylor quoted the eighteenth-century Professor of Law at Oxford, William Blackstone, on the Norman forestry laws 'From this root has sprung a bastard slip, known by the name of the Game Laws.'[80] In Britain reverence for the freedom of forest-dwelling animals was sometimes portrayed as another component element in a freeborn Englishman's liberties linked closely with lost rights. As in the past, freedom dwelt on the margins, and in the forests and woodlands of Old England. These ideas merged in an attack on fox-hunting in the radical journal *Liberty* which declared: 'When we find the country-lanes swarming with hounds, we know there is to be a "meet" and that some free denizen of the forest or moor is to be hunted to death.'[81] Here the fox symbolised the free spirit and endangered carnivalesque ways of the poacher, and the rural community of landless labourers that supported him.[82] Some contemporaries detected a tendency to romanticise poaching on these grounds, noting that the 'poacher's friends' overlooked or excused the cruelty of snare-trapping.[83]

The main point of comments like those made by Salt and Freeman was to expose the despotic tendencies behind the reasonable, consti-tutional face of the court, and to remind the public of the ruling dynasty's familial links with ancestral tyranny and the absolutist 'kaiserism' of Germany. This was in line with the conventional republican position that too much power remained in the hands of a fragment of aristocracy and an over-mighty executive that was ripe for abuse should Victoria transplant continental styles of government to Britain. Her patronage of the exiled Napoleon III after 1870 was represented as an early indication of this intent, and Bonaparte's death in 1873 was celebrated by radicals as the end of French imperialism 'finally buried at Chistlehurst'.[84] In some ways the debate about the traditional royal sport of stag-hunting transmogrified this theme, and it became a constitutional debate about the predilection for tyranny within the executive. Feelings ran high about the hunting of carted stags at Hurlingham by the Royal Buckhounds under the control of the Master of Buckhounds, Lord Ribblesdale, a member of the royal household. This was a political as well as an emotional issue, leading to the first mass petitioning campaign around an animal welfare cause. The Reverend J. Stratton, who had campaigned against the Buckhounds for many years, intimated that the arguments mustered in their defence were a flawed expression of the notion of timeless continuity and ritual that underpinned a moribund constitution. He wrote: 'The lapse of years pleaded in its defence is often the most vulnerable point of an institu-tion.'[85] Queen Victoria liked the ritual surrounding the Buckhounds, but they were a liability compromising the public position of the throne and the higher nobility. Her death in 1901 opened the way to their dispersal. In this case stag-hunting was about far more than simply the preservation of animal life. Instead it opened up a debate about the purpose, function, and bloodline of the country's leading families, including the 'highest in the land'.

In Britain hunting was conventionally seen as the privilege of a narrow, exclusive elite with its apex in the court and amongst royal retainers. In contrast to hunting in France and Germany, where it was a 'people's pastime' wrested from the aristocracy during the revolutions of 1789 and 1848, hunting in England was never associated with notions of breaking down exclusivity and bridging social distance.[86] Whereas European radicals and reformers like Friedrich Engels enjoyed the hunt, seeing it as an annexation of privileges formerly reserved for the aristocracy, in Britain hunting stood for the flouting of immemorial rights of access, the violation of the sanctity of the small property-holder, and a contempt for the rural poor. The British hunt was never quite able to lose its connection with the dispossession of the English *villein* and the usurpation of inherited constitutional liberties. The great hunting estates patronised by society's leaders came to symbolise the loss of ancestral freedoms to traditional English sacred ground. The rural writer Mary Sturge Gretton recalled one old yokel remarking of the fashionably feather-bedecked daughter of the local blacksmith 'them thur feythers be the ruination o'this country'.[87] Charles Bradlaugh complained of land set aside for game preservation, and noted in particular the Chillingham estates in Northumberland reserved: 'for a few wild cattle, in order that a Prince of Wales may now and then drive about it, and from the safe eminence of a cart may have the pleasure of shooting at a bull'.[88] The large pheasant estates in the southern counties of England were bitterly resented. Flocks of tame pheasants roved at will, feasted off their neighbours' crops, and exacted a so called 'bird-tax' from adjoining smaller proprietors.[89] Moreover, the annual burning of moorland heather to create the right conditions for pheasants to breed caused the erosion of topsoil and large-scale ecological damage. Bird carcasses were anyway too riddled with shot to be eaten. Even the later inter-war generation of conservative rural writers were in no doubt that 'the costliness and absenteeism of hunting are incompatible with good husbandry'.[90] In the nineteenth century, at a time of considerable interest in land reform when the ownership of crown land was in contention, a love of hunting exalted the feudal rights of aristocratic huntsman over the small farmer, rambler, or working-poor of the towns. Hunts habitually trampled the crops of small rural proprietors, and made a virtue of these actions in their hunting songs; smallholders were required to overlook such incursions:

> Oh, what were trampled pasture, and oh what was
>   damaged wheat,
> Or poultry raised and fattened which the foxes used to
>   eat?
> Oh, what were broken fences, what was stock all gone
>   astray?
> Great houses brought our produce then, great stables used
>   our hay.
> There was stir and animation, the country-side was gay
> With all the pomp and glitter and pride of a hunting
>   day![91]

Huntsmen then could trespass with impunity on tenant land and were exempt from sabbatarian restrictions on a Sunday; ramblers were subject to the law of trespass, could not obstruct the hunt, and were exiled from their roots in the soil. Henry Salt said of the grouse moors around Kinder Scout in Derbyshire, that 'there is no spot in England which is guarded against intruders with more jealous care!'[92] P.A. Taylor talked of the depredations of 'bands of armed myrmidons . . . armed with cutlasses, guns and flails' who were hired by game preservers to police the moors.[93] On the great shooting estates in Scotland landless labourers lived in poverty unable to touch the bounties that surrounded them, their only occupation, according to ribald contemporary opinion, to manufacture that 'Keep Out' signs that oppressed them.[94] The American land reformer and social crusader Henry George drew on Biblical parables to emphasise the plight of those he saw as little better than 'beasts of burden'. He commented in a speech at Glasgow in 1884: 'You remember how, to feed the hungry Israelites, quail were sent from heaven? If they had been sent into Scotland, your common Scotsman would not have been able to touch them. Here the quail are preserved.'[95] Writing in the *Humane Review* Maurice Adams made the link between hunting and dispossession explicit: 'In England today hunting is an anachronism which survives only because land monopoly and an unjust distribution of the national inheritance have led our "splendid barbarians" in the absence of the need for work, the pressure of social distinctions, and the want of higher mental development to seek release from boredom and fill up an aimless life by the indulgence and artificial stimulation of sub-human instincts.'[96]

Hunting thus appeared as a reincarnation of Norman oppression that took place with royal sanction and touched radical concerns for the reclamation of 'waste' or the non-productive land of the game-preservers.[97]

It was apparent to many radicals that the topography of Britain's fields and ditches established by the acts of dispossession and enclosure that deprived the people of their true rights created the perfect conditions for hunting.[98] Some saw Britain as little better than a 'theme-park' for royal relatives and flunkeys from abroad. Tourist, hunting royals were especially loathed on these grounds. Their presence brought out the followers of the hunt in large numbers. The Empress Elizabeth of Austria rode with the Northamptonshire Rythlings in 1871 and 1878 and hunted in Ireland in 1880. On her visit in 1878 five-hundred horsemen rode with her, and there were nearly 5000 spectators. So impressed was she by British hunting rituals that she established her own kennels at the Habsburg royal palace, the Hofburg, staffed by an English-style hunting retinue.[99] When she again visited Britain in 1882, bringing her retainers with her, *Reynolds's Newspaper* reported:

> True to their sycophantic nature large numbers of the English aristocracy, ladies and gentlemen, before the arrival of the Empress, had begged eagerly to be allowed the distinguished honour of hunting with her. The consequence has been that the fields have been unprecedentedly large and the injuries to the farmers therefore unprecedentedly great. Whole fields of wheat have been wasted. And for what? Simply that a half-frantic woman, whose delight by day is to run horses to death, and whose solace at night is to lie on the sofa and watch the smoke rising from her cigarettes, shall indulge one of her caprices.[100]

From the 1870s the spread of shooting estates in Scotland frequented by visiting dignitaries, which were some two million acres in extent by the end of the decade, caused an answering militancy amongst Lanarkshire miners who formed an Anti-Royalty League and a Labour League to pursue the case against an alien monopoly of Scotland's traditional moorland.[101] The Scottish land agitation was an antidote to the *kitsch* 'Balmoralism' of the Highlands. Writing in 1913 Jane Cobden-Unwin commented on the ferocity of the land war in Scotland, describing a 'revolutionary spirit' that evoked the image of a resurgent Jacobinism.[102] In Lancashire and Yorkshire, radical dialect authors like Allen Clarke and Abraham Stansfield celebrated the moors as a place where the true spirit of unfettered Anglo-Saxon liberties lingered longest: 'In no part of these kingdoms were the regulations of the "New Poor Law" enforced with more difficulty. Nowhere, until within the last few years, have those numerous stalwart fellows who rejoice in the common name of

"Peeler" had so bad a time of it. And in no part are many ancient and obsolete customs destined to die so hard a death.'[103] In their writings the moorland was seen as a plebeian space, untainted by the influence of kings and courtiers, and a former haunt of Chartists, Puritan hedge-preachers and medical botanists, where the free fraternity of the moors that subsisted on its fragile ecology was threatened by the influence of rising numbers of sporting tenants and their guests. Allen Clarke wrote in similar vein:

> Sit down here on a summer's day on the green moorland, under the blue sky, and though you own not a yard of land nor a stick of property you are on a throne, and king of the world, a happier and far more innocent king than any ruler who ever held tinsel court and played havoc with the destiny of nations – you are monarch of all the magic of the moorlands.[104]

In the 1890s the fencing off of these moors by powerful and well-connected game preservers created a context of 'grouse versus humanity' which Solomon Partington, agitator in the celebrated Winter Hill disputes outside Bolton, called 'sport for a handful against the rational enjoyment and recuperation of the many'.[105]

The broader context of empire afforded the opportunity for even greater excesses of royal hunting prowess and display. The killing of exotic animals symbolised social prestige and power. The republican MP, P.A. Taylor, saw hunting as altogether incompatible with civilisation, and its patronage by the nation's social betters as illustrative of a broader degradation of morals amongst colonial administrators and servants. Revisiting the traditional tableau of radical *cause célèbre* that debased the cause of empire for anti-imperialists, he commented: 'It hardens the heart and familiarises the mind with needlessly inflicted suffering. The lash in the British army and navy and the brutalities of the Jamaica massacres and Afghan hangings are all indirectly the result of the cruelties of the hunting-field.'[106] The anti-hunt radical Robert Buchanan concurred, exclaiming: 'moral sanctions are disregarded, the rights of inferior races are forgotten'.[107] The central role of hunting in establishment circles meant that throughout the empire indigenous examples of fox-hunting, pheasant-shooting and similar transplanted country pursuits stood out as badges of imperial privilege. In Kenya and Australia, wide sweeping plains provided the perfect terrain for hunting, whilst a jungle or mountain setting created fresh challenges for determined huntsmen.[108] In Africa the eradication of local wildlife was seen as overcoming impediments to the colonising process, taking hunting out of the hands of the local community, and transforming the sport into an exclusionary pastime emblematic of imperial rule.[109] In the white-settler colonies like Australia hunting was embraced by aspiring aristocrats and self-made men to create a counterfeit of aristocratic life in the shires. J.A. Froude noticed that the colonial elite mimicked 'old-fashioned baronial England' and hunted regularly around their parks in a transported version of English hunting-life.[110] In Queensland 'Botany Bay Baronets' slaughtered indigenous wildlife and re-stocked the countryside with pheasant, foxes, and grouse. Where there was no imported English wildlife to hunt, kangaroos were substituted and hunted with the techniques of the fox-hunting pack or the *battue*.[111] In Kenya, jackals, and in Canada, coyotes, took the place of the more traditional fox and preserved the ritual of the hunt in a colonial setting.

The colonies then were the forcing-ground of the burgeoning sport of big-game hunting. Moreover, taking the practices of hunting abroad on royal tours was seen as an assertion of traditional kingly authority over the vassal states of the empire, recently subdued by an arrogant imperial adventurism reminiscent of the brutality of the Norman Conquest in Britain, and recalling the excesses of the royal family's Plantagenet ancestors. High-profile tours became, in effect, lavish safaris for the courtly circles of retainers, aristocratic hangers-on, and local 'nabobs'. For radicals, anti-imperial sentiments merged with hostility to aristocratic imperial administrators, republicanism, and sympathy for imperial subjects, in press campaigns against royal hunting tours.[112] As with the *battue* there was a military quality to the large-scale hunt or safari in India and Africa. Hunting in India demonstrated that British imperial rule still came from the barrel of a gun.[113] Contemporary descriptions of Prince Edward's hunting camp on a royal visit to India in 1921 describe it as a 'white city in canvas' with a system of listening posts and telephone stations '[that] rendered it practically impossible for a tiger or a rhinoceros to move without its presence being promptly signalled back'.[114] These military undertones were very apparent during the visit of Albert Edward to India in 1875–1876 on the first royal tour since the mutiny. The visit was in part an exercise to pave the way for Victoria's assumption of the title of 'Empress of India'. For many radicals, peasant culture in India represented a world of sturdy yeoman values, long lost in Britain, but surviving in the further reaches of the empire.[115] The notion of an imperial kingship introduced in 1876 evoked the spectre of a French-style imperial despotism, colliding with the fragile world of the traditional Indian rural economy that was romanticised by radicals as a threatened remnant of peasant virtue. As Matt Cartmill points out, there was a clear analogy between the role of the white conqueror and his superiority over subject peoples, and that of the hunter over his prey.[116] The conspicuous presence of members of Edward's 'Marlborough House set' on the trip, and the fact that the disgraced Colonel Valentine Baker has been scheduled to attend the Prince on the visit, confirmed the apparent connection between a dissolute and roving nobility exploiting the spoils of empire, and cruelty to the indigenous animal-life of India. Albert Edward embodied the new imperial man. He hunted from a howdah on the back of an elephant in the traditional Indian fashion, apparently surpassing the shooting feats of local princes. His game-bag included eight tigers, a cheetah, numerous elephants, a crocodile, and several much-prized wild Indian pigs, felled in a noisy barrage described by *Reynolds's Newspaper* as 'waking up all India with his exploits amongst tigers and crocodiles'.[117] In the radical press Edward appeared as a despotic Eastern-style potentate, indigenising his style of dress, and accepting jewels, dancing girls, and hunting specimens as tribute from local rulers. The *People's Advocate* was, despite itself, impressed by his skill in bringing down a cheetah, but declared that 'his victories over pigs and tame elephants we will not dwell upon'.[118] *Reynolds's Newspaper* regarded his shooting escapades as emblematic of the subordinate status of both the people and animal-life of the country and condemned the excesses of 'our pig-sticking prince, and his rowdy associates'.[119] For most radicals the public slaughter of animals in India confirmed the continuing spiral of degradation for England's ruling dynasties: 'Faulty though the Stuarts were, the fall from the Stuarts to the Brunswicks was yet a fall from an Olympus of light to an Avernus of mud, our piggish and pig-sticking Prince of Wales not withstanding.'[120] For middle-class observers it showed the prevalence of sporting customs in the empire that degraded the British imperial mission and carried uncomfortable echoes of other corrupting imperial systems: 'Our contemporary assures us that the sport is far superior to the best run with the Pytchley. We should be exceedingly glad to learn how far it is superior to the Spanish bull fight.'[121]

For urban radicals animal abuse was represented as the traditional occupational pastime of the aristocracy and the court, undermining the governing elite's claim to the moral leadership of the nation. For some critics it was in the character of the court and the flattery that surrounded it to provide a dynamic for ever greater excesses of savagery and cruelty. Some contemporaries noted the relative restraint of British courtiers in the killing of game birds, especially when compared to the ostentatious slaughter of animals by European monarchs. Edward VII, for example, refrained from the continental practice of piling up birds he had not in fact shot in front of his grouse-butt to impress with the size of his game-bag.[122] Nevertheless, a royal or noble presence could sometimes increase a kill by two- or even three-fold. Writing in 1870 George Francis Morant, a pioneer of the Royal Society for the Protection of Birds, high-lighted the slaughter on the shooting estates when visiting dignitaries encouraged sportsmen to competitive frenzies of bloodlust: 'When royal personages join in any sport they are bound to try to excel other performances. *Noblesse Oblige*. It would not be the thing to do less, and the "fierce, white light which beats upon a throne" reveals all, always. So pheasant shooting can be overdone, as when we read in the papers eleven hundred are shot in a few hours in France.'[123] Reformers pointed out that sports involving cruelty to animals flourished most during periods of monarchical and aristocratic ascendency under the patronage of the court. Anti-hunters saw mercy, common humanity, and pity for weaker creatures as characteristics that were representative of a republican view of the world. At the time of Cromwell's Commonwealth, curbs had been introduced on public gatherings convened for the purpose of participating in animal cruelty. In contrast bear-baiting, bull-baiting, and dog-fighting were all revived and flourished as popular pastimes after the Restoration.[124] Critics of the throne pointed out that royal ceremonial, like the 1897 Jubilee, provided the opportunity for opulent public displays dependant on fashions and adornments that required a high degree of suffering in animals. Outraged letters in *The Times* castigated fashions at court that were decorated with feathers from game birds: 'So long as royalty and the elite wear *aigrettes*, more especially the so-called *tocques* – the advocated headgear for the Jubilee – so long will the unfortunate bird be "slaugh-tered" until they may become extinct like the dodo.'[125]

The same theme emerged with regard to European courts; the degen-eracy of the restored Bourbon monarchy in Spain was apparently confirmed by its reintroduction of bull-fighting, which had been banned under the republic of 1873–1874, but was revived by the heir to the throne, Don Alfonso: 'While the country he has been called to rule is destroyed by internal dissension, he has been desporting himself like a *hidalgo* of old days and reviving a sport which is a disgrace to civilisation.'[126] The preservation of wildlife was thus often represented as a feature of virtuous republics where all forms of life were revered and aristocratic pastimes were purged. In the 1870s, at a time when republic-anism was a topic of public discussion, the Puritans were reclaimed as forerunners of the anti-cruelty movement and portrayed as emblematic of the increased concern for animal welfare that accompanied the suspension of royal rule. The icons of anti-hunters were dissident republican Englishmen like Shelley, Byron, and Thomas Paine (or indeed Scotsmen like Burns) whose merciful outlook was portrayed as an expression of indigenous concern for 'fair play' for both animals and humans.[127] Drawing on Thomas More's opposition to hunting in his *Utopia* the anti-hunting radicals construed an alternative reading of Englishness rooted in the romantic tradition and preservation of the soil.[128] In their appropriation of such work radicals looked for a purged England that was a nation reborn, without tyranny, aristocracy, and plutocracy.

By the 1890s the anti-hunting fraternity had established a counter-culture that sought to undermine and erode the traditional rituals surrounding the hunt and the shoot. Hunt-sabotage *per se* remained rare outside Ireland.[129] Nevertheless, hostility to bloodsports was increasingly part of the outlook of the New Lifers, social reformers, and faddists who made up the ranks of the radical intelligentsia. Steeped in Tolstoy and a communistic vegetarianism their views shaded into non-violence, notions of universal brotherhood, and concern for animals in a world without hierarchy.[130] These were the 'malcontents who in the guise of humanitarians, bolshevists or what not crop up at all times and in all the hunting counties' that hunters complained bitterly of throughout this period.[131] In a subversive gesture, their uniform became the Jaeger jacket, designed originally to cool the blood and steady the aim of huntsmen, but appropriated by reformers to represent the advantages of healthy and rational dress.[132] For others, who celebrated a life lived close to the soil, the true heroes were the poachers, who passed through the game preserves at will and whose exploits were applauded as symbols of a stubborn, rebellious primitivism opposed to the fencing-off of the earth by aristocrats and monarchs.[133] The Victorian poacher and freethinker James Hawker paid the greatest compliment he could muster to his hero, the secularist leader Charles Bradlaugh, by comparing him to a poacher, but 'he was not a poacher of game, but a poacher on the privileges of the rich class'.[134] Recalling the part Carlyle attributed to poachers in bringing about the French Revolution, the socialist Jim Connell saw opposition to hunting as a potentially explosive issue, undermining privilege, the stability of landownership, and perhaps threatening the survival of the throne itself.[135] Significantly, experience of trespassing, gamekeeping, and poaching were marked characteristics of many mid-Victorian radicals and of the activists who built the Labour Party.[136] For the early twentieth-century generation of land reformers the possible cessation of hunting symbolised the passing of the feudal order and the restoration of agrarian harmony: 'Some day the whole thing must pass behind the hill, the sum of its interests, its passions, conventions and honours appearing little better worth striving for than a fox's brush. Perhaps when the hunt has passed by, the ploughman may be seen returning home over the fields, or the milkmaid driv[ing] home the kine from the meadows.'[137]

For their critics, the shooting estates of the nineteenth century created an arid, sterile rural landscape 'semi-derelict and manless, fit for the hunting of foxes and the preservation of game' in which few traces remained of the indigenous English.[138] The exiled anarchist author Peter Kropotkin commented that 'in the Weald I could walk for twenty miles without crossing anything but heath or woodland, rented as pheasant-shooting grounds to "London gentlemen" as the labourers said'.[139] The romantic socialist Edward Carpenter blamed the tone set by the court and polite society for the vogue of hunting amongst a new class of aspirational landowners who sought to ape the shooting estates of Edward VII and his retinue.[140] Paradoxically some traditional aristocrats joined in the chorus of criticism of hunting courtiers. Depicting themselves as the true custodians of the soil and its values, they attacked the shifting, rootless plutocrats entertained by Edward on his shooting weekends and, where they could, probed the background and ethnic origins of his circle.[141] New money tainted and degraded a pastime that was in their eyes as much about managing and maintaining the land as about sport, leading to fierce condemnation of: 'rich cads rude to all and sundry, not excluding the owners of the land over which they ride by the kind permission of these same owners, many of whom and of whose ancestors hunted years before these upstarts and their mean families emerged from the gutter'.[142] Radicals also sought to exploit the apparent connection between the upwardly mobile, the Prince of Wales, and the Jewish financiers present in his court. In 1884 the Social Democratic Federation's organ *Justice* brought these themes together in anti-Semitic attacks on the Jewish finance capital believed by some reformers to be behind the British war in Egypt, which it christened 'the bondholders' *battue*'.[143]

The connections between notions of useful toil and the unjust exactions of a pampered *rentier* class meant that early opponents of bloodsports in Britain were closely linked to radicalism and the pioneer Labour movement. At the same time, aristocratic patrons of the sport saw abolition of hunting as a prelude to further incremental and radical change within the political system. Sir Willoughby de Broke recalled the verses:

For I looked into its pages and, and I read the book of fate
And saw fox-hunting abolished by an order of the state

Saw the landlords yield their acres after centuries of wrongs,
Cotton lords turn country gentlemen in patriotic throngs;

Queen, Religion, State abandoned, and the flags of party furled
In the government of Cobden, and the dotage of the world.[144]

Hunting then became a line drawn in the sand around which urban and rural, radical and reactionary sentiments revolved. Outside the countryside hunting was increasingly seen as a cruel pastime that exposed the tensions between the role of nobility as an exemplar to the nation with a concern for the correct family and moral values, and the depraved, degraded aspect of lives devoted solely to indolence and pleasure amongst a *louche* social circle of hunters and sportsmen. For radicals it established a double standard in which laws governing animal abuse were flouted or circumvented by the wealthy. Sporting courtiers revolted even some of the strongest supporters of the throne. Robert Blatchford, for example, made his admiration for monarchy apparent, seeing it as the correct organic governing system for Britain and a manifestation of Bagehotian democracy 'as free as any republic in the world'.[145] At the same time he found it impossible to conceal his revulsion for the presence of sporting earls in the retinue of the king. Whereas ritual traditionally works for the established order in Britain, over this issue aristocratic pastimes clashed in the nineteenth century with expectations of public morality and popular concerns about animal welfare, leaving the notion of *noblesse oblige* compromised, and presenting the image of a callous and uncaring aristocratic dynasty as indifferent to the fate of animals, as to the subjects of the realm.

Plate 1 An apocalyptic image of Landlordism draining the resources of the planet. 'Get off the Earth', cover of *Land Tax Cartoons from the Morning Leader* (London, 1909). (By permission of Chetham's Library, Manchester.)

Plate 2 Aristocracy as a barrier to the land. 'Hands off the Land', from *The Prestwich Division Liberal Almanac* (1908–10). (By permission of Chetham's Library, Manchester.)

CARTOONS ON THE LAND QUESTION.

WORKING-MAN : "Look here, guvnor. I think it's about time you got out and walked."

"On the walls of Mr. Balfour's meeting were the words 'We protest against fraud and folly.' So do I. These things have only been possible up to the present through the fraud of the few and the folly of the millions."—Mr. LLOYD-GEORGE, at Limehouse.

Plate 3 The aristocracy as a national encumbrance. From *Land Tax Cartoons from the Morning Leader* (London, 1909). (By permission of Chetham's Library, Manchester.)

CARTOONS ON THE LAND QUESTION.

"WHAT THEY SAY THEY ARE COMING TO."

"They are now protesting against paying their fair share of the taxation of the land and they are doing so by saying you are burdening the community, you are putting burdens upon the people which they cannot bear."—Mr. LLOYD-GEORGE, at Limehouse.

"The Morning Leader" for best Sports News.

Plate 4 Aristocrats pleading poverty and satirised as impoverished paupers. From *Land Tax Cartoons from the Morning Leader* (London, 1909). (By permission of Chetham's Library, Manchester.)

Why he voted against the Budget!

Earl of Cockshott (4th Earl):

" Because this d — d super- t a x means that I shall have to give up my pheas- ant shooting.'

[N.B.—As his Lordship spent no less than £53 4s. 6d. last season on beaters' wages, the loss to the locality will be heavy.]

11

Printed and Published by Hudson and Son, Livery Street. Birmingham ; and London.

Plate 5   Satire of the uncritical 'huntin' and shootin'' aristocratic opponent of reform of the House of Lords. From *The Peers and the Budget: Why Some of them Voted Against it* (Birmingham, 1910). (By permission of Chetham's Library, Manchester.)

Plate 6 Satire of the dispossession of the English peasantry by the landowning aristocracy. From *The Labour Annual*, 1895, p. 129.

TO
LEGISLATIVE
REFORMS

LORDS

JOHN BULL: "Well, I MUST be an ass to drag these burdens about after me."

Plate 7 John Bull as 'an ass' dragging around the burden of the House of Lords. From the cover of W.T. Stead, *Peers or People? The House of Lords Weighed in the Balance and Found Wanting* (London, 1907). (Author's collection.)

CAPITULATION.

Plate 8 Gladstone as the hunted prey of the House of Lords over the Irish Home Rule Bill in 1885. From *The Gladstone Almanack, 1885* (William Blackwood and Sons, 1885). (Author's collection.)

Plate 9 An indictment of urban landlordism entitled 'The Scapegoat' from 'Cynicus', *Cartoons Social and Political* (1893). (Author's collection.)

Plate 10 Aristocrats and the Tory Party conflated as the party of high food prices during the Tariff Reform Campaign. 'It's Your Food We Want to Tax' (National Liberal Federation, 1909). (By permission of Chetham's Library, Manchester.)

Plate 11 Aristocrats as inefficient leaders of men in 1940. 'Brass Hats in Command of the Armed Forces' from *The Men Behind the War* (CPGB, 1940). (Author's collection.)

Plate 12   An organicist view of the aristocrat and the yeoman united in defence of the countryside. Cover of *The English Countryman* by H.J. Massingham (1942).

4
'Lords of Misrule': Liberalism, the House of Lords, and the Campaign Against Privilege, 1870–1911

Their past conduct has always shown that the peace and tranquillity of the country are to be held as dust in the balance, compared with the preservation of their usurped privileges. And this must always be the case with an assembly of exclusives, who assume political power, by right of inheritance, and, who in consequence of that assumption, can command the resources and wield the physical force of a government ... The question, therefore, that now presents itself to all inquiring minds is this – Is this titled and anti-national oligarchy to retain its wonted political prerogatives, when they have proved so baneful to the well-being of the country?[1]

The representation of the people as it at present exists is a hideous mockery. It is so by the usurpation and encroachments of the aristocracy and landed interests ... It is surely no small matter, that by these usurpations the government of this, a great commercial country, is become the patrimony of two rival factions of aristocratic families. Ruling absolute in their own House, and their brothers and sons, uncles and nephews, relatives and connections in the People's Houses, they are under no necessity to labour for the acquisition of that knowledge and experience which are essential ... Yet they arrogate to themselves ... all the highest offices and dignities whilst numbers of other men of talent and probity ... are perpetually excluded as 'political adventurers'. All that either of these aristocratic factions require, is that a few of them should possess some tact and cleverness in debate ... Even that necessity each faction occasionally ekes out by picking up and using as subservient tools men of intellect – not of their order.[2]

Hostility to privilege, wealth, and the trappings of landed society were at their strongest in campaigns against the House of Lords. Drawing on the same narratives of a traditional radical disdain for leisure, inherited titles, and the idle courtiers that featured in the land campaign and in anti-hunting rhetoric, opponents of the House of Lords sought to circumscribe the unaccountable and non-elective power of landed wealth by laying siege to the Upper Chamber. Dislike of the hereditary principle amongst respectable politicians was most frequently expressed through attacks on the House of Lords. From 1832 onwards the Lords was seen by reformers of all hues as the unacceptable face of landed wealth and naked class interest. Many reformers portrayed knightly titles as quite simply a feudal relic. In their public pronouncements they hoped to excise aristocratic influences from government altogether. For some politicians any assault on hereditary government threatened to undermine the notion of hereditary kingship. Purging aristocracy therefore substituted a war against aristocracy for a war against the royal state. Whereas an attack on monarchy imperilled the foundations of the constitution, reform of the Lords could pass as a legitimate act of party politics used to curb the excesses of a retrograde and permanently Tory element within the legislature. The vast array of manipulative patronage at the disposal of the court, and used by the executive to shore up this system was portrayed by radicals as morally insupportable, and inimical to the ideals of liberty expressed in the struggle between parliament and the executive in the seventeenth century. In this sense opposition to the Lords was depicted as the final act in the purification of British democracy. Joseph Clayton wrote in 1907: 'Power without responsibility has always proved injurious to the commonwealth, and has always been challenged in England. It brought violent death to certain of our kings and ruin to their favourites. Rejecting it has caused the steady passage to a popular government, and will give Great Britain a democracy when women are enfranchised and the veto of the Lords is abolished.'[3] In this way the Liberal 'Peers versus the People' rhetoric of the late nineteenth and early twentieth centuries substituted for an attack upon the monarchical state, and diverted attention away from the monarchy itself. At the same time it drew together existing radical criticisms of privilege to create a Liberal view of the constitution that whilst loyalist in nature, nevertheless sought alternatives to inherited privilege deployed in party interest. The debate about the Lords was sufficiently destabilising to overflow into the world of letters. Algernon Swinburne wrote three anti-lords poems in 1904.[4]

I

The struggle against the House of Lords in 1910–1911 is a canonical moment in the evolution of parliamentary institutions, and in radical campaigns to curb aristocratic influences within the executive. Much of the energy of Liberal governments from the 1880s onwards was expended on taming the Lords. In many ways the Lords were entirely antithetical to parliamentary Liberalism, causing the politics of the period from 1880 onwards to configure around the schism between the House of Lords and a Liberal-led Commons. Up until 1911 this agenda still dominated the dying days of Liberalism on the eve of the Great War. Aristocratic interference in government degraded and defiled the sacred constitution. Moreover, the delinquency of aristocratic misrule in government mirrored the aberrant behaviour of sporting earls on the hunting field and in their private lives. For reformers the Lords were a piratical fragment that usurped the royal prerogative, undermined the Commons, and tyrannised freely elected Liberal governments. Radicals who campaigned against the Upper House were the heirs to a long history of anti-Lords rhetoric. Armed with the authority of Emerson, John Bright, and other opponents of the Upper Chamber, radicals sought to curb or lay low the Lords. For radicals like Charles Bradlaugh, the very existence of the Lords revealed incarnate the inherited pre-disposition towards tyranny that characterised the 'barbarian' outlook of aristocracy. He declared: 'the whole principle of aristocracy is embodied in that House, the whole fatal notion that the accident of birth gives the right to rule'.[5] John Bright called the House 'almost the last refuge of political ignorance and passion'.[6] Drawing together these themes, by the 1900s Liberalism projected itself as the only vehicle capable of curtailing the power of aristocracy. Alarmist and apocalyptic reporting of the conduct of the Lords created the image of a rogue and untamed power that threatened the political health of the body politic. Exaggerating wildly, some radicals saw the attitude of the Lords as undermining the stability of the nation, and sowing the seeds of revolution in the United Kingdom. The ferocity of language used to subvert the Lords on the occasions of Liberal confrontations with them, shattered the decorous and civilised pretensions of British politics, as well as injecting a note of fierce class hostility into the debate that recalled the social and political divisions of the 1830s and 1840s. Josiah Wedgwood, for example, implored his audience at a meeting in Staffordshire in 1908: 'Were they going to give them the power to screw the neck of the House of Lords?'[7] W.T. Stead claimed that the invective used against the Lords in 1884 was so effective that it convinced other European powers that Britain was about to succumb to revolution, scaring 'the Emperors of Germany, Russia and Austria into the Three Emperors' League against the triumph of republicanism in England'.[8] Queen Victoria was alarmed by the fiery language used about the peers. She saw it as an encroachment on all hereditary office-holding, and a campaign that might imperil the foundations of property itself. In her private correspondence she condemned Lord Rosebery's speeches on the Lords issue as 'radical to a degree to be almost communistic'.[9] Some scholars still see the intensity of party conflict over the Lords between 1909 and 1911 as undermining British democracy, and finally contributing to the fragmentation of the Liberal coalition in a 'strange death' of Liberal England.

Liberal strategies to tame the Lords received the support of the traditional radical constituency, both inside and outside Liberalism. Anti-Lords hostility was deeply entrenched in popular politics. Amongst radicals there were long-standing grievances against attempts by the Lords to stall the progress of popular enfranchisement bills. Often these interventions by the Lords dictated the rhythm of agitations for parliamentary reform. In 1831 and 1866 the Lords held up the progress of reform bills. On both occasions interventions by the Lords strengthened the impulse towards reform and helped foster an atmosphere of crisis. In 1866 radical anger was directed towards the House of Lords when their posturings imperilled Gladstone's reform measure, prompting discussion of extreme measures and strategies in radical circles. At the time of the 1866 Reform Act, interference by the Lords promoted increased working-class unity in the face of an incoming Tory ministry and an intrusive House of Lords. Thereafter, the Lords were portrayed as an instrument of obstruction and a bulwark that held up the momentum towards manhood suffrage. For radicals there was a Peers' 'Hall of Shame' in which numerous measures that had the potential to alleviate the lot of the working-poor were mutilated or rejected outright.[10] Some reformers were disappointed that despite the various reform bill crises, the subsequent reform acts were only partial successes, leaving the legislative function of the upper house untouched. The close association between the House of Lords and landed wealth meant that the issues raised by the Upper Chamber also became intertwined with the land debate. In 1884 Henry George endorsed the agitation against the House of Lords from afar.[11] In addition, W.T. Stead wrote: 'The House of Lords question is at bottom the land question, and land reformers of all shades who are in serious earnest will probably discover that it is sound policy to sink their differences and unite in a great combined attack upon the common enemy.'[12] L.T. Hobhouse concurred, arguing in 1907 that the land 'is the true battleground for a struggle with the Lords'.[13] Chartists like Ernest Jones who campaigned against the excessive waste of fertile land involved in conventional farming methods became part of an acceptable radical pedigree on this issue. In 1910 his speech on 'The Hereditary Landed Aristocracy' from 1856 featured prominently in Liberal election leaflets.[14] After 1909 Liberals attempted to unblock the constitution by embracing a strategy of land reform that increased taxation of land values for the very rich. It was intended that this project would cause the wealthy landowners who monopolised the Lords to simply fade away and so resolve the problems posed by a predominantly landed Second Chamber.

Reform of the House of Lords is frequently portrayed by political historians as an unpopular issue that lacked real momentum and generated no lasting public debate. Traditionally Lords reform is reduced to the level of a mere re-ordering of the legislature.[15] Here the popular politics of the campaign against privilege is ignored. For historians of Liberalism it is inextricably linked with the decline of the Liberal Party and the changes to the constitution resulting from the 1911 Parliament Act. On this reading Liberal criticisms of the Lords after 1884 are seen as an ineffectual rhetoric that did little to arrest the steady decline of the party in the early part of the twentieth century. Indeed the 1909–1911 campaign against the peers is sometimes represented as a backward-looking exercise that demonstrated Liberalism's failure to devise an agenda for the early twentieth century, or to address the labour versus capital issues that were beginning to undermine the position of Liberalism and provide a platform for an emergent Labour Party. According to this analysis the campaign against the Lords was a product of confusion and uncertainty, impelled simply by the weight of Liberalism's history and traditions. This view is compounded by the early socialist press's dismissive treatment of the Lords issue, and its occasional questioning of the Liberals' reasons for embracing it.[16]

For some radical newspapers the issue was simply a distraction. The *Christian Socialist* wrote: 'royalty and the House of Lords both bear their character conspicuously on their foreheads, but the House of Commons is more likely of all to prove dangerous to the people's liberties, when it is essentially a class governing body...'.[17] Many contemporary sources claim that the issue was greeted with apathy by the electorate in 1910.[18]

In addition the Lords issue is linked to the long-term structural weaknesses of the Liberal Party. With Henry Campbell-Bannerman's comment 'when in doubt, slang the Lords' in mind, it is frequently represented as a blocking tactic that prevented the emergence of other more divisive policies that might upset the balance of interests within the Liberal coalition. The Fabian Socialist Cecil Chesterton was in no doubt that the campaign against the Lords was another variant of Liberal 'faddism'. For him, House of Lords reform appeased 'faddist' groups within the party, but did not enthuse electorally. In 1905 he wrote: 'the objection to the House of Lords is not a reformer's objection, but a Liberal partisan's objection ... With us, to whom it is a matter of supreme indifference by which party reforms are carries, this consideration need not weigh.'[19] Paradoxically the charge of 'opportunism' is sometimes levelled against Lloyd George's radical Liberalism over this issue. Such a view acknowledges the popularity of the campaign, but never satisfactorily explains the popular basis of its support. Only Eugenio Biagini has noted the strength of public hostility against the Lords as a significant component in a still vigorous popular Gladstonianism after 1884.[20] This chapter argues that far from being the last gasp of an exhausted Liberalism, Lords reform was a strong popular issue that created the basis for a working partnership with the Labour Party in the early twentieth century and cemented the progressivist politics of 1906–1914. Moreover, the example of Liberal reform of the Lords provided a working model for Labour in office, in which an acceptable rhetoric of opposition to aristocracy kept the Lords in check.

II

Aristocracy was situated at the heart of the British state through the royal bloodline, by traditions of service, and through the outward forms of court protocol. An aristocratic presence at court and in parliament conferred a historic dignity and splendour on the offices of the crown. Aristocrats were accordingly present at all significant state occasions and during the public rituals of monarchy. Their centrality to the rites of passage that characterised the parliamentary year continued to unnerve reformers into the nineteenth century. In 1850 George Julian Harney's *Freethinker's Magazine* condemned them as 'attendant flunkeys of the genus aristocratic' and wrote of their decorative function in parliament: 'the peers are like a volume bound in calf and splendidly "got-up" – the Commons like a people's edition of the self-same book'.[21] Queen Victoria's funeral re-iterated the importance of the British aristocracy at the beginning of the Edwardian period. Their assembled strength, alongside the forty-two archdukes and two emperors of the royal houses of Europe, demonstrated the still very narrow concentration of wealth, power, and land in the hands of a small number of landed and titled families. Radicals at the turn of the century remained conscious of this social aberration and frequently levelled charges of oligarchy against the great territorial aristocracy. Moreover, radicalism realised that the survival of an unchanged and unchallenged aristocracy was conditional upon the persistence of an enduring and unruly court at the heart of government. The *Radical* commented in 1888:

> On inquiry it will be found that in connection with our monarchical institutions there is an aristocracy, founded upon favouritism, and sustained by the royal will, an aristocracy of idlers, doing nothing to enrich the state, but absorbing much of its treasure – the result of the hard and patient toil of thousands of workers.[22]

Such criticisms were part of a long tradition. 'Greedy peers' had figured prominently in radical rhetoric since the 1790s. Most reformers viewed them as part of a hierarchy of wealth and influence that conspired to deprive the people of their just rights. In the 1830s the *Poor Man's Guardian*, which campaigned vigorously against aristocratic influence in politics and in public life, dismissed the House of Lords as a 'hereditary band of bigots, antiquaries and imbeciles'. Richard Carlile christened it 'The Lump'; still others saw the aristocratic system it embodied as a 'huge octopus dragging you and your children down to the depths of misery'.[23] Viewed in these terms, the House of Lords acted as a bulwark against liberty that shielded the reactionary element within the constitution. The Chartists sought to challenge their inviolable position within the executive, and undermined them with a rhetoric of insults. Ernest Jones criticised the entrenched aristocratic composition of the Upper House at the time of the 1858 debates surrounding the Jewish Disabilities Relief Bill which was delayed several times in the Lords: 'the House of Lords as at present constituted is part of our glorious constitution. Touch it with an infant's hand and you sully its purity. Take the possibility of a Jew becoming a lord – it is horrible!'[24] The peers were an easier target than the monarchy or the Anglican Church. Throughout the nineteenth century the House of Lords was more overtly self-serving and nakedly opportunistic in its dealings with reformers than the crown. As a result it never inspired the same demonstrations of popular loyalty as monarchism. This gave radicals a pretext for attacks on aristocracy, and a firm basis of support for their actions that, unlike hostility to the throne, was not dependant on the periodic unpopularity of individual monarchs. For many radicals it was possible to exonerate the monarchy from charges of unduly selfish behaviour, whereas the Lords were portrayed as rampant and unrestrained. The radical journalist William Howitt wrote in 1848 'With our own worthy Queen we have no quarrel. We believe that from her no exercise of popular right would receive a check. But there is another power which has a huge debt to discharge to the nation, that is the aristocracy. This power has usurped everything in this country which can be called natural right as private property. It engrosses the throne, the church, and the property of the people.'[25] Here the Lords were portrayed as shackling Crown and Church in a manner that produced deformed government, weakened the throne, and unbalanced the constitution. Radical pamphleteers like W.T. Stead claimed that the Lords 'itself the creation of the crown, has usurped some of the prerogatives of its creator'.[26] This was a common view. A pamphlet produced by the Financial Reform Association in Liverpool during the Reform Bill crisis posited that the power formerly concentrated in royal hands was now the preserve of an unchecked aristocracy that ruled without restraint through its instrument of the Lords.[27] There were elements of the mindset of the Medieval peasant revolt in the determination by radicals to restrain an ungovernable aristocratic revolt that kept royal power caged, and worked in the interests of the First Estate against Crown and people co-joined. Joseph Clayton made the link with peasant *jacquerie* explicit, writing in 1910: 'The leaders of the Labour Party, in their speeches at public meetings, use much of the old revolutionary talk of John Ball and Robert Ket, and the arguments of Winstanley for the popular ownership of the land.'[28]

From the 1870s onwards an increased momentum built up against the Lords. In 1872 a conference of radicals in Birmingham declared for abolition of the Second Chamber in a measure that 'would equal a change greater than 1688'.[29] Anti-Lords hostility was particularly marked in the radical press and grew in line with the Lords' ungovernability. *Reynolds's Newspaper* and George Standring's *The Republican* revived an older political tradition of invective against the Lords. *Reynolds's* rejoiced in the exposure of the disreputable hidden history of the peerage. Its 'Reynolds's Peerage', which directly lampooned 'Debrett's Peerage', the 'Bible of the Aristocracy', divulged the historical wrongdoings and misdeeds of eminent landed families. In 1897 it exposed the family link of the Earl of Bradford, Lord Chamberlain of the Queen's household, to the President of the Court of Regicides, responsible for the exhumation and violation of Oliver

Cromwell's corpse. In later editions there were similar revelations about the Marquis of Bute and other landed dynasties.[30] The centrality of this form of rhetoric has often been overlooked. Contemporary accounts of the formation of the Democratic Federation, the precursor to the Social Democratic Federation (SDF), demonstrate that it was originally established not for the purposes of disseminating socialism, but rather to campaign for the outright abolition of the House of Lords.[31] Here a recovered popular radicalism reminiscent of the 1830s lived on as a vital element in a vigorous fantasy of plebeian democracy. Opposition to the Lords provided an initiation into popular politics for a new generation of militant radicals throughout this period. The generation of reformers who built the Labour Party, were radicalised by the campaigns against the Lords from the 1860s onwards and set their faces against the Upper Chamber. The Labour MP, John Hodge, recalled as a young boy watching the Great Franchise Demonstration against the Lords on Glasgow Green in 1866: 'There was an iron cage in which was a man dressed so as to represent a peer, and, of course, placards stating "what the people would do with the peers".' Philip Snowden, later Labour Chancellor in the 1920s, remembered demonstrating against the Lords in 1889: 'I remember when the House of Lords suspended the "County Franchise Bill", walking in a procession holding aloft a banner with the words: "Down with the House of Lords" inscribed on it. That was fifty years ago, and the House of Lords is still like Johnny Walker. It has not been my lot to help in "ending" this archaic institution, so I have made my personal contribution to "mending" it.'[32]

Within Liberalism a crude rhetoric of popular egalitarianism also surfaced from the 1860s. By the beginning of his first ministry in 1868 Gladstone had become a shrewd operator in the political brinkmanship required to steer complicated measures through the House of Lords. As Chancellor of the Exchequer in 1860 he had already faced fierce opposition from the Lords for his budget abolishing the excise duty on paper, so making a cheap press possible. The Lords opposed this measure on the grounds that it enabled radicals to further their ideas through the production of inexpensive printed literature. Subsequently Gladstone's first ministry presaged later Liberal attacks on landed and aristocratic privilege. Gladstone's reform programme struck directly at landed society by measures to prevent the purchase of army commissions in 1871, to extend rights of ownership to tenant farmers in Ireland, and to disestablish the Church of Ireland. These latter measures posed a threat to the landed Anglican establishment in Ireland. They were also measures that appealed strongly to a radical audience. High Gladstonianism appeared to be implementing older reform agendas that had traditionally opposed the Church of England as the backbone of the establishment. Here it was in touch with the shade of an existing radical style of agitation. Furthermore, such measures brought the Liberal Party into direct conflict with the House of Lords over issues that had a strong basis of popular support. Both the Church Disestablishment Bill of 1869 and the Irish Land Act of 1870 were mutilated or delayed by the Lords, causing outcry in the popular press.

Traditionally Gladstone's Irish policy has been dismissed as a mere distraction that simply obstructed the evolution of broader social welfare agendas within the Liberal Party. In reality Ireland enabled Gladstone to portray the Liberal Party as radical in focus, and provided the opportunity for a change in direction that held out the prospect for similar land and church reforms on the English mainland. In fact there was sleight of hand here and many radicals in the 1860s were unconvinced by the vague promises made by Liberals during and after Gladstone's first government.[33] Ireland remained Ireland, and the sphere of Irish politics for most Liberals an entirely separate arena of political debate. Gladstone was never radical enough to contemplate significant land reform in England or disestablishment of the Church of England on the Irish model. Rather he embraced a conservative agenda, that trimmed off the worst excesses of privilege in church and state to make established institutions more easily defensible. I have argued elsewhere that before the 1880s there is no real evidence for any lasting accord between Liberalism and working-class radicalism on the basis of a shared and compatible reform agenda.[34] Indeed, such a policy appeared impossible whilst Gladstone continued in place as leader of the Liberal Party and remained true to his conservative inclinations. Nor would I wish to revive John Morley's argument that Gladstone became more radical as he grew older; this is now generally accepted as a product of Morley's wishful thinking.[35] After 1884, however, Gladstone's confrontation with the House of Lords created a continuing demand for significant constitutional reform measures that laid the groundwork for later Liberal successes against the Upper House. As Gladstone's hold on the party weakened, these came increasingly to dominate a shared discourse between radicals and Liberals that paved the way for the fused politics of Progressivism in the years before the First World War. Gladstone himself featured as an icon of these Liberal/radical reforming impulses. Considering himself an outsider he always resisted the notion of a peerage and elevation to the Upper House after his retirement. This delighted his working-class radical following. After his death *The Single Tax* wrote: '"The Great Commoner", to the joy of all democrats, has passed away without the tinsel ornaments of monarchy so dear to the hearts of men of feebler mind... [his title is] greater than that of a king.'[36] Disraeli acted as a counterweight to Gladstone in this respect; his assumption of an earldom and his elevation to the House of Lords in 1876 reinforced the association of Gladstonianism with democratic virtues, and of Toryism with narrow privilege and a system of honours. In Disraeli's case the peerage was seen as favouring the interests of a non-English outsider.

Nevertheless, Gladstone's conservatism emerged most strongly over the issue of the constitution and the role of the House of Lords. Despite continuing obstruction of Liberal policies by the Lords into the 1880s, Gladstone was reluctant to open the doorway to reform of the Upper House or to seriously consider modification of their powers. For him the basis of the House of Lords and the grounding of monarchy in the hereditary principle meant that these institutions were too inextricably intertwined to make any such programme possible. In his view, Lords reform would imperil the very foundations of the monarchy itself. He wrote to Queen Victoria in 1884 that he would resist any attack on hereditary power 'for the avoidance of greater evils' and that: 'organic change of this kind in the House of Lords may strip and lay bare, and in laying bare may weaken, the foundations even of the throne'.[37] Whilst countenancing a public reform campaign against the House of Lords following its rejection of the 1884 reform bill and condemning the institution as an 'irresponsible power' in his stump oratory, Gladstone was still not prepared to go the whole hog and propose a blueprint for a reformed Second Chamber. Indeed his politics remained strongly coloured by his own aristocratic background. Throughout his career the substance of his oratory about the Upper House, whilst critical, never really progressed beyond the view he expressed strongly in 1869 that the real problem with the Lords was the chamber's remoteness from the legislative process. He commented then that: 'from the great eminence on which they sit they can no more discuss the minute particulars of our transactions than could a man in a balloon'.[38] After 1893 when Gladstone encountered fresh obstruction from the Lords over his second Irish Home Rule Bill he strenuously resisted pressure from radical Liberals to embrace a popular crusade against them. Gladstone's 1892–1894 government reflected his aristocratic preferences in this regard. His second Home Rule Bill contained provision for an unelected Upper Chamber in Ireland made up of Irish peers, and in cabinet he promoted peers to high office over the heads of long-standing reform Liberals. Moreover, in 1895 he sought to deter his successor, Lord Rosebery, from fighting a general election with Lords reform as its theme. Gladstone counselled John Morley that Liberals should learn to live with the Lords. Rather than seeking to abolish the Upper House altogether, Gladstone instead proposed keeping the Lords busy by wrongfooting them with a constant stream of small measures: 'like pistols at the heads of the Lords...bills that the opposition in the commons would find it embarrassing to obstruct or oppose'.[39] Symbolically, the final speech of Gladstone's career in the House of Commons in 1894 was on the issue of the Lords' amendment of the Parish Councils Bill for the counties, and constituted a retreat from the notion of an election fought solely on the Lords issue.[40] Toryism shared the concerns of Gladstonian Liberalism that tampering with the Lords imperilled the fabric of the constitution. During the 1909–1911 House of Lords crisis, Tories repeatedly claimed that the issue placed the throne under greater threat than at any time in recent British history. The death of Edward VII in May 1910 apparently confirmed the mortal danger to the constitution posed by Liberal policies, prompting angry scenes in the Commons when Asquith next spoke and shouts of 'who killed the king?' from the opposition benches.[41]

This chapter re-examines Gladstone's contemporary reputation as a timid reformer by reference to his position on the monarchy and the House of Lords. It draws particularly on the 1884 reform bill crisis and Gladstone's reluctance to tackle the issue of reform of the Upper House either in 1884, or in 1892–1894 over his second Irish Home Rule bill. Many advanced radicals understood and were troubled by the contradictions raised by political reform that left the formal structures of hereditary privilege underpinning the royal state and the constitution untouched. Some were prepared to contemplate modification of the monarchy and outright abolition of the Lords. This issue was raised repeatedly by working-class reformers both within and outside Liberalism. Gladstone, however, was reluctant to countenance such changes. For him, tampering with the fabric of the hereditary Second Chamber imperilled the foundations of monarchy and the church. This created unfinished business over the Lords issue for the Rosebery government of 1894–1895 and the Progressivist Liberal administration of 1906–1914. I seek to rehabilitate the Lords issue within Liberalism, by suggesting that far from posing a distraction to the Liberal Party, it was actually central to the preoccupations of many reformers who saw Gladstone not as a constitutional reformer, but rather as a brake on the process of change. This was not a dead end for Liberals or a further way of blocking social reform legislation. Rather it constituted a genuine expression of discontent with a hereditary caste system that thwarted the will of the people. Nevertheless, the strength of Liberal grassroots opinion on this issue was something Gladstone refused to recognise. The Lords issue demonstrates Gladstone's profound constitutional caution. As the Lords increased their resistance to Liberal measure, the conventions governing the relationship between the Upper and Lower House broke down. This meant that the instinctive constitutional caution of many Liberals was overcome, and a more resolute attitude became apparent on the Lords issue. After 1894 Lord Rosebery was prepared to campaign around the issue, and made reform of the Upper Chamber a plank of the Liberal platform.[42] For the majority of mainstream Liberals the House of Lords issue was about the partisan exercise of power by a branch of the legislature. Liberals saw this as promoting the interests of the Tory Party, reducing the Second Chamber to an arm of political Conservatism, and impoverishing the constitution. In his Premier's battle cry on the eve of the general election of November 1910 Asquith condemned the existing system as fostering the 'yoke of [a] Single Chamber – tyranny'.[43] Tory refusals to accept Lords reform accelerated the political confrontation emerging from the issues surrounding the entrenched power of the peerage in the Upper House. In 1884 at the time of the Third Reform Bill, the peers re-emerged as the enemies of progress, reform, and the rights of the people. Again in 1909 Lloyd George likened the Lords to a waiter who: 'if the cook is a Liberal one . . . insists upon showing the dish and ascertaining the views of the customer . . . until it gets quite cold. But if the cook happens to be a Tory one, [he] never ascertains the views of the customer. He has to take it.'[44] Many Liberals concluded that they 'found themselves in office only, but not in power'.[45]

In the early 1880s radical and Liberal attitudes diverged significantly on issues of privilege and a hereditary Second Chamber. For working-class radicals, reform of the Lords was seen as the thin end of the wedge, holding out the prospect of a more substantive amendment and renewal of government. Moreover, radicals were untroubled by the implied threat to monarchy that emerged from proposals to reform the hereditary element within the legislature. Many radicals believed that reform of the monarchy might follow on naturally from the dismantling of the aristocratic superstructure that cushioned the throne and the court. For the reform community this was a development to be welcomed. At a lecture to the Paddington branch of the National Secular Society, J.E. Woolacott asserted:

It is urged by some that the arguments used against the Lords apply equally to the crown. If this is so, and these arguments are good arguments, all I have to say is 'so much the worse for the crown'. I have but little sympathy with lords and kings. I believe in government for the people, and by the people.[46]

Challenging the notion that the House of Lords acted as a bulwark and first line of defence for the monarchy the orator Mackenzie commented in similar vein at the time of the 1884 Reform Bill:

Unwise, I think, at least from a conservative point of view, are those who in these days, admit that the monarchy stands in need of any institution which is in itself prejudicial to the interests of the whole community. Our present sovereign may continue to reside quietly by the lovely shores of Osborne or her Highland house of Balmoral, but depend upon it, the days of monarchy are numbered, and as Shelley says: 'Kingly glare/will lose its power to dazzle, its authority/will silently pass by'.[47]

Implicit in these arguments was the notion, frequently reiterated elsewhere, that the monarchy and the House of Lords would sink or swim together. Some radicals argued during the franchise bill crisis of 1884 that once the initiative passed out of the hands of ministers and was taken up by the populace as a public issue then, 'however they may put a bold face on the matter, [it] must make the hereditary legislators look to themselves, and to the preservation of their privileges'.[48] Many ultra-radical pamphlets bore variations on the theme of 'What shall We Do With It?' in their titles, in conscious emulation of the diatribes against monarchy from the 1870s.[49] For Liberals, in contrast, a wider reform of the royal state was only accidentally implied by the rhetorical assaults on the Upper Chamber that occurred with increasing frequency from 1884 onwards. In 1884, during the anti-Lords demonstration in Hyde Park, the Whig flank of the party was eager that anti-Lords protesters should demonstrate their loyalty to the throne. Lord Carrington urged them to cheer the spectators who included the Prince and Princess of Wales:

I had invited visitors to see the demonstration from my house ... and I heard that the Prince and Princess of Wales would come to see the demonstration. I suggested to one of the organisers that it would serve to show the loyalty of the Liberal Party if, as the procession passed, it should take off its hats and cheer loudly. This happened and the procession took three and a half hours to pass the window...[50]

A common opposition to privilege helped, however, overcome the deep cleavages between Liberal and advanced radical culture. Radical images of the Lords as malign and interfering, projected a different impression of the Upper Chamber from the benign and impotent one sometimes evoked in popular culture.[51] Such narratives united Liberal Nonconformist opposition to indolence and dislike of Church of England bishops resident in the Upper House, with a broader radical hostility to non-productive wealth and inherited social status. Nonconformists had long campaigned against the Lords Spiritual and their role as defenders of the interests of the Church of England within the executive. Even some Anglicans agreed, seeing the role of bishops within the House of Lord as inimical to civil and religious liberties.[52] The Lords' rejection of the 1908 Licensing Bill, which sought to increase licensing and spirit duties, confirmed the vision of the peers and the Tory brewers working in tandem against the Nonconformist interest and the temperance crusade.[53] The anti-Lords slogan of 'The Peerage and the Beerage' epitomises the debased moral vision that radicals believed they shared. Between 1909 and 1911 Liberals campaigned to undercut the moral authority of the Upper House by highlighting the defects that disfigured the moral landscape of aristocracy. During this period hatred of a restrictive, idle, drunken aristocratic presence retarding constitutional advance crystallised around hostility to the Upper Chamber, and enabled the Liberal Party to posture as the leveller of the Lords. The temperance campaigner and Liberal MP, Wilfred Lawson, brought these issues of drink and 'calling time' on the hereditaries together: 'He had been accused of a desire to rob the poor man of his beer, and now he was going to rob the poor man of his peer.'[54] Fused Nonconformist and radical inspired notions of virtue, temperance, and self-improvement also underpinned Lloyd George's remark in a speech at Newcastle that the House of Lords constituted: 'five hundred men...chosen accidentally from among the unemployed'.[55] The image of the Lords presented here and viewed from the perspective of a Welsh 'outsider' in politics was one of moral laxity and malaise. Indeed the campaign against the Lords was suffused with a marked sense of moral earnestness throughout. Condemning the 'Lords of Misrule' one Liberal pamphlet from 1884 drew attention to the image of the peerage that emerged from the aristocracy's own journals, advising that anyone who wished to know their true character: 'will then learn what a compound of gossip, frivolity, conceit and superciliousness is the literature specially composed for them. . . . If he wants to know anything of their moral influence let him turn to the turf, and to the divorce court'.[56] For Lloyd George such failings were in the nature of hereditary rule. He described members of the peerage as 'the ennobled indiscretions of kings'.[57] Fraudulent bloodlines equalled the degraded and the illegitimate authority of delinquent legislators. In a familiar image some Liberals traded in the established rhetoric of opposition to hunting that featured strongly in anti-aristocratic sentiment. The Lords' preoccupation with hunting came to symbolise governmental inertia, and blocking tactics within the legislature.[58] Given that a Mountain Trap Pigeon Shooting Bill passed without amendment immediately prior to the rejection of the 1884 reform bill, such comparisons seemed appropriate. The Lords quite literally shot down prospective Liberal reforming legislation. One pamphleteer wrote: 'killing vermin and shooting birds is the work which they do perform; but what shall we say of the work they do not perform?'.[59] Allegations that the Lords interrupted or suspended important legislation in their exodus to the grouse moors on the 'Glorious Twelfth' were a common charge. The 1872 Secret Ballot Act was almost lost when the peers' preoccupation with shooting led to an early dissolution of parliament and a near collapse of the legislation. The Liberal *Wigan Observer* wrote: 'Of course, the Lords thought of the grouse, and as they hold that birds must be shot, the country could wait for the Ballot.'[60] In 1894 the Lords' opposition to a Liberal death duties bill apparently confirmed their role as a selfish class bent only on self-preservation. The topsy-turvy images of carnival were deployed here to illustrate this theme. Peers were depicted as immoral tramps with begging bowls, demanding handouts from the state and the public purse. The contemporary language of 'hereditary pauperdom' for those who were habitual burdens on the parish made this an appropriate image. Such representations of the Upper Chamber were in a long tradition as a way of highlighting the selfishness of aristocrats. In 1857 Ernest Jones told an audience 'Titled paupers have their workhouses, and you pay for them. Their workhouses are Downing Street, and Somerset House, the Admiralty and Horse Guards, Buckingham Palace, and Whitehall, Chancery and the Church.'[61] In 1898 *The Single Tax* showed the Irish peerage taking money from the pockets of a blindfolded John Bull with the connivance of Lord Salisbury and the Tory party under the caption 'out-door relief for the aristocracy'.[62] After 1906 Progressivist Liberalism bridged the gap between radicalism and Liberalism still further, and accentuated the tendency towards distrust of aristocratic values. The New Liberalism celebrated the notion of a community of producers and encouraged a pan-class alliance of the middling sort and the respectable working-class against an idle rich, and an equally idle poor, incapable of responsibility, and lacking any real stake in society. The political partnership of Asquith and Lloyd George was central to this message. Asquith provided a reassuring anchor for the voters of Middle England, whilst Lloyd George acted as the conduit for a more robust criticism of aristocracy rooted in the Welsh experience of high land rents, an alien Anglican Church and absentee landlordism.[63]

There were sufficient shared concerns and common reference points to make an alliance between radicalism and Liberalism desirable during the highpoints of anti-Lords hostility in 1884 and 1909–1911. This co-operation drew its strength from a common vision of the constitution, an ongoing narrative of national liberty, and a perception of Lords reform as a further stage in the battles for English rights and freedoms. The Lords reform campaigns were constructed around a memory of past achievements arising from the inherited highpoints of the national past. They were grounded particularly in memories of the victory over the Upper Chamber during the debates surrounding the 1832 Reform Bill. The 1832 measure, like the 1884 Reform Bill, was subject to delaying and blocking tactics in the Lords that were overcome by a popular campaign of political agitation throughout Britain's towns and cities. Memories of the 1832 Reform Bill riots were irresistibly stirred by an outbreak of disorder at Aston Lower Ground in Birmingham during a Tory meeting in support of the peers' actions.[64] Even at the start of the campaign the radical *Newcastle Weekly Chronicle* discovered parallels between the 1832 riots and obstructionism in the Lords in 1884: 'the House of Lords in 1832 brought the country to the verge of revolution by their hostility to reform, and the motion which Earl Cairns is to introduce on Monday is simply a repetition of their tactics at that time'.[65] Between 1909 and 1911 contemporaries were also reminded of the three close-fought elections waged and won against vested interests in 1830–1832 that presaged later Liberal electoral confrontation with the Lords during the constitutional crisis.[66] There was, however, more than just an appeal to constitutional precedent at work in the 1884 crusade against privilege. According to a Whig reading of constitutional evolution the bill made progress only as a consequence of a shared alliance between middle-class and working-class radical reformers working in tandem against an unrestrained and unjust power. Here it was the notion of the people locked in a struggle against a narrow 'caste' interest that mattered most to a later generation of Liberal/radical reformers. The 1884 anti-Lords campaign was perceived as a renewal of past radical fervour against a common enemy, and an attempt to regain freedoms that seemed endangered by the peers. As part of this process of 'remembering', veterans of 1832 paraded at popular demonstrations, surviving banners were unfurled, and the theatre of popular street display made repeated reference to this earlier sequence of events. One old Warwickshire veteran of 1832 appeared on public platforms with the traditional fasces, or bundle of sticks, that from the time of the French Revolution symbolised the united will and determination of the people.[67] The 1832 slogan 'the bill, the whole bill, and nothing but the bill' was also revived and displayed on placards at the July 1884 demonstration against the Lords in Hyde Park, where coffins marked 'In Memory of the House of Lords A.D. 1884' featured prominently in the procession. At this protest meeting, pride of place was given to: 'a Brobdingnagian representation of Mr. Gladstone holding in his palm a peer wearing his coronet and with 50 [the majority in the Lords against the bill] dangling from his hand ... [this] excited great mirth'.[68] In the regions provincial Liberal culture solidified around an anti-Lords position. At nation-wide demonstrations in the late summer of 1884 radical memories of previous struggles against Lordly misrule were exhumed. A rally in Bolton included a parade by Peterloo veterans, and a model of the Upper Chamber was dragged through the town with the words:

> Mourn not because the Lords are gone,
>   Their light it never brilliant shone,
> A brainless race to honour lost,
>   Who knew them best, despised them most.[69]

At Failsworth near Manchester in 1884, a banner borne by Samuel Bamford and the Middleton contingent at Peterloo proudly flew at the head of a parade of veterans from 1819. Banners from 1832 were again on display at demonstrations on Glasgow Green in 1909 in protest at the rejection of Lloyd George's budget.[70]

Similar historical visions of the people versus privilege emerged from the attempt by the Lords to amend or restrict the Liberal budget in 1909. By convention money bills were in the control of the House of Commons alone. Moreover, the budget was a hallowed fiscal institution for Gladstonians, evoking the financial probity and restraint of the High Victorian state.[71] As a consequence Liberal budgets became the touchstone of the social contract between governors and the governed. Budget day was above all a day of great national reckoning in which the compact between state and people was renewed annually before the public gaze. As part of this process budgets and the theatricality that surrounded them served as reaffirmations of public and political accountability through a commonly recognised set of rituals and display. It was this compact that the Lords disrupted in 1909 with tactics that undermined the sanctity of mutual obligations between the tax-payer and the government.[72] Liberal election leaflets in the two general elections fought against the influence of the peers in 1910 underlined this point. In National Reform Union leaflets Sir Wilfred Lawson was quoted as saying:

> So long as the House of Commons has in its hands the power of the purse, it is strong enough to deal with the Lords whenever it is backed up by public opinion in doing so. Surely that is constitutional enough for anyone; for 'grievance before supply' is a kind of Com-mons Magna Charta, and there is, and can be, no greater grievance than the House of Lords.[73]

The vision of the battles for English liberty and their role in overcoming the narrow Second Chamber animated Liberals into the middle years of the twentieth century and underpinned the party's declaration in 1927 that: 'Liberals stand for the supremacy of the House of Commons, on the fundamental ground that the people must govern themselves – whether for good or ill...nobody can tax the people except themselves.'[74]

Such joint memories knitted together the language of the Whiggery of the 1830s, Nonconformity, radical invective, and the vision of a pure and undiluted constitutionalism with its roots deep in the British past. The peers acknowledged the unanimity of sentiment around the anti-Lords platform and identified a composite 'Jacobinism' as the true threat to the history and traditions of the existing order.[75] In practice radicalism and Liberalism were indistinguishable over this issue. In the absence of any model for an alternative constitution within radicalism there were no clear guidelines over the 'ending or mending it' debate. It is certainly difficult to chart lines of demarcation that separated one camp off from another. For Liberals, notions of 'divided powers' rooted in the discourse of the American and French Revolutions were not imperilled by proposals to reform the Upper House by merely ridding it of its hereditary dimension.[76] Those Liberals who suggested creating an elective Upper Chamber on the American model found many sup-porters within a broader radical culture that still sought inspiration in American democratic precedent. Above all it was older notions of the 'Norman Yoke' that found their strongest expression in rhetoric of this kind. The most evocative appeals were to shared historical memories of 'The Bloody Conqueror' and the oppressive Normanism that featured strongly in both radicalism and the Whig history of the period. For radicals the Norman invasion established a framework of injustice, for Liberals it created a separate hereditary caste that, not for the first time, was engaged in upsetting the delicate balance between king, lords, and commons. Both believed in the powerful myth of a post-Hastings elimination of native freedoms that accelerated the progress of feudalism and was preserved in the Norman heraldic crests and archaic Norman French ceremonial language of the Lords. One pamphleteer wrote of the Conquest: 'The Normans not only planted their feet upon the necks of the English people, but their feet are still there.'[77] Restricting the power of the Lords offered the prospect of redressing this imbalance. In 1893 the Parish Councils Bill creating parish assemblies was represented by both radicals and Liberals as a reassertion of the Anglo-Saxon folk-moot against lordly Norman rule in the counties. This was to be 'the labourer's Magna Charta, designed to give him back the land which in some way had been stolen from his ancestors by the great landlords'.[78] Study of the Norman origins of the Upper House also helped illuminate the Second Chamber's historical role in regard to the mixed constitution, and shattered the peers' own myths about their legislative function. A 1910 Liberal election leaflet quoted the radical Goldwin Smith on this issue:

The House of Lords has been taken everywhere for a second chamber or senate. It is nothing of the kind. It is one of the estates of the feudal realm, reduced by the decay of feudalism to comparative impotence, such influence as it retains being that not of legislative authority, but of hereditary wealth. It has never acted as, what it is imagined by the political architects of Europe to be, an Upper Chamber revising with maturer wisdom, and in an impartial spirit, the hasty or ultra-democratic legislation of the more popular house. It has always acted as what it is, a privileged order in a state of decay and jeopardy, resisting as far as it dare each measure of change, not political only, but legal, social and of every kind...[79]

The alien and un-English character of the Lords was confirmed by the presence of significant numbers of Irish peers in the Upper Chamber. Irish peerages were the debased coinage of aristocracy. Worth far less in social terms than equivalent titles in Britain, they suffered from their past reputation as easy rewards for administrators and bureaucrats supportive of the Ascendancy in Ireland. The origins of many were morally dubious, or sometimes venal. For most radicals, they were an enduring symbol of the malign effects of patronage, political favouritism, and court corruption in Ireland. W.T. Stead wrote: 'Titles have been given to men for deeds for which they deserved whipping at the cart's tail.'[80] Absentee landlords like Lord Lucan in County Mayo ruled by fear, and expelled large numbers of tenants. Despite his exploits at Balaclava, he was known locally as 'The Old Exterminator'.[81] The Irish peers were the shock troops of the House of Lords. Mobilised to vote down measures that might alleviate the lot of the Irish peasantry, critics depicted them as a drag anchor on the process of British government, habitually blocking attempts to resolve the Irish Question, and clouding the debate about British reform measures at home. Over Irish matters they exerted considerable power to hold back the progress of land reform, to retard advancement towards Home Rule, and to buttress the position of the Anglican Church. The catalogue of the House of Lords' infamy included numerous attempts to mutilate or delay measures that improved the lot of the Irish peasantry, amongst them the 1870 Irish Land Act (which was delayed and softened), and the 1880 Compensation for Disturbances Bill, as well as the Irish Evicted Tenants Bill of 1893. Both the latter were rejected in their entirety (see Appendix 3). These joint Anglo-Irish concerns, created a pan-UK alliance, in which British and Irish land reformers marched shoulder to shoulder towards the goal of land reform. For many reformers the Irish peers symbolised constitutional paralysis and the hold exerted by non-English outsiders over the legislative affairs of the Upper House. Moreover, the worst excesses of landlordism were believed to occur in Ireland, where they provoked rebellion, and provided a harbinger of events unfolding in the English countryside.[82]

The persistence of memories of the Norman Conquest, and the presence of the Irish peers in the Upper Chamber created an inverse patriotism amongst reformers, in which they, rather than the nation's natural leaders, became the upholders of the traditions of the 'Freeborn Englishman'. Reformers sought to reclaim the birthright of every Englishman by clearing away the remnants of foreign occupation, and removing the elements grafted onto the Upper Chamber by the political struggle in Ireland. In their own terms they were the patriots, whereas the Lords served the interests of outsiders and aliens. H.J. Wilson fulminated against the support in the Upper Chamber for grants given to royal offspring and foreign princes who married into the royal family. He remarked of Prince Battenberg's Naturalisation Bill 'no-one could tell Sir Wilfred Lawson what better he would be for it'.[83] When the Lords apparently tampered with issues arising from national defence and prosperity, they were particularly vulnerable to criticisms that highlighted their lack of patriotism. In 1875 they were bitterly attacked for endangering the lives of honest British seamen by holding up the Plimsoll legislation, and amending the Unseaworthy Ships Bill. Long an emblem of the prosperity brought by trade, empire, and independence from the Continent, radicals were able to portray the imperilled sailor as a martyr to the Lords' self-interest and political meddling.[84] W.T. Stead saw the influence of the Lords on foreign policy as even more insidious. They refused to censure unjust foreign wars in Afghanistan in 1878 and Zululand in 1879, and in 1871 sought to suppress the Cardwell reforms which broke down aristocratic monopoly of the officer corps and reformed army bureaucracy to streamline the military: 'The House of Commons has sometimes been for peace. The House of Lords has always been for war!'[85] Underpinning the anti-Lords legislation then, was a vein of patriotism in which the Lords, not the Liberals, sought to hasten the disintegration of the nation and encouraged unjustified adventurism abroad against the interests of Britain. In 1884, anti-Lords meetings began with the singing of the national anthem as an assertion of their patriotic intent. Strong memories of 'Old Corruption' suffused the anti-Lords platform, and the peers were portrayed as the linchpin of a network of corrupt practice that deformed office-holding and the constitution. At a demonstration in Bolton in 1884 one man wielded an axe, and carried a placard 'By this sign we conquer.' 'It had been made "not to kill the Tories, but to kill the wrongs of Old England".'[86] John Bull, the icon of Britishness, was drafted in to help the campaign. In much anti-Lords rhetoric he stood on one side, a baffled observer not yet daring to flex his muscles against the peers, but concerned about the privileges of aristocrats and their retainers. Howard Evans wrote: 'John Bull is a very patient animal; but some day perhaps, he will begin to compare the relative proportions of taxation borne by such leviathans as the Duke of Westminster and by struggling professional men, and then he will wonder that he could have been such a fool as to uphold the injustice so long.'[87]

III

The career of Henry Labouchere, former editor of the Liberal *Daily News* and MP for Northampton, symbolises this radical/Liberal fusion over constitutional ideas and demonstrates the ways in which Liberals and radicals united in defence of a legislative structure that was seen as 'historically' constructed. Labouchere became the most vocal Liberal opponent of the Lords, proposing private members bills to abolish the hereditary element in the Upper House on three separate occasions between 1884 and 1888. He stated in the Commons in 1884: 'members of the House of Lords were neither elected nor selected for their merits. They sat by the merits of their ancestors, and, if we looked into the merits of some of those ancestors, we should agree that the less said about them the better.'[88] Such sentiments legitimised Henry Labouchere's personal radical journey from Huguenot Protestant stock, through exposure to English history, American democracy, and French Republicanism, to radical reformer intent on Lords reform.[89] Labouchere was a herculean figure for many radicals. Like David, he took on the Goliath of the Lords in regular debates, motions made during the Queen's Speech, and in barbed reminders of the unaccountability of the Upper Chamber. These became enjoyable occasions, almost akin to carnival, when parliamentary colleagues gathered to hear the exchanges. On one such occasion he declared 'The Conservatives at their meetings always shouted "Thank God we have a House of Lords!". Radicals had no intention to remain any longer supinely like toads under the harrow of the House of Lords. They intended to agitate until they could say: "Thank God we have not an hereditary House of Lords".'[90] In addition, Labouchere created the possibility for a working partnership with groups like the SDF who supported him over his stance on the Lords.[91] These campaigns against the peers came at a time when the steady leakage of landed and urban proprietors away from Liberalism into Toryism increased the influence of radical Liberals within the party. The Newcastle Programme of 1891, which also highlighted Lords reform, marked a highpoint of their significance.[92] During the 1892–1895 Liberal Government, Rosebery's personal Whig legacy as the son of a member of Lord Grey's reforming ministry of the 1830s conferred a marked radical pedigree on this anti-Lords issue. For some radical Liberals, pedigree was as much about inherited dislike of aristocracy and hereditary systems, as about the descent in land and titles along the family line. Sir Charles Dilke saw himself as an ancestral republican with a family tradition of opposing hereditary office-holding.[93] Furthermore the National Liberal Federation, which comprised the strong radical backbone of much Liberal organisation in the regions, gave the campaign against the Lords their wholehearted backing in 1884, and again during the 1895 election. Thereafter, the Liberal attacks on the House of Lords created a generalised narrative of liberty that knitted together the opposing expectations of Liberals and working-class radicals, and provided the framework for a fused vocabulary of co-operation culminating in Progressivism. Here the notion of wielding power on the basis of birth was challenged directly. Between 1910 and 1911 the role of 'the Ditchers' in resisting reform of the Lords to the bitter end confirmed the worst impression of the peers current amongst radicals.

In addition, in the two elections of 1910 members of the House of Lords like Lansdowne, Curzon, Cromer, and Dunraven emerged from their previous seclusion to argue their case publicly on the campaign trail.[94] The raised public profile of individual lords caused an avalanche of satirical squibs, cartoons, and election posters on a scale unrivalled for some years in popular politics. Lord Willoughby de Broke recalled that 'The Peers had been held up to derision on the Liberal hoardings dressed in robes and coronets, like the peers in *Iolanthe*, and it is quite likely that some of the audience thought that we should appear on the platform as we appear at a coronation.'[95] The image of 'the coronet' in satire and the Labourist press became the lasting symbol of this 'nation within a nation' that defied the will of the people.[96] Liberal election posters from the 1895 general election went further and used the image of St George locked in mortal combat with the dragon, surmounted with the coronet of the peerage, to symbolise the eternal struggle between democratic imperatives and caste interests. For its opponents, the 'die-hard' opposition of the Lords was emblematic of the introverted and introspective constitutional world of the Upper Chamber. Lord Willoughby de Broke quoted the antiquated style of the 'backwoodsmen' as emblematic of their obsolescence and redundancy: 'The backwoodsmen came to town in large numbers, some of them redolent of the countryside, bucolic in aspect, many of them wearing the early Victorian stock [*sic*], and in their antique dress and old-fashioned manners recalling a bygone generation.'[97] In cartoons the peers were frequently shown in eighteenth-century styles of dress. Ermine, elaborate robes, knee breeches and hose compounded this vision of a retrograde class, living in antiquarian splendour, and oblivious to the true needs of the nation, but determined to resist the groundswell in favour of reform at any cost. For critics, their decayed and fossilised state was expressed through their obsession with the symbols of office, competition for minor positions at the court, and interest in the trivial trappings of hierarchy and precedence. One radical orator lampooned the 'ancient and sublime mysteries of plush, lords-in-waiting, grooms of this, that, and the other, the difference between gold stick and silver stick, and the duties of [the] Hereditary Grand Falconer'.[98]

This vocal Liberal hostility to the Lords, far from imperilling the throne, confounded Gladstone's prediction of the hereditary principle's vulnerability to scrutiny, and created an acceptable enemy that diverted attention away from a monarchy that rose above mere party conflict. Under the patronage of the Liberal government royal events like the coronation of George V and the 1911 Investiture of the Prince of Wales stabilised the crown during a period in which the foundations of the dignified element within the constitution seemed open to question. In these ceremonies the Liberal vision of the United Kingdom was projected as decentralised, devolved, and diverse, but nevertheless united, under the 'Liberal' monarch, George V.[99] It might also be argued that far from promoting the cause of anti-monarchism, the creation of an acceptable Liberal opposition to privilege actually retarded the prospects of republicanism still further, making it seem irrelevant to the real struggle that arose from the peers versus the people campaigns. For Liberals, House of Lords reform was a safe project, displacing the necessity for a broader revision of the constitution. Moreover, it lifted the monarchy out of the mire of everyday politics and set up a false comparison in which the monarchy remained resolutely aloof from politics, whereas the Lords retained an interest in deploying hereditary privilege in favour of the Tory interest. Here the Lords committed a cardinal sin and hastened their own demise, whilst the fiction of royal impartiality was maintained.[100] In this way the Liberal Party managed to square the circle and laid the groundwork for a future Lib/Lab alliance rooted in a loyalism vision of the constitution in the years before 1914. Radicals like John Burns who favoured a republic realised Liberalism's limited potential as a vehicle for reform of the royal state, and were highly critical of Lloyd George's close relationship with George V during the planning of the Investiture at Caernarfon; 'he's had house maid's knee ever since' was his cynical comment on Lloyd George's first meetings with royalty.[101]

None the less, a notion of democracy and democratic participation was central to the combined vision of Liberalism and Labourism. Recent research on the historical antecedents of turn-of-the-century Labourism have emphasised the strength of such democratic appeals.[102] Here conceptions of democracy, freedom, and political accountability have been reclaimed from Liberalism and Toryism, and made integral to the experience of the early Labour movement. It is now acknowledged that the roots of Liberalism and Labourism are inextricably intertwined. This new scholarship revises existing understandings of the Labour Party as a trade union dominated crusade, intent upon the amelioration of economic and social grievances, and geared towards the goal of redis-tribution of wealth.[103] Instead, the new reading of the Labour tradition emphasises Labourism's debt to Liberalism and an inheritance that was inclusive of those strands of opinion that sought reform of the con-stitution, rather than simple modification of the economic superstructure. Labourism was never, however, simply a client in its turn-of-century relationship with the Liberal Party. The Progressivist project of 1906–1914, underpinned by the Lib/Lab alliance of 1903, is now accepted as a fundamental part of a joint culture that provided a working partnership of ideas and a coherent strategy with consequences that still shaped the direction of Labour policy after 1945.[104]

No longer simply dismissed as a distraction from the forward march of Labour, this period of co-operation has been rediscovered as a profitable interchange and evolution for both sides of the alliance. Without Labour's votes after 1910, when Asquith led a minority government, Progressivism would have been dead in the water. The strength and mutually beneficial nature of this partnership on the ground also explains Labour's failure to make progress on its own terms in by-elections between 1906 and 1914.[105] The House of Lords issue provides a further opportunity to reprise the politics of 1909–1911 and to deepen our understanding of the importance of constitutional reform to the Labour pioneers. Asquith's 1910 declaration of war on the Lords in the second general election of the year signalled a convergence of intent on this subject between Labourism and Liberalism. Radical Liberals, radicals who owed a debt to the Chartist tradition, and Labourites were able to unite around a com-mon strand of belief that saw the existence of the Lords as detrimental to the will of the people. For reformers whose views were moulded by an older radical milieu and who saw English and Irish democracy as co-joined, deliberate attempts by the Lords to overturn reform in Ire-land perpetuated a vision of the country as difficult and unmanageable, whilst further accentuating the differences with the mainland. Many radicals and Irish nationalists saw the presence of Irish peers in the Lords as constituting the major barrier to the resolution of the Irish Question. George Standring noted even the 'blind, the lame and the halt' hurrying to Westminster 'in bath chairs and ambulances' to vote down the Com-pensation for Disturbances in Ireland Bill in 1880.[106] There was also a point of contact here for mainstream Liberals exclusively preoccupied with the Irish issue. W.T. Stead wrote:

It may be said that the House of Lords has been unable to persevere in its opposition to popular reforms excepting in the case of Ireland;

and in the case of Ireland its success has been as signal as it has been pernicious. In England and Scotland it has delayed and marred measures of reform; in Ireland alone has it rejected them.[107]

For socialists within Labourism, the abolition of the Lords was similarly an essential 'clearing away' of a body that thwarted the potential for eventual reform in England itself, and whose defeat made the realisation of true socialism possible. Against this background, advanced radicals were willing to overcome their initial doubts about the Liberal intention to transform the Lords into a Liberal 'House of Patronage', and embrace the reform crusade of 1909–1911. In the eyes of Labour activists like Ramsay MacDonald, steeped in a Chamberlainite radical tradition, it was the actions of the Lords, not the reformers, which upset the delicate balance of the constitution.[108] In part such Labourist notions of a direct democracy were formulated in response to Conservative referendal theories of the House of Lords as a supreme arbiter, expressive of the true will of the people, that occupied the constitutional high-ground of politics in battles with the Commons. According to this argument, the Lords had a constitutional duty to refer measures directly to the electorate for its decision where the government of the day seemingly lacked a full electoral mandate. This reflected an instinctive distrust of the caucus politics of the Commons and in effect openly invited the Lords to rebuff legislation of which they disapproved.[109] Labourist notions of a direct democracy forcefully contested this retrograde vision of the constitution. Devolved democratic participation was central to Labourist concerns. In the 1890s many Labour papers campaigned vigorously for referenda on all council and borough matters as a defence of local autonomy in the face of parliamentary intervention in local affairs. As Ian Bullock and Sian Reynolds have pointed out, the years after 1894 saw something of a vogue for referenda in Labourist circles.[110] For some Labourites referenda provided an opportunity to circumvent the power of the Lords in 'The Mangling House'; J. Morrison Davidson advocated a referendum based on the Australian model in which two consecutive referrals of legislation by the Upper Chamber automatically triggered a ballot of the electorate.[111] Asquith sought to appease this tradition within Labourism in 1910 at the height of the House of Lords crisis when he suggested an immediate referendum on the position of the Lords.

Joint declarations and activity between Labourism and Liberalism against the Lords was strongest at the grassroots. Officially the embryonic Labour Party remained aloof from attempts to reform the Lords. In 1910

Keir Hardie denounced the Liberals for seeking to enhance and consolidate the power of a Liberal-dominated Commons at the expense of the second tier of the executive: 'thus taking away the odium which inevitably attaches to obstructive powers and tactics when continuously exercised by a body of irresponsible legislators'.[112] For many working men, however, the Lords appeared as much a symbol of the ability of local employers to augment their wealth with estates and stately homes, as of landed privilege *per se*. From the turn of the century onwards, the social transformation in the Lords from a house of ancient pedigree to a bastion of former businessmen and 'parvenu peers' had become a common theme amongst radicals.[113] Newly ennobled peers were a 'mushroom aristocracy' that had sprung up like fungus overnight. Defenders of the existing Upper Chamber were perplexed by such arguments. William Charteris Macpherson declared: 'It is remarkable, certainly, that one of the oldest of our institutions should be attacked by the party of "progress" on the ground that for the members of that party it is too new. The bitter cry of the Liberation Society that the House of Lords is insufficiently Medieval is, to the Tory ear, not a little bewildering.'[114] Nevertheless, the merging of the two issues of employment rights and hostility to the Lords paved the way for a common constitutional reform agenda. Responding to the Liberal notion of flooding the Lords with new peers sympathetic to the government, the Fabian and Guild Socialist *New Age* demonstrated an abhorrence of new money and a strong tinge of anti-Semitism in its attacks on: 'the prospect of a second chamber crowded with Jew stock-brokers, wealthy soap-boilers, men who have made their pile in the South African "swindle" and who [have] set up as "gentlemen of England"'.[115] At local level, Labour periodicals in the West Riding fulminated against: 'the [existing] assembly of successful lawyers, slum owners and varnished soap-boilers styled, surely in joke, the "Upper House"'.[116] The Lords' amendment and delay of the 1894 Employers Liabilities Bill did much to mobilise a constituency of trades unionists and the disaffected within Liberalism who sought a final reckoning with the Upper House. During the election of 1895, whilst Keir Hardie cautioned in a speech at Sowerby Bridge against an excessive enthusiasm for Lords reform that might detract from the 'social question', West Riding radicals warmly embraced Lord Rosebery's crusade against the Upper House at an ecstatic meeting in Bradford.[117] In a strong appeal to the West Riding radical tradition the Liberal *Bradford Observer* spoke of enthusiastic demonstrations from the crowd that: 'expressed the long-smouldering fires of Old Liberal as well as New Liberal discontent [and] the long restrained revolt forced upon it by decades of arbitrary and despotic treatment'.[118] Post-Gladstone, many Liberal and Labour activists felt liberated by the end of Liberal policies of tentative and uneasy co-existence with the Lords. Subsequently much pent up anger and frustration was released by the radical activity surrounding Rosebery's campaign. Even Keir Hardie praised Gladstone at the time of his death in 1898 for his role in initiating these later attempts to curb the Lords; in an obituary in the *Labour Leader* he gave the campaign his retrospective blessing and condemned the last Gladstone Cabinet for a lack of nerve in standing up to the peers:

> The old warrior was thirsting for a fray with the Lords...The proud commoner would not brook that the haughty lordlings, themselves bankrupt of prestige and with no power behind them, mere shadows of things which had been, should thwart his will. But the little-souled crew who surrounded him, shrank in dismay from the contest and the consequences...[119]

In the general elections of 1910 fought on the Lords issue, the anti-peers campaign, whilst denting the Liberal majority of 1906, allowed the Liberals to consolidate their strength in working-class districts in Lancashire, Yorkshire, South Wales, Scotland, and London on a high turnout of 46.8 per cent.[120]

The 1911 Parliament Act, which limited the ability of the Lords to retard Commons legislation, stopped short of a full root and branch reform of the Upper House. Liberal intentions of making the Second Chamber an elective body were never fulfilled. Progressivism was not a levelling creed, either in Britain or the US. Instead it advocated a notion of social justice that sought to inform the propertied of their true responsibilities and obligations to the poor. In Britain it never contemplated a full assault on the existing order, rather it hoped simply to humanise the establishment's role as guardian of a Liberal-led status quo.

From the 1880s onwards opponents of the Lords plundered British historical memory to provide a justification for action against them, and precedents for their platform of reform.[121] For reformers the Lords were an army of occupation. As James Vernon has pointed out, images of bondage and imprisonment were the stock motifs of the radical critique of landed influence.[122] The events of the English Civil War, however, provided a model for curtailing the power and persistence of landowners and their lackeys. In 1899, the tercentenary of Cromwell's birth, debates about commemorating his life in Britain's towns and cities led to a re-examination of the Civil War period. Recovered memories of a radical Cromwellianism began a process of reappraisal of the English Civil War in which Cromwell's influence emerged as benign, rather than dictatorial. These retrospective readings of the British national past were debated and mapped out on the pages of radical newspapers of the period. Here 'The Great Commoner' was rehabilitated as a stern and fair dispenser of justice. Traditionally a reworked Cromwellianism had always sustained an oppositional stance critical of unrestrained regal and aristocratic power. In the poetry of Algernon Swinburne, Cromwell was immortalised as one who needed no physical reminders of his importance: 'How should Cromwell stand / With kinglets and with queenlings hewn in stone?'[123] He lived on instead as part of popular historical memory. Joseph Arch had long celebrated the role of the sturdy English yeoman at the side of Cromwell during the English Civil War and England's other tribulations, describing them as: 'The sons of sires who fought at Cressy and Waterloo, and struck for freedom at Naseby and Dunbar.'[124] Such recollections featured strongly in the anti-Lords demonstrations of 1884. Reformers pointed out that the constitutional models for the abolition of the Second Chamber were Cromwellian ones.[125] In 1649 the Commonwealth Parliament had taken the unprecedented step of dismissing the Lords, an action that demonstrated to radicals the effectiveness of resolute action on the constitution. Recalling the words used by Cromwell on that occasion the radical Sheffield MP, H.J. Wilson, told an audience at Doncaster that the Lords: 'Should, in the words of Oliver Cromwell, make way for "better and honester men".'[126] To those who hoped for a broader assault on privilege the anti-Lords campaign raised the possibility of modification or abolition of royal power in a similar style. *Reynolds's Newspaper* noted the memories stirred on the day of the radical demonstration in Hyde Park in July 1884 by the procession passing the site of Charles I's execution at the Banqueting House, Whitehall:

No man with the feelings of an Englishman seeing the procession traversing the historic roads of Whitehall, Charing-Cross and Piccadilly could not but be impressed with the recollection of another crowd that stood there in 1648 [*sic*] to witness the last act in a contest with the people. Except that Englishmen are now much more inclined to employ scorn and contempt rather than the scaffold and the headsman, they are very much what their forefathers were when privilege chose to attack the sacred rights of the people.[127]

Reformers depicted the conflict with the Lords as a new Civil War, taking up the work Cromwell had left unfinished. It particularly united Nonconformist Liberals and reformist radicals who cohered around a 'Solemn League and Covenant' rooted in hostility to unbridled aristocracy.[128] Exponents of a revived Cromwellianism reached deep into the past to reclaim the code of the seventeenth-century Puritan movement. Summoning up the spirit of Puritanism in 1912, Ramsay MacDonald equated it with the inheritance of liberty from the Germanic tribes and commented of its levelling tendency: 'For the relief of its conscience it must occasionally demonstrate the equality of kings and men by chopping off the heads of King Charleses.'[129] The image of 'The Man from Huntingdon' as a figure of unsullied radical zeal and integrity emerged powerfully from this vision. He was portrayed primarily as an anti-aristocratic figure, who strove against 'delusive' aristocratic values and outworn and counterfeit chivalric codes.[130] Inspired by this historical memory, the language used by reformers was a confrontational and pugnacious one. Writing at the height of the budget crisis in 1909 *Our Land* quoted Cromwell's words on the House of Lords 'lay it aside' and depicted the opponents of the Lords as a New Model Army in training for war. It remarked: 'We may not win the first battle; the "interests" against us are strong. Our scythes and pruning hooks have still to be turned into swords, our need for drill and discipline may yet be apparent. But those of us whose electoral life has been stultified and neutralised welcome the call to arms, and, as we have already said, death is better than slavery.'[131] For most radicals, the real threat posed by aristocracy was as a social system, controlling and retarding the progress towards the realisation of true democracy. Some reformers saw the various House of Lords crises as opportune moments to assault the political excesses of landownership in patronage, political preferment, and control of tenants in pocket boroughs. Other reformers warned balefully that the House of Lords was capable of mobilising a vast army of vassals and flunkeys in its defence. There was more than a hint of the royalist cavaliers about this army of reaction. Josiah Wedgwood told a Labour Party conference at Portsmouth: 'From the times of the *Gracchi* to that of the Black Hundreds, the dependants are always more dangerous than their masters in opposition to every form of liberty.'[132] This cluster of forces was the harbinger of the coming apocalyptic struggle with the forces of landlordism. For other radicals the Commonwealth period offered a generalised narrative of liberty. Groups like the Levellers and the Diggers became immensely sympathetic figures for a new generation of

Labourites at the turn of the twentieth century. Their advocacy of franchise extension, land reform, and communal living mirrored the concerns of Georgeite land reformers, millenarian socialism, and radicals of all hues.[133]

The House of Lords crisis then, offered two distinctive views of English politics, English history, and the English state. It pitted the forces of progressivism against the scions of the hereditary aristocracy, ranged the upholders of liberty against the advocates of the status quo, and put advocates of freedom in opposition to defenders of monopoly. For radicals and Liberals involved in this campaign it was a patriotic movement, cleansing the remnants of Norman feudalism from the legislature. In 1911 Lords reform was long overdue. Thereafter, the debates surrounding it dented the image of a venerable and unchanging continuity embodied by the Lords. At the beginning of the twentieth century the House of Lords issue provided a more significant and contentious political moment than hitherto realised by historians. In simple constitutional terms the 1911 Parliament Act merely turned the convention of Lords non-interference in money bills into enforceable statute. Much conventional historiography has therefore concentrated on the long-term constitutional implications of the 1911 Act for the balance of power between the Lords and the Commons. This is to miss the point. Above all Lords reform provided the opportunity for unity between the contending factions of radicalism, Labourism, and the New Liberalism behind a common purpose. The project of modernising the state was as much a concern of early Labourism and later radicalism as it was of Liberalism. Re-visiting their common Enlightenment legacy and drawing together themes of public service, civic reform, and popular accountability, Lords reform propelled the divided forces of radicalism, Labourism, and Liberalism into a communality of ideas. In so doing it drew the sting of popular anti-monarchism from radicalism, and provided the framework for future Labourist co-operation with the establishment. Moreover, rather than weakening or challenging the throne, the Liberal House of Lords crisis confounded Gladstone's predictions of the 1880s, with the result that the monarchy emerged from the dispute with the Commons revived, and with its prestige enhanced in the years before the outbreak of the Great War.

5
Plutocracy

I am of a savage and envious nature – I like to see these two
humbugs which, dividing, as they do, the social empire of this
kingdom between them, hate each other naturally, making
truce and uniting, for the sordid interests of either. I like to see
an old aristocrat, swelling with pride of race, the descendant of
illustrious Norman robbers, whose blood has been pure for
centuries, and who looks down upon common Englishmen
as a freeborn American does on a nigger – I like to see an old
Stiffneck obliged to bow down his head and swallow his infernal
pride, and drink the cup of humiliation poured out by Pump and
Aldgate's butler...I despise you, but I want money; and I will
sell you my beloved daughter, Blanche Stiffneck, for a hundred
thousand pound, to pay off my mortgages. Let your son marry
her, and she shall become Lady Blanche Pump and Aldgate.[1]

It is a brutal thought, but we cannot refrain from the reflection
that, if all the contemporary payers of supertax on unearned
incomes – meaning the property-owners of £5.000 a year and
upwards – were to go down in a new *Titanic* disaster, whatever
else the United Kingdom might lose, it would, in respect of artists,
scientists, authors, poets, musicians, composers or religious
teachers of any distinction, be none the poorer.[2]

He saw aristocracy dead at the root, and plutocracy enthroned
to 'reign till it rotted'.[3]

The withering of the British aristocracy provided testimony to a lost
England. For contemporaries the 1920s and 1930s were characterised by

images of a declining and decadent aristocratic presence bent on its own self-destruction. For some authors, the inter-war aristocracy inhabited the wreckage of its former grandeur, plundered and undermined by the forces of an emergent plutocracy. The aristocracy's inevitable decline was hastened by a collapse of the virtues of gentility, restraint, and the *espirit de corps* that in the nineteenth century had traditionally charac-terised the closed caste of the British 'upper ten thousand'. In a period of rapid social change, aristocracy seemed to be celebrating its own decline in the hedonistic excess of the 1920s. The overriding image of the period was of the decay of the country home, the decline of aristocratic manners, and the disruption of the social hierarchies that had held life together on the land. The literature of the inter-war years were thus marked by a nostalgia for a national past of social stability and elite patrician values, imperilled by a 'new barbarism' in which values of *noblesse oblige* were abandoned and disregarded, and a caste, formerly characterised by stoicism and self-restraint, fell into reckless abandon. For defenders of the aristocracy the castle of the constitution, both figuratively and literally, had been overwhelmed by philistinism and materialism.

During these years discussion of aristocracy's decline became a regular feature of literary treatments of inter-war culture. The 1920s were the height of the literary boom that featured lost and self-destructive aristocratic figures. For Huxley the aristocracy had turned in on itself. In his writings the superficiality of inter-war society was a measure of the lack of guidance and leadership provided by a now uncertain and regressive class. The aspiring aristocrat, John Buchan, evaluating the impact of the Great War on British society, saw the failure of aristocratic leadership in the trenches, and the rough egalitarianism of wartime as diminishing the reverence and respect due to social superiors. In a decade marked by the death of deference, there was little place for the more traditional forms of aristocratic display. Aldous Huxley, Evelyn Waugh, and others composed an epitaph to pre-1914 values that discussed the aristocracy in terms of its decline and rapid disintegration. In Waugh's *Work Suspended*, Plant's father remains obsessed by the expropriatory policies of Lloyd George and believes in an 'open conspiracy for the destruction of himself and his class'. He remarks: 'Seventy years ago the politicians and the tradesmen were in alliance; they destroyed the gentry by destroying the value of the land; some of the gentry became politicians themselves, others tradesmen; out of what was left they created a new class, into which I was born, the moneyless, landless, educated gentry who managed the country for them. My grandfather was a Canon of Christchurch, my father was in the Bengal Civil Service. All the capital they left their sons was education and moral principle.'[4] Lacking direction, Waugh portrayed younger members of the aristocracy burning themselves up in an orgy of self-indulgent and excessive behaviour in the over-heated atmosphere of the 1920s and 1930s. For historians like David Cannadine, the inter-war aristocracy had quite simply lost its way. Bereaved by the loss of many of its younger sons in the trenches, and destabilised by a collective collapse of self-confidence following its defeat over the Lords issue, the aristocratic politics of the 1930s in particular was marked by a tendency towards extremist posturing, or an introspective self-absorption. For many contemporaries this was quite simply a doomed class with little merit, and no discernible future. Critics saw a closing of the book on traditional aristocratic values that paved the way for the emergence of new social forces and the evolution of society along more meritocratic, egalitarian lines.

These images of a decadent and debauched social elite found strong resonances in the popular politics of the 1920s and 1930s. The years between 1900 and 1940 were marked by increasing concerns about the 'plutocratisation' of the British aristocracy. There was a deliberate irony in the choice of title for Howard Evans' critique of the aristocracy, *Our Old Nobility*. In it, he revealed that 'The family tree of the Duke of Leeds, Earl Fitzwilliam, the Earl of Radnor, the Earl of Ancaster, the Marquess of Northampton, and many another noble, has its roots not in some crusading warrior, but in a money grubbing alderman.'[5] In 1912 Arthur Ponsonby, a former page to Queen Victoria and a brother to the Edwardian courtier Fritz Ponsonby, and thereby sensitive to social-climbers around the throne, alerted his readers to the threat of invasive plutocratic values, and the degree to which they undermined and eroded the gentility of high society: 'The advent of a plutocracy, we devoutly hope, is only a nightmare.'[6] Beatrice Webb's nightmare was fulfilled in the shape of her plutocratic brother-in-law, Daniel Meinertzhagen, who predicted a future in which the City was 'an island of capital in a sea of foreign investment' and the land was given over to game preservation.[7] The Edwardian period and the years after the Great War were the high-point of plutocratic influences, in which their values and example were seen as 'warrening' the edifice of aristocratic culture. These were the years of the 'Nitrate King', the 'Silver King', and the 'Gold King' who aped and simultaneously eroded the values of the titles they emulated and aspired to.[8] Writing in 1935 at the time of the death of George V, John Buchan attributed the period of labour unrest before the Great War to the increased visibility of plutocrats in the entourage of Edward

VII: 'The power of plutocracies was everywhere in the ascendant, and the aristocracies, even the most ancient and respectable, found their prestige dwindling. In Britain the great families were still in the governing class, and the great houses were still maintained, but they counted for less. The catholic tastes of King Edward had opened fashionable society to many who a generation earlier would have knocked at the door in vain.' In his view their high-profile public presence, opulence, and acquisition of vast sums of unearned wealth tended to 'coarsen and vulgarise the public mood', stoking up the fires of social envy, and encouraging acquisitiveness and social discontent.[9] Prominent in his novels were just such characters, educated, cosmopolitan, with exotic connections, at work in organised conspiracies to diminish and discredit society. In his writings Britain is subverted by 'the whole gang of Jew speculators and vulgarians who would corrupt a great country'.[10] Such criticisms were in a long tradition. A framework of aristocracy, 'refilled' with new members had transformed landed society into 'a scarcely venerable ruin of the Feudal aristocracy' in 'the days of Newton and Kepler'.[11] In the 1850s, however, concerns about the degeneration of aristocratic stock, new money, and 'vulgar' incomers had solidified around the idea of a plutocracy that was neither entirely landed, nor entirely industrial or commercial. The trades unionist George Potter recorded the use of the term by Gladstone but saw it as 'a softer but less generally understood word' than 'money-bags'.[12] The word itself was often used to describe those social forces that had cohered around the defence of land and property at the time of the 1867 and 1884 Reform Acts.[13] Many aristocrats were concerned about the influx of individuals who sported the outward social trappings of aristocracy, but lacked all the social graces that went with power and position. At the same time, the exodus of traditional families from the land seemed to sound the death knell of the 'county set'. James Wentworth Day, editor of the *Illustrated Sporting and Dramatic News* lamented the trend: 'During the last twenty-five years, many men whose families were founded in the land, and their children made human and great thereby, have sold their acres and gone into a world of paper speculation from which little appears to result, except anxiety, topsy-turvy riches, and a mercurial sense of values.'[14]

The term 'plutocracy' as a category of social description prospered from the 1890s onwards. For some these were the new, cosmopolitan social forces that inspired an urban-centred, anti-landlord Liberalism, and fostered the sale of venal peerages at the time of Lloyd George's 'Honours Scandal'.[15] At one level the term was simply an insult directed towards the vulgar and the unmannered. James Lees-Milne recorded in his diaries of the conspicuous consumption of former aristocratic friends: 'I did not enjoy this visit because I do not belong to their plutocratic, bullion-broking, racing, gambling set.'[16] Nevertheless, the word lost none of its power by force of repetition. It operated both as a criticism of aspiring industrialists, as a thinly-veiled insult with racial undertones, and as an explanation for the unmerited rise of certain key families and individuals. Moreover, it was able to unite critics both of the Left and of the Right. For defenders of the existing order it created a measure of social change and decline, explained the loss of estates and the erosion of land values, and provided a marker for the diversification of commercial wealth. The organicist and Far Right fellow traveller, Rolf Gardiner wrote: 'During the last century or so whence has much of this newer blood come from? From the filters of alien races, the courts of the money-chasers, the halls of the luxury trades and industries, the offices of the asphalt-minded Press. It is these elements which have destroyed the British aristocracy from within, this upstart section.'[17] Hilaire Belloc discerned 'a corrupt bargain for the defence of privileged or personal interests' grounded in plutocratic, vested concerns.[18] For radicals and socialists, the term undermined the integrity of the existing order, and held out the prospect of the old enemy of capital reinvented in a new guise. J.B. Priestly referred to 'a plutocracy disguised as an aristocracy' inspiring the image of emergent new wealth encased in the 'moth-eaten garb' of the old traditional families.[19] For the conservationist movement, the plutocrats exacerbated the dispossession of the Englishman from his birthright in moors and mountains, creating the circumstances in which 'the plutocrat wants a solitude for himself and his friends, and our curious British land system gives him unique facilities for creating one'.[20]

The increasing centrality of notions of plutocracy provided one response to the changing nature of aristocracy in the inter-war years. The image of an 'upper class' diluted by wealth and riches gained ground as a response to the evident entryism by commercial magnates and financiers into the hitherto landed bastions of the peerage. The acceleration of this process indicated the degree to which the ramparts protecting landed wealth and the peerage had been breached, undermining the traditional territorial aristocracy. As Ross Mckibben has pointed out, in the period 1921–1930 only 13 out of 93 newly created peers had landed backgrounds.[21] For some contemporaries this signalled that the traditional rural aristocracy was in decline. Even older landed families saw them as increasingly marginalised. The Tory MP, socialite and celebrated gossip,

Chips Channon, expressed a common view of the declining county aristocracy as poor relations to their metropolitan cousins when he wrote 'Honor and I went to dine locally with the "county" in a ghastly house smelling of gentry – china in cabinets higgledy-piggledy [*sic*], water-colours in gilt frames on the walls. Horror'.[22] With no new blood, and fewer links to the land, 'society' was increasingly reshaped around the vested interests of the power elite of newspaper proprietors, party functionaries, socially ascendant lawyers, and the 'hard-faced men' who had contributed to victory in the Great War. A common complaint at inter-war society functions related to the decline of the traditional gentry, now perceived as giving way to a hybridised 'fast-set' of Americans, 'men-on-the-make', and a group of barely-gentrified 'hangers-on'.[23] Opponents of the monarchy saw these influences as instrumental in the consolidation of a new breed of courtiers that put their own power and position above simple loyalty to the crown. When Edward VIII's position became compromised by his relationship with Mrs Simpson, they had little scruple in agitating for his removal. Reflecting on the Abdication Crisis, the ILP pamphlet *Cant and Humbug* remarked: 'The ruling class know no loyalty. As long as the King served their interests, they would keep the King. When the King failed to serve their interests, out the King would go.'[24] From his position in exile, the Duke of Windsor echoed many of these sentiments. Fossilised in a permanent 1930s-style existence in Paris, he lamented the decline of the traditional aristocracy, and the descent into penury and superficiality of the great noble houses. Ruminating on the fallen state of the high aristocracy at the time of Elizabeth's coronation in 1953, he measured their reduced circumstances in terms of coronation robes trimmed not with the traditional ermine, but with rabbit skin.[25] For him there was a clear falling off from the days of the great shooting weekends with the Marlboroughs at Blenheim Palace, the Duke of Portland at Welbrook Abbey, and the Duke of Sutherland at Dunrobin Castle. Comparing their former greatness with the current situation he brooded on the reasons for the impoverishment of the public ceremonial surrounding the coronation.

> How different the picture is now! Many of the stately homes of Britain have passed under the auctioneer's hammer or been taken over by the National Trust. In many others the squire and his family have retreated perhaps to one of the wings, or to the housekeeper's old quarters, the lodgekeeper's or the gardener's cottage, or in more fortunate circumstances to the dower house. What is left of the shooting has in most cases been let. The retainers – those

who have not been pensioned off – have scattered to the factories and farms.[26]

In political terms, the stock of aristocracy remained low in the inter-war years. Images of immorality and decadence still clung around the great aristocratic houses, causing the radical and labourist press to recoil from their excesses. Marcus Collins has suggested that after 1918 the cult of the gentleman was in abeyance, leading to a decline in the values of gentility and self-restraint.[27] For many critics of the landed elite, the prevalence of scandal in 'high society' indicated that the aristocracy had quite simply outlived its usefulness. From a position of Catholic reaction, Hilaire Belloc became preoccupied with the phenomenon of a once-mighty caste losing its chivalric values, and descending into dissipation and scandal. He wrote: 'There are many signs that aristocracy is in the last stages of dying, or is actually dead, in England today.'[28] Such notions echoed G.K. Chesterton's view that without the pretext of war and service to the nation the aristocracy had degenerated into the boisterousness of 'an army without an enemy billeted on the people'.[29] There was a 'downstairs revolt' quality to the writings of reformers who had the effrontery to scrutinise and expose the doings of their social superiors. Labour leaders nurtured in a long radical tradition of anti-aristocracy, highlighted the arrogance of a caste that left most of its historical misdemeanours unconcealed, and played out its internal dysfunction and sexual promiscuity in the full glare of the media spotlight. *Lansbury's Labour Weekly* commented: 'The governing classes should never have allowed us to dig into history and read from the records of the noble houses of this country.'[30] Speeding duchesses who had failed to renew their driving licences and titled 'old boys' of Eton and Sandhurst, convicted of passing dud cheques, remained the staples of the labourist press.[31] Prudishly scrutinising aristocracy's affairs, *Lansbury's Labour Weekly* reminded its readers:

Sexual looseness is common to all ages and all nations. But it seems to have burst all bounds in 'society' now. There is nothing to compare it to but the records of the eighteenth century, and the debauchery of the aristocracy then. The aristocrats then mucked about because they were idle, wealthy parasites who had no useful functions, and really had nothing else to do. So now, a governing class that has become idle and parasitic has nothing left to do but run after other people's wives. And like George IV's Regency Bucks, they are near the end of their lease of power, which is just as well, for what all these people want is a job of work.[32]

By the 1930s, the antics of high society stood out in stark relief against a decade of mass unemployment and financial rectitude. Chips Channon had a front-row seat at some of the society scandals of the 1930s. Observing the trial of Lord de Clifford for manslaughter in front of a jury of his peers in 1934, he depicted him as a type of the '*déclassé* night-club peer' and observed one old aristocratic roué noting down the address of an attractive female witness.[33] For J.F. Kennedy, son of the American ambassador to Britain, Joseph Kennedy, the image of a ruling and imperial caste disporting themselves in a social world of empty and predatory sexual conquests became the template of elite behaviour for his own court, constructed around memories of the manners and morals of the declining inter-war aristocracy in Britain.[34] The depredations of aimless and witless aristocrats, deprived of their social function by the meritocratic impulses of the post-war years, became an accepted feature of inter-war and post-war fiction. Describing the debagging of Paul Pennyfeather by a mob of upper-class hearties in *Decline and Fall*, Evelyn Waugh wrote: 'Any who have heard that sound will shrink from the recollection of it; it is the sound of English county families baying for glass.'[35] At the beginning of the Second World War, the Communist Party of Great Britain traded in images of a frivolous, irrelevant, and flighty class, lacking the true qualities of leadership, and devoting its war effort to profiteering, and filling in empty leisure time. These were the 'wealthy and extravagant relations of our aristocracy' and 'society women', appointed to committees, and profiting from '...a form of corruption, but this corruption is only the symptom of a greater evil...which permits a small class of wealthy men to rule the country, and to lead the country into war'.[36] Without the rationale of exclusive service to the empire, stripped of the exercise of their military function by a career open to talent in the army and the opportunity to display their *espirit de corps* on the field of honour, and undermined by parvenu imposters, the traditional aristocracy had lapsed into aimless 'prankery' and lame acts of student bravado.

For many on the Left, however, the persistence of connection, and ties of blood and kinship meant that the aristocracy had far from run its course. For them aristocracy functioned as a screen behind which the forces of trade, industry, and commerce had re-aligned themselves. Large numbers of radicals believed that this 'cousinhood', as Simon Haxey described it, posed a threat to all core democratic values. Haxey's *Tory MP*, published by the Left Bookclub in 1939, set out to expose continuing aristocratic power, and the degree to which it had been supplanted and reinvigorated by plutocratic influences.[37] Moving beyond the traditional Edwardian preoccupations with the House of

Lords, it viewed the Tory Party as little more than a militant arm of a neo-feudal oligarchy, entrenched within the party system, and wielding undisputed political control. For Haxey, the aristocracy had entered willingly into a compact with industry that paved the way for a combined social block on political progress, and a re-ordered social structure in the United Kingdom that favoured its own narrow interests. His book re-evaluated the significance not just of landownership, but also of the control of main-line railway companies, the banks, and the insurance companies:

> During the struggle which inevitably occurred between interests in one sort of property and interests in another, some noble families remained obstinately on the wrong side of the fence. These families have tended to lose their position in the governing class and to be replaced by new commoners. But the majority of the British aristocracy have survived any such struggle by attaching themselves to, and identifying themselves with, the winning side. Indeed, our aristocracy have always shown an extraordinary acuteness in economic matters, and are remarkably long-sighted whenever it is a question of the retention of their leadership.[38]

Titles, Haxey suggested, were a mere 'reflex' of property, 'and in an age when the wealth of the community consists of stocks and shares in big industrial concerns, our titled aristocracy is composed of big business men'.[39] Reviewing the individual histories of the great titled families who had allied themselves with new money, Haxey concluded that the soft ermine of aristocracy, the robes, tinsel, and orbs with which they bedecked themselves, softened the outlines of wealth derived from the brutal processes of industry and manufacture, and made the acquisition of personal fortunes palatable and acceptable to the aspirational bourgeosie, and the rising lower middle class. As evidence for this view he suggested that the individual currency of titles had declined. Whereas once, gradations of status were very marked within the peerage, by the 1930s their social function had changed. Rather than setting out orders of precedence at state functions and royal ceremonial, the value of titles had now degraded and acted purely to delineate the boundaries of the rich.[40] The aristocracy highlighted by Haxey was no longer recognisable as the body that had provided the leadership for Victorian England. Rather than standing still, critics of aristocracy believed that the caste had mutated, to encompass aspiring parvenus from below, with the effect of consolidating the wealth of the country in even fewer hands. For Hilaire Belloc, the traditional disdain for trade had been about the self-preservation of the landed elite, keen to keep the corrupting and socially debilitating influence of commerce at arm's length: 'The men who, if England was still Aristocratic, would govern, now tolerate an easy domestic equality with adventurers and rapscallions whom their fathers would not have admitted beyond the doorstep, and with most of whom their fathers would not even have conversed in the street. The old reason for a gentleman despising the rapscallion was not a particularly moral reason. It came rather from an instinct of self-preservation: the preservation of the Aristocratic State as a whole.' For Belloc, lassitude and the 'tired need for money' had taken aristocracy in a new direction, away from the virtues of the old gentry.[41] Some Conservative writers became reconciled to the emergence of a new social order that by fusing the virtues of industry and enterprise, tamed the worst excesses of unbridled capitalism, and created a disparate caste less overtly ambitious than the rich of the United States, and restrained in its naked ambition by the aristocracy's traditions of service. Some saw the 'new men of wealth' as a benign 'pleasant plutocracy' taking on the paternalistic responsibilities of the old nobility on the land and in village communities that the benighted aristocracy were no longer in a position to exercise.[42] Writing in 1944, the Tory MP and academic Christopher Hollis detected positive benefits to the aristocracy from the emergence of 'new men of wealth', and lauded a system in which freedom and harmony apparently flowed from the balance of social forces that made up the British state:

> Wiser Americans say that, in spite of these [feudal] relics, there is far more freedom and far less oppression in England than America. The wisest Americans are those who understand that this freedom and absence of oppression in England are largely because of, rather than in spite of, our illogicalities and our traditions. In the totalitarian country there is but one hierarchy – that of the party. In the purely capitalist society there is but one hierarchy – that of the plutocracy. But in a traditional society the whole virtue of life is in its variety. One order reigns over one department of its life and another over another. The plutocrat is kept in his place by the aristocrat, and the aristocrat by the plutocrat, to the benefit of society at large and of the underprivileged.[43]

For most inter-war Labour supporters, however, the diversified patterns of wealth that characterised plutocratic influence remained the true expression of the enemy. In mining in particular the trade union militancy of the 1920s was fuelled by a continuing resentment of ancestral aristocratic influences consolidated around control of the coal-fields. In the North-East the large mine owners were dukes and aristocrats who had exploited the potential of the mineral rights on the estates they owned. There the great aristocratic families were responsible for the sinking of deeper and deeper shafts, and the spread of mining into the colliery villages of County Durham. The Lambtons, the Northumberlands, the Londonderrys, and the Hamiltons were mining dynasts who drew substantial annual incomes from the mines, exacted semi-feudal dues from the pit villages, and cultivated traditions of deference and near-reverential attitudes towards their exalted position in the region. The Duke of Northumberland was especially despised, becoming a figure of opprobrium in Labour and Communist circles. He and his 'brother robber barons' were classed as monopolists and tyrants, who employed the coercive traditions of the great feudal households to enforce discipline on the coal-fields.[44] *Lansbury's Labour Weekly* castigated Northumberland for refusing to debate landownership with his critics on a public platform, and for his self-serving testimony in front of the Coal Commission in 1926. It commented ironically on his evidence: 'that God intended dukes to pocket £200 a day in royalties on coal that less deserving men risk their lives in getting for two pounds odd a week'.[45] Paradoxically, the miners, who were the backbone of the modern and class-conscious Communist Party in the inter-war years espoused an archaic strand of anti-aristocratic rhetoric that had persisted almost unchanged from the radical campaigns of the middle years of the nineteenth century. Bob Smillie, standing at a by-election in Morpeth as a Labour candidate in 1924 with the support of the Communist Party, attacked a system persisting in mining in the North-East in which profits for individual aristocratic coal-owners 'flourished on the unpaid wages of workers'. Both the Duke of Hamilton and the Duke of Northumberland emerged as emblems of unjust land monopoly who by inflating excessive rents and royalties on coal-production, lined their own pockets: 'The first tub filled goes to the Duke, the second to the coal owner, and the third is for the miner.'[46]

Undermined by plutocracy, frustrated by their loss of position, and often living in reduced circumstances, the traditional aristocracy was now depicted as a hollow and bedraggled remnant of its former glory. Contemporaries saw the collapse of the Anglo-Irish aristocracy after the formation of the Irish Free State in 1922 as presaging a broader disintegration of the traditional titled families of the realm. By uncoupling the great houses from their Irish possessions and estates, Irish separatism posed further problems for the financial viability of the big land-holdings.

For their part, the Ascendency families were plunged into a world of penury and make-believe. In the case of W.B. Yeats' impoverished family, the fictions and mythologies that were traditionally woven around bloodlines and inheritance translated into an obsession with occultism and Irish folk-tale, and settled around a make-believe Ascendancy pedigree.[47] With the walls of its exclusivity breached, the aristocracy has been depicted by David Cannadine as having no coherent political position following the resolution of the House of Lords issue in 1911. From 1919 onwards, the politics of the aristocracy fragmented. He accuses it of embracing a 'politics of paranoia' that projected an almost apocalyptic sense of loss and social decay.[48] Thereafter, it accommodated, as best it could, to the changed social and political climate. Some Labour supporters detected a strategy on the part of the traditional aristocracy to re-establish their position at the helm of British politics by infiltrating the new political party of organised Labour. Critics of aristocratic influences saw this as a policy of 'buying up', and even taming, the Labour Party. Paradoxically, one such convert Oswald Mosley, noted that aristocratic 'turn-coats' like Charles Buxton, Arthur Ponsonby, and Charles Trevelyan were often a disappointment to the Labour leadership, tacking to the extreme Left to validate their political credentials, rather than conferring respectability and stability on the party hierarchy.[49] Generally the Labour intelligentsia despised these apostate aristocrats and 'Red Marquesses'.[50] Particular spleen was reserved for the Countess of Warwick, despite the donation of her stately home, Easton Lodge, to the party for meetings and functions. There seemed an incongruity about a congress of the industrial masses meeting in a grand aristocratic house.[51] Writing in *Lansbury's Labour Weekly*, Hugh Gemmell suggested that the party had been 'invaded' by lords and ladies: 'When the aristocracy come forward the people fall backwards, but when the people come forward, the aristocracy, fearful of being left behind, insinuate themselves into positions of trust and timid leadership...It is unfortunately true that the path of progress is paved with the slaughtered bodies of the working class, betrayed by the broken bonds of the blue-bloodied aristocrats.'[52] Despite herself, Beatrice Webb was won over by some of these aristocratic infiltrators. She excused the entry of her nephew, 'the Red Squire' Stafford Cripps into the party, on the grounds that he came from the 'country gentleman and public service families'.[53] She also expressed particular admiration for Oswald Mosley 'the perfect politician who is also the perfect gentleman' and reported that some members of the party detected distinct advantages in apostate figures who embraced a pro-Labour stance:

It is, by the way, interesting to note that the Scottish Covenanters are prejudiced in favour of anyone who is particularly hated by the other side. 'There are three men in the House who are detested and reviled by the Tories', says Johnston, the editor of *Forward*, who is himself in the House – Sidney Webb, Patrick Webb and Oswald Mosley – a remark that accounts for the growing popularity among the extremists of the two very 'bourgeois' figures and the one super-aristocrat. 'Why are they so hated?' asks *Forward*; 'because they are traitors to their class,' he answers triumphantly, as if he were canonising them![54]

For defenders of aristocracy like Christopher Hollis, the move by aristo-crats and landed wealth into the Labour Party demonstrated the persist-ence of notions of 'unpaid public service' within the ruling elite, and the degree to which even the Left might benefit from residual traditions of *noblesse oblige*. He wrote in 1944 against the democratic temper of the war years: 'The working-man, on the whole, and other things being equal, prefers to be represented in Parliament by a member who has received the advantages of a privileged education. Nowhere is this more notable than in the Labour Party, where its recruits from the public schools have received and accepted positions on the public bench far in excess of what could be justified by their numbers or, so it would appear to an outsider, by their talent.'[55] For those to the left of Labour, the party's links with the Establishment indicated the lengths it was prepared to go in pursuit of compromise. For them, Ramsay MacDonald symbolised the degree to which socialist principles were tarnished by exposure to the aristocratic embrace and the lure of the great houses. Such entryism alarmed a party permanently scarred by the defection of Ramsay MacDonald, and the formation of the National Government in 1931. Chips Channon wrote of MacDonald: 'He had a disarming smile and aristocratic appearance which lent colour to the legend of his birth – an illegitimate Dalhousie!...I saw him sometimes in those early months of the first Labour Government when London society wisely decided to take him up rather than ignore him. Defiant at first he soon took to grandeur and high life and wallowed in it like a man who has been starving all his life.'[56] Mosley and other aristocratic defectors were depicted with gold spoons in their mouths, or in one famous cartoon of Mosley following a successful election campaign, trading in his working-men's clothes for a topper and tails with the caption 'after the bawl'.[57] The Glasgow anarchist Guy Aldred condemned the 'obsequiousness' demonstrated by Labour leaders who cultivated close ties with the social elite, and deriding the pretensions of some within the party, quoted with approval the *Daily Herald's* satirical story that 'socialist debutantes' presented at Court were only a matter of time.[58]

Some critics believed that the desperate period of the 1930s encouraged the traditional aristocracy to embrace reactive and counter-revolutionary styles of politics. In Aldous Huxley's novel of inter-war society, *Antic Hay*, the decadent aristocrat Bruin seeks refuge in fantasies of former aristocratic greatness. Confronted with the poor and lower middle class on a jaunt through London, he reaches back into the past to recall his grandfather's opposition to the democratic progress of the people: 'I remember when I was a little boy . . . my old grandfather used to tell me stories about his childhood. He told me that when he was about five or six, just before the passing of the Reform Bill of 'thirty-two, there was a song which all right-thinking people used to sing, with a chorus that went like this: "Rot the people, blast the people, damn the Lower Classes". I wish I knew the rest of the words and the tune. It must have been a good song.'[59] Such attitudes were consonant with the findings of radicals and those on the Left who detected evidence of a retreat by high society into anti-democratic posturings during these years. The Labour Party's Research Department implied a strong connection between extremism of the Right and an embattled aristocracy. This reflected the view, widely articulated in Labour circles, that there was much covert sympathy for British Fascism in elite society.[60] Labour opponents of the New Party pointed out that Mosley, despite his former role in the Labour Cabinet, was irreparably marred by his membership of the patrician class. Under his sophisticated, urbane, political exterior, they argued, he was heir to many of the defects of his aristocratic past. Delving deep into his family history, anti-Fascists uncovered a discreditable story of support for the royalist side in the English Civil War, enclosures, slum-landlordism, absenteeism, and profiteering from the sale of the Manor of Manchester to the City Corporation in 1846.[61] Here the many *exposés* of aristocratic misdeeds in the nineteenth century bore fruit in reproaches to Mosley's integrity over his family's role in Peterloo and the misgovernment of Manchester.[62] Attacks on Mosley in the 1930s continued this theme. In *Who Backs Mosley* the Labour Research Department highlighted the social origins of Oswald Mosley and his key lieutenants, exposing the society patrons who provided much of the financial backing for the New Party and the BUF. Society hostesses like Lady Cunard and Mrs Greville were depicted as entranced by wealthy Blackshirts and visiting Nazi dignitaries.[63] Listing titled backers and supporters of the movement in the Blackshirt January Club, *Who Backs*

Mosley commented: 'The January Club holds its dinners at the Savoy and the Hotel Splendide. The Tatler shows pictures of the club assemblies, distinguished by evening dress, wines, flowers and a general air of luxury. The leader is enjoying himself amongst his own class. A striking feature of the British Union of Fascists and the January Club is the large number of army officers in their personnel. "Many Blackshirts are RAF men" boasts Rothermere's *Sunday Dispatch* (29.4.34). The next most striking thing is the amount of land and money represented.'[64] The elite social status of a number of leading Blackshirts and their leader's links with high society rekindled suspicions that the law courts looked favourably on Blackshirt offenders. Contemporaries suggested that whereas the police more often than not protected Blackshirt demonstrations, Communists and anti-Fascists frequently found themselves on the receiving end of police brutality. This, then, was apparently a 'gentlemanly Fascism', which was distinguished by its genteel status, and which enjoyed a tacit collaboration from large sections within the landed Establishment. Such an interpretation is consonant with the historiography of British Fascism. Richard Thurlow and Robert Skidelsky note British Fascism's links to the Edwardian 'Die-Hards' and their platform appeal to a disaffected and recalcitrant gentry.[65] Traditions of service, leadership, and hierarchy anchor the Fascist movement even more securely within the mainstream of aristocratic values. Patrician styles, a showy opulence, and unquestioning near-feudal obedience demonstrated that British Fascism provided a vector for declining aristocratic sentiments. Mosley's own family were the dispossessed and rootless remnants of a formerly mighty dynasty, reduced to a single mouldering country manor at Rolleston in Staffordshire. British Fascism's obsession with plutocracy as a cover for the importation of alien and 'un-British' capital is also in a long tradition. Complaints against a rootless and cosmopolitan 'money power' that undermined the traditional social elite in Britain gave an anti-Semitic inflection to Fascist rhetoric, and drew on the long-established aristocratic resentment towards 'new money'.

Sinister dining circles like the Cliveden Set became a distillation of the fears and resentments that traditionally surrounded titled, foreigner-favouring high society. The prevalence of appeasement and the apparent lack of enthusiasm on the part of the political Establishment for a war against Hitlerism led many on the Left to suspect a compact between Fascism and a declining landed elite, hopeful of consolidating its position under foreign rule. This was most strongly expressed in the stories of plots and pro-German sentiments amongst the leaders of society that were cultivated by Communist and Left-wing journalists.[66] The image of a landed Establishment that was unenthusiastic in its pursuit of war seemed a judgement on the decline and loss of energy of the traditional ruling families. The accusation that they favoured German expansionism, and sought to undermine British foreign policy was in a long tradition of viewing the aristocracy as both un-British and opposed to the national interest. The Astors, owners of the stately home at Cliveden, were particular objects of suspicion. Viscount Astor, of American and German extraction, whose father had been ennobled by a purchased Lloyd George peerage in 1917, was 'a member of what was once regarded as the very vulgar plutocracy'.[67] A classic plutocrat, cut adrift from national loyalties and sympathies, his family became central to the mythology of the Cliveden Set. In the intrigues at the stately home he was portrayed as a cosmopolitan and ruthless manipulator of the fading aristocracy. The shallowness and superficiality of traditional aristocratic families like the Astors, the Mitfords and the Londonderrys was believed to lay them open to manipulation by foreign agencies. A Communist Party pamphlet wrote: 'The Astors and the Lothians are not traitors to their nation of the ruling class, city magnates, landed aristocrats and industrial bosses. But they are to our nation, the nation of the common peace-loving, liberty-respecting people.'[68] These were place hunters and professional political intriguers 'supported by a group of henchmen great and small who carry the trail of intrigue against democracy wide and deep into the mansions of land and money baronage'. *Tribune* saw the functions of the traditionally aristocratic foreign office as now usurped and 'transferred to the palatial residence of the Astor family at Taplow, Bucks. Diplomatically, therefore, both Britain and Europe are now in the hands of the higher peerage.'[69] Moreover, scrutiny of the ancestry of the Londonderrys demonstrated a predisposition towards anti-democratic and extremist sentiments. Quoting Howard Evans, *Tribune* exposed their familial connection with the scion of the Addington clan, Lord Castlereagh, architect of the Holy Alliance in Europe in the aftermath of the Napoleonic Wars, *bête noire* of Byron and Shelley, apologist for Peterloo, and opponent of parliamentary reform at home. It remarked: '[He] was one of the chief promoters of the gagging coercion bills by which the Tories of that day sought to stifle the cry of freedom...And now, the ruling head of the house of Castlereagh, Lord Londonderry, carries on the tradition by supporting the Fascist dictatorships in Europe, who smash trade union organisation, destroy culture, and bomb defenceless people in Spain and Abyssinia.'[70] Inspired by the Cliveden Set, a wily and untrustworthy aristocracy lived on in the popular memory of wartime. In the Ealing propaganda film 'Went the Day Well' directed by Cavalcanti in 1943, the villainous Squire Welsford schemes to help the invading Germans. Ruthless and amoral, he places his own considerations above patriotism and duty to his tenants. His plans are foiled by the observant villagers and by his traditional enemy, the village poacher who emerges as an unlikely hero. Shot by his mistress when his treachery is revealed, the film ends with the symbolic destruction of his gated manor house and the traditional privileges that went with it.[71] Similarly, in J.B. Priestly's *Blackout in Gretley*, the sinister Colonel Tarlington is the head of a circle of collaborators and spies. In the denouement at the symbolic Oakenfield Manor, the wounded hero, Humphrey Neyland, takes the opportunity to lambaste Tarlington in an indignant peroration that recalled the many suspicions of pro-appeasement aristocrats intent only in securing their own position in the event of a British defeat:

> You see yourself as a rightly privileged person, quite different from the common crowd, and you're ready to pay a big price to keep your privileges. You hate democracy and all it means. There's something fundamentally stiff-necked, arrogant, dominating and conceited about you that just can't take it. When Hess flew over here he was looking for people like you. It isn't that you're pro-German, unpatriotic in the ordinary sense. In the last war, which seemed to you a straightforward nationalistic affair, I've no doubt that you did a good job. But this war, which is quite different, is too much for you. I heard you speak the other night. You only said what a lot of people of your kind keep on saying – telling the people to keep in their old place, to fight and work, and suffer to maintain something they no longer believe in – and, if you ask me, every word of this stuff is worth another gun or whip to Hitler and his gang. But you're a bit more intelligent and a bit more unscrupulous than most of your kind, and so you realised that to keep all you wanted to keep, it meant that the people mustn't win and that Fascism mustn't lose. So they persuaded you that a Nazi victory only meant that you'd have the sort of England you've always wanted, with yourself and a few others securely on top, and the common people kept in their place forever.[72]

Shooting himself in the time-honoured manner, the final verdict on Tarlington is of an immoral aristocrat, unable to overcome his own narrow self-interest and unwilling to throw in his lot with a national and potentially levelling 'people's war'.

The rootless impoverished aristocracy of the inter-war years sought stability through a retrospective view of its successes in the past. Increasingly the Elizabethan period was identified as the era in which aristocracy was most truly at the height of its political, social, and cultural significance. From the diminished perspective of the 1930s, there had been a considerable falling off from the years when aristocracy set the standard in terms of style, taste, martial values, and courtly protocol. As Peter Mandler has pointed out, from the nineteenth century onwards the reign of the Tudors was re-invented as an age when England most truly came into its own as a major naval power, an empire, and a Protestant nation capable of vanquishing Catholic Spain. Marked out by the Reformation, victory in the Wars of the Roses, and the ruthless suppression of internal dissent, the Tudor period came to embody the correct religious and expansionist virtues that prefigured the Victorians and the Edwardian mission of Empire.[73] In the 1920s and 1930s, Tudor precedents were increasingly mined by a nervous aristocracy, critics of the rising plutocracy, and plutocrats themselves, eager to consolidate their own position within the annals of the nation. References back to the lost greatness and might of the first Elizabethan empire became the stock-in-trade of Fascist orators like Mosley, who emphasised the vital quality of the Tudor court, and the manliness of the gentry who hunted, and were trained in challenging and dangerous sports.[74] For many British Fascists, the Tudor state displayed a strong leadership principle enshrined in the rule of William Cecil, and provided the model for a nationally integrated society rooted in economic self-sufficiency. One British Union of Fascists (BUF) propagandist wrote:

> Those who see in Fascism a force destructive of culture should examine this period of our history. Like the dawning Fascist era, it was an age of popular dictatorship and national integration, an age in which individualism was not suffered to degenerate into anarchy, an age when men did not hesitate when necessary to meet force with force. It was the epoch of Hawkins, Drake and Raleigh. And yet it was in this 'barbarous' period that England experienced a cultural Renaissance unequalled in her previous or subsequent history. The Elizabethan had hot blood and a ready hand, but he was none the less a great artist. Culture is not a monopoly of the 'Bloomsbury Intellectual' type.[75]

In similar vein, Mosley's admirers saw him as a throwback to his landed Elizabethan forebears, and the last true incarnation of the Elizabethan gentleman:

Oswald Mosley, indeed, would scarcely have failed to come into his own had he been born a subject of Elizabeth. One can picture him striding across the landscape of that time as though an artist had designed it for him – a superb physical and mental specimen of a race rapturously discovering its own vigour amidst the thousand-fold possibilities of the new life then being unfolded for its opportunity and triumph. Had he been able to stay the course with the Queen (which is improbable) he would have blazed his way to victory in precisely those directions in which Essex stumbled to the block, and in any event, an age of adventurous idealism and practical patriotism must certainly have marked him down for high leadership.[76]

For critics of plutocracy and defenders of aristocratic mores, the Tudor period constituted the last era in which the aristocracy truly flourished, uncompromised and uncorrupted by the taint of trade and commerce. Under the Tudors, the gentry of England reached an apogee of courtly refinement characterised by aristocratic manners derived from the Renaissance that became the outward expression of an educated, land-owning elite. For Mosley, the family estate and his childhood home at Rolleston in Staffordshire provided the model for a benevolent aristocratic Caesarism rooted in property accrued under the Tudors and traditional feudal values. He described its household as: 'A remarkable, truly feudal survival...In feudal fashion the warmest and most intimate friendships developed between us and these people, so characteristic of traditional England, not only in their daily occupations, but in the strong bonds of sympathy of life's events, birth, marriage, death, occasions sad and festive; this really was a classless society.'[77] Thereafter trade undermined aristocracy and the social and cultural world it had created. Arthur Bryant, popular historian and erstwhile Fascist sympathiser, chronicled the historical story of aristocracy as one of fragmentation and decline following the Napoleonic Wars, and the repeal of the Corn Laws.[78] In his view *laissez-faire* had made the fortunes of the gentry class untenable, killing off the great landed estates. For him, industrialisation, trade, and commerce were a blight that undermined the true rural values of England, typified by the ruddy-faced squire. In his morale-raising *English Saga* of 1940 he catalogued a story of the decline of the 'squirearchy', priced out of the market by wealthy *arriviste* parvenus, and unwise governmental measures dictated by urban, rather than rural, considerations. Here the narrative of aristocracy and its decline became interwoven with an Island story suffused with nostalgia, regret, and loss in wartime:

The older, smaller type of squire was also departing – killed by the violent fluctuations which followed in the wake of the Napoleonic Wars and by the rising standards of social expenses set by rich neighbours... To him and his kind, defying the sombre black of the encroaching towns [the] landscape owed at least part of its enchantment. He supplied it with pageantry. The lovely primary colours of the English past that to-day only survive in the dress uniform of the guards and the huntsman's coat shone in front of the vivid greenery of May or glowed through the mists of autumn.[79]

From the late 1930s, the proliferation of narratives of this nature meant that the restoration of English greatness became inextricably intertwined with a revival of traditional aristocratic values, position, and status. In an echo of Bryant, Mosley himself was characterised as 'a man predisposed to look upon the triumphs of nineteenth century economic liberalism as placing a false and perilous emphasis upon industrialism and usury at the expense of agriculture, and creating a lop-sided economy... even while the towns decay with the general decline of the countryside'.[80]

In the aftermath of two world wars, some writers traced the collapse of the traditional way of life on the land to the contraction of the established aristocracy. Such notions derived from an increasing accommodation with the images of a nostalgic, chivalrous, and 'squierarchical' past. The wholesale slaughter of young heirs in the Great War, apparently crippling death duties, and the impoverishment of landed wealth, provided the opportunity for parvenus to buy up the rotting and neglected property of the ancient landed families, and accelerated the decline of the 'great houses' of the eighteenth and nineteenth centuries. Images of crumbling and derelict aristocratic accommodation accentuated the image of a vacant countryside, bereft of the leadership of the rural squire, and exposed to the ravening depredations of the new generation of landed plutocrats. The prevailing tone was of sadness and regret for a passing era on the land. In this sense the deserted country house and decaying aristocratic property that was such a potent image in inter-war fiction became an emblem not just of the reduced circumstances of the older territorial families, but also a symbol for the death of a whole social system.[81] J. Wentworth Day wrote:

To-day the Hall stands grey and empty, a voiceless shell. The house and park which once gave steady employment to two hundred and forty men and women, to-day employs perhaps a dozen. There are no deer in the park. I have not seen six pheasants in two years nor a score of rabbits nor half a score of hares. The urban golfer plods his way where once the great red stags belled under October moons. Daws and jays, crows and foxes, stoats and rats, in their verminous scores infest the woods, where once six guns could shoot two hundred and fifty brace of pheasants in a day and the men and boys of two villages had a good day's fun and a full day's pay, with lunch and beer at 'brushing'.[82]

Such notions were echoed by the Dorset landowner, Rolf Gardiner. He wrote: '...Death itself was already in the house quite aside from the inane absorption of some of the inmates in "nothing but bridge and lawn-tennis, lawn-tennis and bridge, until death parts them even from their cards and their racquets". The social apparel was torn from the economic flesh, and the economic flesh from the religious bones. The whole context had disintegrated.'[83] The fate of most country houses, lamented C.E.M. Joad, during the war years, was to decline into arid, contextless parkland or 'to subside into schools, hospitals, homes and permanently evacuated offices'.[84] As Malcolm Chase has pointed out, there is a tension in such ideas. The same aristocracy that now faced political and economic marginalisation, bore the responsibility in the first instance for many of the excesses of enclosure and the novel farming methods that had consigned the old ways to oblivion and accelerated the decline of the English yeoman.[85] Scrutiny of plutocratic and financial interests resolved this issue of blame. New wealth, not traditional aristocracy, had ruined the land. The land movement's particular bile was reserved for the 'money power' and 'usury' which Henry Massingham saw as antipathetical to English virtues, and promoted by a noxious troupe who had thrown English history off course, amongst them: '...an obese autocrat concerned with his conscience, the Ironsides after him, Dutch William who sold his purse to the Bank of England, the great lords of the Enclosures, the Victorian frock-coats headed by Adam Smith, Malthus, Cobden and Darwin, and bringing up the rear the metal juggernaut whose fuel is human blood'.[86] Memories of enclosure and the expulsion of the poor from the land coloured this sense of a lost arcadian idyll. The augmentation of old money by new sources of power and wealth was seen by contemporary observers as instrumental in the problems of inter-war agriculture. In such literature blame was apportioned to the un-English plutocrats, both for the exodus from rural England and for the decline of the English yeoman smallholder. This was a natural consequence of a 'commercial plutocracy vaunting the plumes of a displaced aristocracy'.[87] The rural writer Henry Massingham wrote of the historical dominance by a 'new squirearchy ... recruited from courtiers, members of the Privy Council, City of London merchants and land speculators whose rapacity and contempt for customary rights earned them the name of "caterpillars of the Commonwealth"'. Such notions had their inspiration in a Tawneyesque view of an aristocracy undermined and eroded by new wealth, and the importation of commercial and economic methods of farming management into the countryside. Under the inspiration of Puritan ideas of money-management and commercial greed: 'These were the new rich who inoculated the countryside with the commercial spirit, to be championed in the next century by the Puritans.'[88] For Massingham, writing under the tutelage of his father's New Liberal ideas expressed during his editorship of *The Nation* in the 1890s, the continuing power of the Puritan Revolution lay in 'closing the gap between religion and plutocracy' thus creating a new social system that was both urban-centred, and dismissive of the established aristocracy, its estates, its religion, and its core chivalric values.[89]

Informed by such conceptions, inter-war rural writers constructed an idealised arcadian model for an England reborn out of the wreckage of war. Drawing on new Georgeian notions of a pastoral idyll in poetry and song, they looked to the countryside for a renewal of authentic English values.[90] In the eyes of their critics, new money bore the responsibility for the erosion of the embattled and declining smallholder class, which proved the repository for all the correct and now endangered English characteristics. This was an all-embracing and barbarous 'pluto-bureaucratic system' that smothered the English yeomanry.[91] In this vision, the resurrection of the smallholder held the key to the economic regeneration of the countryside. Such notions were in a long tradition that spanned the political divide. Arthur Bryant's retrospective image of the sunlit uplands of the past as an ordered hierarchy harmonised well with the attitude of a new generation of rural writers who hoped to preserve intact the values of the old aristocracy, as part of a broader renewal of traditional English rural life. Such attitudes often gravitated towards reaction. Lord Lymington and Rolf Gardiner were amongst the many aristocrats prominent in these movements. Their dalliances with *volkisch* 'back-to-the-land' organisations and the extreme Right were symptomatic of the direction taken by rogue aristocrats disillusioned by the fate of rural culture, and seeking solace in an imagined, nostalgic past of hierarchy and order.[92] For Gardiner, Nazism, though worthy of praise, was essentially a vulgar, lower middle-class movement. The values it aspired to were innately elitist and more properly featured in a traditional aristocratic outlook. His objective, then, was the revival of the organic aristocracy, rooted in the rich loam of England, to provide leadership to the simple swains of the countryside. As part of the project of reinvigorating landed society, the inter-war organic movement campaigned for a revival of notions of 'good stewardship' growing out of the traditional 'Great Estate' and 'exorcising the curse of the enclosures'.[93] For organicists like Gardiner and Henry Massingham, the model of Bismarckian Germany provided the blueprint for a strong and vigorous aristocracy, immersed in landed wealth, profiting from a protected agricultural yield, and resistant to the blandishments of trade and commerce. They argued that the decline of the small proprietor class had led to a spiritual suppression of the values of the 'countryman' rooted in a life on the land and a mystical contemplation of plant and animal life. For some, the recreation of the gentry, purged of the influence of commercial wealth, held out the prospect of a new spirituality based around traditional rural hierarchies. For others it provided the opportunity for a restoration of the reassuring intimacies of the rural community, and of the agrarian harmony and social balance of the shires.[94] Only a traditional and robust landlordism of the kind that characterised the nineteenth century, it was felt, could re-invigorate the land, and the system of small tenant proprietorships that drew its strength from the great estates.

Once this agitation for the rediscovery of the English yeoman was uncoupled from the platform of anti-landlordism that had characterised the Liberal-inspired movement of small rural proprietors in the 1880s, it drifted steadily away from its roots on the radical progressivist flank of the political spectrum. The inter-war organic movement symbolised this tendency. Movements like Social Credit, the English Array, and the Catholic Land Movement proposed programmes that were a distillation of the disillusionments arising from the decline of landed wealth and traditional deferential rural society.[95] Agitations like the Catholic-inspired Distributionist movements followed the doctrines of Pope Leo XIII in his encyclical letter of 1891, and preached a diffusion of rural property-holding to counteract the spread of socialism and Bolshevism. These were associations that were, above all, accepting of hierarchy. They shared a zeal for orthodox models of spade-husbandry, sympathy for the great landowners, devolved regional cultures, and a Catholic-centred obsession with the methods of charity and poor relief rooted in the abbeys and monasteries of pre-Reformation England. The re-emergence of such notions was matched by a revival of interest in William Cobbett.

Indeed, William Stafford has christened these ideas 'Cobbett Syndrome' and linked them with concerns for the resurrection of an 'England ... secretly slain'.[96] A number of conflicting ideological strands merged around this platform. The ideas of Tawney lived on in attempts to promote governmental investment in small-holdings, and in campaigns to redress the problems of rural poverty.[97] There was also a residue of Left-wing land idealism. The apostate Communist Douglas Hyde, who turned his back on the party to become an organic soil militant, saw little contradiction between his commitment to William Morris and the 'crypto-medievalism' of early socialism, and his zealotry on behalf of what he termed 'muck and mysticism'.[98] Such attitudes crossed the political divide, uniting former socialists and soil activists, and fetching up on the political margins. Even the Communist Party was involved in agitations to defend village life and culture in England. Anarchist elements too were apparent. The Anarchist writer Herbert Read declaimed:

> In spite of my intellectual pretensions, I am by birth and tradition a peasant. I remain essentially a peasant. I despise this foul industrial epoch – not only the plutocracy which it has raised to power, but also the industrial proletariat which it has drained from the land and proliferated in hovels of indifferent brick. The class in the community for which I feel a natural sympathy is the agricultural class, including the genuine remnants of a landed aristocracy. This perhaps explains my early attraction to Bakunin, Kropotkin, and Tolstoy, who were also of the land, aristocrats and peasants. A man cultivating the earth – that is the elementary economic fact; and as a poet I am only concerned with elementary facts.[99]

Talk of 'Just Prices' echoed the vocabulary of craftsmen and the Guilds that were seen as central to this pre-modern order. As part of an attempt to invoke this spirit, the organic movement sought to reclaim the 'work gospel of the craft guilds' readapted to the modern world.[100] At the same time, it traded in a distinctive brand of 'country-wise' nationalism that accentuated the patriotic benefits to be gained from a return to the land, and attempted to hold back the strident call for land nationalisation through a 'National Estate' programme.[101] The agitation saw its mission as the recovery of the authentic spirit of England from under the accretions of industrial civilisation, the 'money power' and a commercial reliance on foreign-produced food.[102] There was an apocalyptic tone to its ideas. Devotees saw it as a last opportunity to rescue England from tourism, suburbia, poor jerry-built housing, and commercialised leisure-activities.

For Henry Massingham, it sought to rectify a dispossession from the land that, against the background of 1940, was as savage as the Nazi suppression of the liberties of Poland and Bohemia.[103] Peter Howard wrote:

> Did God give Britons their soil, the finest in all the world, to use and develop, or to waste if that suits the pockets of the financiers? Britain's growing arable acreage could provide life-work for hundreds and thousands of families, and a life-work calling for all that the best of work does offer – craftsmanship, character and courage... We could and should become a healthier nation and recapture the joy and soundness of heart which made other nations call us 'Merrie England' in the days before cinemas, central heating and garden suburbs were created to keep us happy.[104]

The organic movement elevated the traditional aristocratic families of England, re-inventing them as a shield for long-established English values against the alien, invasive presence of un-English plutocrats. This image of the aristocracy as a delicate and endangered fragment of British culture lived on in the post-war years, until appropriated by the preservationist movement of the 1960s. At its fringes, this outlook meshed with a conservationist enthusiasm for a restoration of the Gothic, and a zealotry for country-house living. The legacy the conservationists sought to preserve was one of contoured rolling pastures with its epicentre in the country house, and the farm estate. In the popular perception of the aristocracy's traditional role, this provided the chief bequest of the aristocracy to the landscape and the topographical appearance of England. James Lees-Milne wrote, 'God, what England owes to the landed gentry for the trim appearance of their estates.'[105] In the 1950s the aristocracy was commonly characterised as an impotent relic, and a quaint semi-feudal survival. With its disappearance much heralded, but never quite fulfilled, the 'falling leaves' of the British political establishment displayed a remarkable longevity, and a strong instinct for survival.[106] The apparent powerlessness and political impotence of aristocracy converted the feared landed power of the nineteenth century into a mere adornment of the countryside. Landowners now celebrated their role not as 'wreckers' of the constitution, but rather as custodians of the virtues of continuity and timeless ancestral tradition. Inspired by their position as 'eco-toffs' and by 'eco-feudalism' in the organic movement, and as the preservers of distinguished collections of art and traditional pedigrees, they re-invented themselves as the guardians of the nation's heritage. Some dynasties made restitution for the past misdeeds of the aristocracy by displaying an enthusiasm for forestry and park renovation.[107] By the 1950s, a new justification for the 'lords of the shires' had emerged in which they appeared as cultural custodians of traditional British values. The inter-war depression augmented by the wartime decline of landed wealth, and the collapse of agricultural prices created a new climate for the British conservation movement, in which the fruits of the *Grand Tour* in aristocratic houses and art galleries across the country were given precedence over the preservation of moorlands, open spaces, and lower-class dwellings. In 1937 and 1939 parliament passed legislation enabling country-house proprietors to donate their properties to the National Trust. In return for tax concessions, continued residence, and in some cases state money for renovation, they gave permission for limited public access by visitors and tourists in the summer months.[108] Run by idealistic patricians like G.M. Trevelyan and Lord Zetland, the governing committee of the Trust was staffed by a social elite that stamped the imprint of aristocratic conservation ideas on the organisation. The prevalence of hunting on Trust land and the continued use of 'Keep Out' signs that recalled the 'Wooden Liars' or 'Trespassers will be Prosecuted' notices of the game preserves showed that the traditional proprieties of the great estate system were observed even under National Trust ownership.[109] For Vita Sackville-West this re-invented the culture of aristocracy as a mausoleum, in which landownership was preserved, pickled in aspic, and presented permanently on display to voyeuristic visitors.[110] For critics of the new 'heritage industry' it created a situation in which a nostalgic vision of the past was promoted, snobbery flourished, and the remnants of aristocracy were celebrated for their role as the nation's cultural curators. From the 1950s onwards, country-house visiting became synonymous with improving rational recreation, 'Englishness', and a sepia-tinted memory of 'times past'.[111]

Contemporaries have often been surprised by the resilience and survival instinct of the British aristocracy. The major theme of the twentieth century in the United Kingdom has been one of the persistence of aristocracy. Despite the deep-seated social change of the 1960s, analysis of the apparent decline of aristocratic power and influence demonstrates that it is largely illusory.[112] The conventional view of aristocracy is that it waned after the collapse of the stable, hierarchical world of the Edwardian era. From the 1920s onwards the aristocracy was regarded as fragmenting. Dissipated, indolent, and broken by war it was portrayed as undermined by plutocracy and incapable of adapting to the straightened circumstances of the post-1919 world. In the post-war years it played the part of mere adornment or backdrop to the changing social trends of the period. During this period aristocracy became accepted and tolerated, rather than despised. After 1945 aristocrats were increasingly relegated to the status of custodians of national tradition, the natural world, and traditional values. This was a more passive and compliant role for aristocracy, but one that still masked considerable hidden powers over land, investments, and the countryside that existed undimmed by the seismic political change of 1945. Under the aegis of the National Trust, heritage culture intertwined the country home and the narrative of the national past into a relatively benign vision of British social history. Country-house living was now seen as gracious and cultured, rather than dissipated and immoral. In this process of re-invention, the history of opposition to the great landed families was lost. They were now protectors of the landscape, rather than despoilers of the land.

Conclusions

> Frederick William John Augustus Harvey is a genuine throw-back to the old raucous days of high-born, high-living low life. His method of opening a stuck refrigerator full of champagne, by blasting the door with a shotgun, could have been done a century ago by any number of landed gentry.[1]

In 1959 Harold Macmillan declared 'the class war obsolete', but formed a government that included a duke, three earls, and a marquess. Under Macmillan, the eleventh Duke of Devonshire could still acquire a string of state offices from his uncle in a promotion which he himself described as 'the greatest act of nepotism ever'.[2] Thereafter, the Labour Party framed its hostility to Conservatism in terms of its opposition to the old entrenched elites. 'Wilsonianism' was a self-consciously modern creed, that disavowed the 'economics of the grouse-moors' and maligned the closed political world of Conservatism. Wilson, with links to Beveridge and the New Liberalism, symbolised something of the 'little man' locked in conflict with the unelected and unaccountable power of the great Tory grandees. For many Labour supporters, the victory in 1964 over the Tories personified by the land-owning Sir Alec Douglas-Home, symbolised a final sweeping away of unelected and ancestral power.

Such enthusiasm was, however, premature. The 1960s failed to break the power of aristocracy. It remains at the heart of British society and culture. It persists both as an exemplar, and as a target. From the middle years of the nineteenth century onwards, aristocracy was the *bête noire* of radicals and progressives of all political stripes. Declamatory hostility towards the aristocracy and an avowed intent to reform land tenure or break up the great estates remained a recurrent feature of the political programmes of radical organisations into the middle years of the twentieth century. The Land Campaign and House of Lords crisis of 1909–1911 are only the most visible aspects of a long and protracted agitation against landownership and aristocratic power that has roots deep in the political past. For most radicals there was a lineage of anti-aristocratic sentiment deriving from Paine, Ricardo, and Adam Smith, and revived by the saintly Henry George, that transcended the divisions between capital and labour, Liberals and socialists, reformers and revolutionaries. Indeed, the one factor that united Labour, Liberals, and radicals was their dislike of the encumbrances aristocracy placed on the British people. As G.R. Searle has pointed out, the momentum of British Liberalism in the first decade of the twentieth century was sustained by attacks on hereditary wealth that far eclipsed Labour's platform utterances in the bitterness and rancour of its rhetoric.[3] For most political groupings motivated by reforming zeal, the declaration to restrict or abolish the aristocracy provided an article of faith in political progress. Anti-aristocratic fervour was thus a totem of modernity that reformers embraced to sanctify their mission to purify and purge the political system of the inherited relics of a barbarous and feudal caste.

Nineteenth-century land campaigners succeeded in placing the issue of the land at the heart of the relationship between property and power. Thereafter matters of land reform have never lost their centrality. In the wake of the 1875 *Return on Owners of Land, exposés* of landownership have continued to yield information about the restricted nature of land-owning. Much of this material has a revelatory aspect that demonstrates the retrograde nature of English land-holding patterns and reveals the arcane nature of Britain's position within Europe as an unreformed 'Old Order' state. The tensions within the political system posed by inequities in landownership remain apparent despite the aristocracy's perceived loss of power and position in the inter-war years. From the 1920s onwards, revelations about the closed world of landownership revealed little change in the distribution of landed proprietorship from the characteristic land-holding patterns of the Edwardian period. The work of Howard Evans, William Howitt, and W.T. Stead was complemented by further research that proved conclusively that the same handful of Anglo-Scottish families remained at the apex of land-owning in Great Britain. Such injustices were most apparent on the margins in outworks of landed influence. Scotland in particular remains the country with the highest concentration of private landownership in the world. Three hundred and forty three people or bodies own more than half of all private rural land there.[4] Despite universal suffrage, changing demography, immigration, and the emergence of an aspirational classless middle rank, 'the club has not bothered to welcome too many newcomers'.[5] For some critics the aristocracy provided the raw material for a 'new corruption', in which the wealth of the great estates was augmented by extravagant farm subsidies from the Common Agricultural Policy, rewarding large landed proprietors for intensive farming methods that had a damaging impact on the environment, whilst adding to Europe's growing food mountains.[6]

The executive role of legislative and unelected power also provides a constant reminder of continuing aristocratic influences within government. When Liberal and Labour governments pursue a progressivist crusade they assume the mantle of Lords reform as an antidote to the Conservative usurpation of the national interest. Reforming the Lords is a long-standing policy ambition of non-Tory governments intended to remove the built-in institutional bias against progressivist legislation, and to provide a concrete expression of the pledge to modernise and purify the political system. For most reformers such intentions are couched in much the same terms as the Edwardian 'End it or Mend it' debate. When in 1996 in the aftermath of the Dunblane Massacre, members of the Lords spoke out against gun control legislation that might interfere with rural sporting pursuits, they evoked the spirit of the closed Edwardian 'huntin', shootin' and fishin'' fraternity much derided in the parliament of 1906–1914.[7] Reform of the Lords remains one of the Labour Party's oldest policy commitments. The issue of House of Lords reform returns the Labour Party to its origins, and touches the hem of the sacred garments of its pioneers. Keir Hardie campaigned on the issue in the famous West Ham election which took him to parliament as the first independent Labour MP in 1892. For most progressive reform governments, the persistence of aristocracy signalled unfinished business. In 1999 a cull of hereditary peers marked a historic break with tradition by expelling all but a rump of 92 survivors of the peerage who remain in place until a new system can be agreed. In 2003 a free vote on various blueprints for the Second Chamber established that a majority of MPs favoured an elected Upper House, although they failed to reach agreement on any particular model. Still unresolved to everyone's satisfaction, reform of the Second Chamber remains the longest-running constitutional debate in British politics. For better or for worse, the aristocracy stamped their imprint on the Upper Chamber during long years of domination. Despite recent attempts to resolve the issues arising from reform of the Lords, suspicions remain that something of the style and clubbable gentlemanly appeal of the peerage, if not the actual personages of the great hereditary dynasts themselves, will survive in the reformed Second Chamber.[8]

The legacy of the campaign against aristocracy has also left significant trace elements within political rhetoric and broader British culture. It survives particularly in newspaper journalism where it furnishes material for titillation and condescension towards the nation's social superiors. The famous case of 'The Headless Man' typifies this tendency. In 1963 a photograph of Margaret, Duchess of Argyll, showing her performing an act of fellatio on a man whose identity was concealed by the angle of the lens, was used by her husband in open court as grounds for adultery in the celebrated Argyll divorce case. Variously identified as the actor Douglas Fairbanks Jr, or the Conservative MP, Duncan Sandys, the photograph caused a sensation, and the affair became one of the society scandals that defined the 1960s. The episode added to the contemporary view of aristocracy as jaded and outmoded.[9] The raucous, condemnatory quality of this kind of journalism creates the vision of a louche, philistine, and degraded aristocracy whose image recurs in the lurid tabloid tales of the misbehaviour of our social betters. Images of cocaine-fuelled aristocrats and crude, rude, swaggering nobles who live lives of hedonistic excess have their origins in many of the stereotypes that became the speciality of land and parliamentary reformers in the late nineteenth century. Colonel Valentine Baker and the scions of other debauched elite families bequeathed a legacy of misbehaviour that became a cliché, and has long echoes in popular culture. In 1963 the scandal surrounding the Conservative defence minister John Profumo that led to the defeat of Sir Alec Douglas-Home's Conservative government began at a party at the Astors' home of Cliveden, site of much mythology about a degraded aristocracy, where Profumo was first introduced to Christine Keeler. In the 1990s, the Marquess of Bristol, who allegedly had drugs flown in by helicopter, and the heroin-addicted Marquess of Blandford, heir to the Marlborough estates, illustrated the same fundamental issue – that the aristocracy, with its penchant for giving way to its unbridled lusts and desires, had forfeited the right to rule.[10] In traditional radical rhetoric, these were errant dynasties tainted by bad blood. The Blandford case revived long-standing slurs about the devious, immoral, and discreditable behaviour of the Marlboroughs inspired by the decision of Winston Churchill MP to 'sell' his grandfather's wartime papers to the nation for a considerable sum.[11] For other commentators, the death of Lady Diana Mosley in 2003 revived memories of the links between the aristocracy and extremism.[12] The Marques of Bristol's father was a gun-runner for Franco, who also served time for his involvement in a Mayfair jewel robbery.[13] Aristocracy, then, was venal as well as immoral, corrupt as well as dissolute, with a personal history that intertwined with the darker aspects of the European past.

Moreover, recently there has been renewed interest in the role and position of aristocracy, following the emergence of pressure groups organised to defend their pastimes and privileges. Tony Blair's strongest concession to the Labour past is in his antipathy to 'the forces of conservatism', sometimes defined as synonymous with adamantine attitudes on legislative, sporting, and local government reform. Some doubt the strength of his commitment to fox-hunting and Lords reform, although he clearly recognises the totemic significance of fox-hunting both to its opponents and to its supporters. As on other occasions when non-Tory governments have been elected, since 1997 the aristocracy has rallied in opposition to legislative attempts to undermine their influence. Fox-hunting, reform of the Lords, the Countryside Right of Way Act in 2000, and a crofters' protection bill passed by the Holyrood Parliament in Scotland all provide apparent opportunities to erode the fabric of aristocratic life and diminish their traditional position. Defenders of aristocracy have decried measures as diverse as the crofters' land bill, which gives crofters the right to buy their own land, and a new register of parish councillors' interests as inimical to the position of landowners. In a now notorious outburst, landowners in the Scottish Assembly declared the land act akin to President Mugabe's sequestration of white farmers' land in Zimbabwe.[14] Suspicions also remain that the Countryside Right of Way Act does not go far enough. It gives the public access to a mere 12 per cent of England and Wales and was much criticised at public meetings in April 2002 to honour the seventieth anniversary of the fabled Kinder Scout trespass.[15] As a counterweight to a perceived urban disdain for all things rustic, aristocrats have reconstituted themselves as the custodians of rural life. Groups like the Countryside Alliance serve as a front for aristocratic vested interests. As David Cox remarks: 'Hunting is actually the touchstone not for the countryside's overall concerns, but for the longstanding hegemony over our homeland of the land-owning class.'[16] Some commentators echo the point made by nineteenth-century opponents of aristocracy, that the true heritage reflected in the story of the great British noble families is not the one the Countryside Alliance seeks to preserve, but rather the narrative of dispossession, and impoverishment that disfigures the history of the English small yeoman proprietor.[17]

In the nineteenth and early twentieth centuries, radicals defined themselves in terms of opposition to landownership and aristocratic influences. They detected an excessive deference for nobility and ancestral landownership that stamped its imprint on the fabric of British government. Radicals were fundamentally accurate in their estimate of the causes and consequences of landed power. In the nineteenth century, campaigners were united in their summation that many of Britain's most entrenched economic and social problems were rooted in the lingering power and position of the aristocracy. Reformers considered rule by the 'acreocracy' and the sanction it gave to the worst aspects of hereditary power, inappropriate for a modern, advanced, industrial nation. For them the great radical campaigns of the late nineteenth and early twentieth centuries were a corrective to a governing structure that was undermined by the British people's excessive tolerance for nobility and ancestral landownership. Subsequently, the death knell of the British aristocracy has been frequently sounded. For contemporaries, the Reform Acts, the Corn Laws, and capital transfer taxation provided ammunition for both the defenders and the opponents of aristocracy, both unanimous in their interpretation that such measures hastened the imminent end of landed society. The demise of aristocracy, however, remains much anticipated, but ultimately never realised. Although their wealth now rests less in land and property, and has diversified into bonds, trusts, and investments, the power and position of titled society persists. Concluding his ironic obituary of the Duke of Hamilton in 1895, Keir Hardie remarked 'Liberal may succeed Tory, and Tory succeed Liberal in the seat of power – all of them representing the common people – and yet the power of territorial magnates such as the one in question will remain unchecked. Truly we are a great people, democratically governed.'[18]

Appendix 1

The most amazing exhibition of inconsistency of national character in the whole history of the world is in that of the people of England. The most active, the most shrewd, the most practical and matter-of-fact, and at the same time the most adventurous and successful of people on the face of the earth, it cannot fail to strike every reader of their annuals with unfeigned astonishment, to see how at all times, but still more as they advance towards the summit of national greatness, in wealth, in ingenuity, in commerce, and vastness of empire, they have totally neglected the one means of securing to themselves the fruits of their own labours and genius – that of good and self-government. We behold them with unspeakable surprise, piling up with indefatigable energy advantage on advantage, and glory on glory, and suffering, with the most one-eyed unconsciousness, a race of lazy but cunning drones to filch from them the product of their toils and triumphs. We see them destroying tyrants, chasing them from the throne when in the shape of kings, but suffering them in legions when in the shape of lords. When a king seeks to destroy their constitution, they start up at once, and take off his head; but when an aristocracy does the very same thing, they tolerate, nay, they are accused by foreigners of even worshipping it. From the hour that that aristocracy contrived to secure a majority in the House of Commons, the constitution was as completely at an end as when Charles Stuart entered there and demanded, with armed troopers at his back, that the opposers of ship-money should be given up to him. Yet the acute and high-spirited British people have gone on for a hundred and fifty years dreaming of their constitution when it was in its grave, and the aristocratic usurpers were enriched at their expense, and revelling in the profits of their trade, their manufacturers, and their colonies.

Had this English people been a more plodding and labouring people, dense and dull of brain, but ready to execute, like good Chinese, any piece of business or mechanism that the bright and inventive genius of a *really higher class* had originated; had the aristocracy of England been the party which struck out and built up arts, science and philosophy; which had constructed ships, and discovered and planted new lands; had invented machinery, and brought to light steam, and gas, and all the chemical agents that have vitalised our stupendous structure of manufacturing and social existence; *then* there would have been no wonder in that matter! *Then* we might have seen the aristocracy playing strange pranks, and arrogating strange honours and emoluments at the popular cost, and however we might have lamented, we could not have marvelled. But the paradox of the thing is, that when we look at the two classes, and ask which is the originating class – the class of genius and of projective as well as executive energy, we stand in blank amaze [*sic*] to discover that the aristocracy are as barren as the desert sand, and as absorbent of all good. The people are the fruitful soil of all genius, of all imagination, of all constructiveness, of all valour, daring, enterprise, success and national glory. The aristocracy are the mere vermin that ride in the lion's mane, because they have clearly located themselves out of reach of his paws.

The following catechism is pointed and vigorous:

'Who laid the foundations of our free institutions, Parliaments, representation, and trial by jury?' – The old Anglo-Saxon people.

'Who destroyed these, to a great practical extent, and rent the soil from its ancient possessors, by the introduction of feudalism?' – The aristocracy of the Danish Normans.

'Who attempted to wring the Magna Charta from King John and failed?' – The Barons.

'Who won it?' – The bowmen of England, who drove John and the barons too, and their invited French King, before them, and compelled Henry III to give them a still better Charter.

'Who tore the kingdom to pieces by cruel wars and wranglings for the crown, till the reign of Henry VII?' – The aristocracy.

'Who meantime, cultivated the ground, originated trade, raised the country in wealth, strength, and respect, spite of its internal aristocratic dissonance?' – The people.

'Who trembled before the Tudors, and became their instruments even to the commission of systematic murders in Scotland and at home?' – The aristocracy.

'Who made the Tudor Elizabeth tremble in the midst of her haughtiness and retract her arbitrary commands?' – The people in their Parliament.

'Who joined with the Stuarts to destroy the liberties of the nation, and to rule by a standing army?' – The aristocracy.

'Who put down king and aristocracy, and made the first example in the world of a headless king, for the warning of bad monarchs, and the encouragement of injured nations?' – The people of England.

'Who recalled the debauched Charles II to this country, and bargained with him for their own profit and the popular wrong?' – The aristocracy.

'Who again drove the Stuarts from the throne?' – The people.

'Who got the credit of it?' – Seven bishops, whose 'Diana of the Ephesians,' the Church, was in danger by the king's plan of restoring Popery, and some dozen or two of the aristocracy, who called in the Dutch king to rule and rob him.

'Who, from that time to 1815, went on spending the national funds in foreign wars, for the establishment of foreign tyrants, till the cost of bloodshed amounted to three thousand millions?' – The aristocracy.

'Who, meantime, raised the wind? Who ploughed and sowed, dug and hoed, spun and wove, and sailed and traded, and raised England to such a pitch of power and wealth as withstood all immediate ruin, but left an awful heap of debt to look at?' – The people of England.

'Who planted America?' – The people.

'Who lost it?' – The imbecile aristocracy.

'Who invented all improvements in agriculture, mechanics, and manufacturers, which ingenuity produced national wealth? Who made roads, cut canals, called into knowledge and use gas and steam; built steam-engines and steam-ships; laid down rail-roads, and put in motion spinning-jennies and power-looms, the grand sources of our national ascendancy?' – The people.

'Who invented the National Debt?' – The aristocracy.

Founders and inventors

Commoners	Lords
Founders and inventors	*Founders and inventors*
Paterson, founder of the Bank of England	
Gunter, inventor of Logarithmical scale	
Arkwright, introducer of the water-power for spinning cotton	
Watt, improver of the steam engine	
Bolton, ditto, and of coining	
Hargrave, inventor of the spinning-jenny	
Compton, inventor of the mule-jenny for cotton spinning	
Brindley, constructor of canals, locks, &c	
Smeaton, engineer, builder of Eddystone Lighthouse	
John Lombe, introducer of silk-throwing, and builder of the first silk mill in England at Derby	
Lee, inventor of the stocking-loom	Earl of Rosse, improver of the telescope
Strutt, improver of the stocking-loom	
William Ged, inventor of stereotype printing	
Josiah Wedgwood, improver of earthenware	
Harrison, improver of the chronometer	
James Gregory, inventor of the reflecting telescope	
Dr Roebuck, improver of iron-founding. Founder of Carron Works	
Napier, inventor of logarithms	
Dolland, inventor of the Achromatic telescope	
Brown, founder of the Brunonian system of medicine	
Bakewell, improver of sheep and cattle	As agriculturists, the nobility have shown themselves more laudable than in any other character; and we may name the Duke of Portland, Lord Althorpe, Lord Western, and many other zealous cattle breeders and farmers; but rather following the Bakewells, Cullys &c. than leading the way in invention
Cully, ditto, and of agriculture	
Arthur Young, ditto	
T.W. Coke of Holkham, made Lord Leicester	
Miller, Taylor, and Symington, first starters of a steam boat on Dalswinton Lake, Scotland	
Henry Bell, first runner of a steamer for passengers on the Clyde	

Trevithic and Vivian, first runners of
a steam-engine on a tram-road at
Merthyr-Tydvil

Tilloch, first effectual introducer of
stereotype printing

Cont, improver of iron-founding

Huntsman of Attercliffe, discoverer of the
art of converting cast-iron into steel

Dr Edmund Cartwright, inventor of the
power-loom

Robert Frost, inventor or great improver
of the lace-loom and machinery for
wool-combing

Holmes, inventor of point-net

Wissett, promoter of silk-growing in
Bengal, and of silk-throwing in England

Philip James Knight, a great improver of
the Norwich shawls

Watt, Henry and Tennant, introducers of
chemical bleaching

Bell, inventor of the cylindrical machine
for printing calicoes

M'Adam, introducer of a new system of
road-making

Sir Humphrey Davy, inventor of the safety
lamp, and author of many chemical
discoveries

Hutton, inventor of the Huttonian theory
of the earth

Dr Birkbeck, founder of Mechanics'
Institutes

Robert Raikes, founder of Sunday schools

Dr Jenner, introducer of vaccination

Bell and Lancaster, founders of the
school-systems bearing their names

Rev. Mr Bailley, of Sheffield, founder of
People's Colleges

Discoverers

John Cabot and Sebastian Cabot,
father and son, the first discoverers of
Newfoundland, and the mainland of
America

Martin Frobisher, explorer of the Arctic
coast of America, and discoverer of the
straits bearing his name

Francis Drake, discoverer of New Albion

Discoverers

Duke of Norfolk, discoverer of the
hitherto unknown properties of
curry-powder, by which roast-beef,
plum-pudding, and such heavy and
dyspeptic articles of food are likely
to grow eventually out of use, to the
signal relief of mankind

Appendix 1   (Continued)

Commoners	Lords
Thomas Cavendish, discoverer of various portions of South America, and the South Sea; and circumnavigator	
John Davis, discoverer of Davis's Straits; explorer of the coasts of Greenland, Iceland, &c.	
Commodore Byron, discoverer of the Isles of Danger and Duke of York's Island	
Captain Wallis, discoverer of the Island of Otaheite	
Captain Cook, discoverer of New South Wales, New Caledonia, Sandwich Isles, and rediscoverer of New Zealand	
Harvey, discoverer of the circulation of the blood	
Dr Black, discoverer of latent heat	
Bradley, discoverer of the aberration of light	
William Murdoch, a Cornish man, who first used gas to light his own house	
Watt and Boulton, first lit with Soho with it	
Sandby, introducer of water colour painting	

We say

Look on this picture, and on that!

And what do we see? Immense columns of stirring, active, able men, inventing, contriving, constructing and building up the nation in arts, sciences, discoveries, laws, colonies, and all manner of new and great things. Nay, the numbers we have taken are but a mere fragment; any reader knows that the very names of the whole body of meritorious men and women of England would make a large volume.

Amongst philosophers there is no name of a born lord. Amongst great churchmen and religionists, the fact is the same, though they have the whole church as a heritage; the distinguished are, almost to a man, those who are sprung of 'earth's best blood', the blood of the middle classes. In the mighty catalogue of the poets, the name of Lord Byron is the only one that stands out in his class as a first-rate man, and how he came to prove such is easily explained by the fact that, though born to the prospect of a peerage, he was born poor, and left to wander amid the wild majesty of mountains in his boyhood, instead of being swathed and swaddled in aristocratic luxury. He made acquaintance with nature before he knew too much of man, and it unfolded the inward eye, and developed that power which is clogged and overlaid by aristocratic ease. But as he grew up, and had passed through the aristocratic hot-beds of Harrow and Cambridge, and entered the aristocratic circles of London, he acquired so much of the spirit of 'the order', that his principles and his feelings were for ever after at variance. His principles were thoroughly radical, his feelings were haughty and aristocratic.

From William Howitt, *The Aristocracy of England* (London, 1856), ch. XXVI (pp. 306–23).

Appendix 2

Henry George: *Progress and Poverty*

Our boasted freedom necessarily involves slavery, so long as we recognise private property in land. Until that is abolished, Declarations of Independence and Acts of Emancipation are in vain. So long as one man can claim the exclusive ownership of the land from which other men must live, slavery will exist, and as material progress goes on, must grow and deepen! . . .

Mr Mill's plan for nationalising the future 'unearned increase in the value of land' by fixing the present market value of all lands and appropriating to the state future increase of value, would not add to the injustice of the present distribution of wealth, but it would not remedy it. . . .

Herbert Spencer says: 'Had we to deal with the parties who originally robbed the human race of its heritage, we might make short work of the matter.' Why not make short work of the matter anyhow? For this robbery is not like the robbery of a horse or a sum of money, that ceases with the act. It is a fresh and continuous robbery, that goes on every day and every hour. It is not from the produce of the past that rent is drawn; it is from the produce of the present. It is a toll levied upon labour constantly and continuously. Every blow of the hammer, every stroke of the pick, every thrust of the shuttle, every throb of the steam engine pay it tribute. It levies upon the earnings of the men who, deep underground, risk their lives . . . it claims the just reward of the capitalist and the fruits of the inventor's patient effort . . . it robs the shivering of warmth; the hungry, of food; the sick, of medicine; the anxious, of peace . . . It crowds families of eight and ten into a single squalid room . . .

It is not merely a robbery in the past; it is a robbery in the present – a robbery that deprives of their birth-right the infants that are now coming into the world! Why should we hesitate about making short work of such a system? Because I was robbed yesterday, and the day before, and the day before that, is it any reason that I should suffer myself to be robbed to-day and to-morrow? Any reason that I should conclude that the robber has acquired a vested right to rob me? . . .

What more than anything else prevents the realisation of the essential injustice of private property in land . . . is that mental habit which makes anything that has long existed seem natural and necessary . . . If it were true that land had always been treated as private property, that would not prove the justice or necessity of continuing so to treat it . . . but . . . this is *not* true. On the contrary, the common right to land has everywhere been primarily recognised, and private ownership has nowhere grown up save as the result of usurpation. Historically, as ethically, private property in land is robbery. It nowhere springs from contract; it can nowhere be traced to perceptions of justice or expediency; it has everywhere had its birth in war and conquest, and in the selfish use which the cunning have made of superstition and law . . .

This is clear – that in Great Britain to-day the right of the people as a whole to the soil of their native country is much less fully acknowledged than it was in feudal times. A much smaller proportion of the people own the soil, and their ownership is much more absolute. The commons...have, all but a small remnant of yet worthless land, been appropriated to individual ownership and inclosed; the great estates of the church...have been diverted from that trust to enrich individuals; the dues of the military tenants have been shaken off, and the cost of maintaining the military establishment and paying the interest upon an immense debt accumulated by wars has been saddled upon the whole people...The crown lands have mostly passed into private possession, and for the support of the royal family and all the petty princelings who marry into it, the British workman must pay in the price of his mug of beer and pipe of tobacco. The English yeoman – the sturdy breed who won Crecy, and Poitiers, and Agincourt – are as extinct as the mastodon. The Scottish clansman, whose right to the soil of his native hills was then as undisputed as that of his chieftain, has been driven out to make room for the sheep ranges or deerparks of that chieftain's descendant; the tribal right of the Irishman has been turned into a tenancy-at-will. Thirty thousand men have legal power to expel the whole population from five-sixths of the British Islands, and the vast majority of the British people have no right whatsoever to their native land save to walk the streets or trudge the roads...

(This extract is taken from the English edition of 1890, pp. 256–71.)

Appendix 3

National Reform Union Leaflet – No. 120

The House of Lords:
Its Cup of Iniquity

Arthur G. Symonds

Here is a List of Good and Popular Measures which the Lords have Rejected, Mutilated, or Delayed during the last hundred years.

I – PARLIAMENTARY REFORM

Reform Bill, 1831.
Disfranchisement of Five Corrupt Boroughs, 1834.
Bribery Prevention Bill, 1834.
Vote by Ballot, 1871.
Reform Bill, 1884.
Plural Voting Bill, 1906.
London Elections Bill, 1909.

II – MUNICIPAL REFORM

English Municipal Reform Bill, 1835.
Irish Municipal Reform Bill, 1837, 1838, 1839.

III – IRELAND

Catholic Emancipation, 1821–1826.
Arterial Drainage Bill, 1829.
Irish Church Temporalities Bill, 1833.
Irish Church Tithes Bill, 1837–1858.
Penal Laws Repeal Bill, 1844.
Compensation for Tenants' Improvements Bill, 1845–1870.
Irish Church Disestablishment Resolutions, 1868.
Irish Church Disestablishment Bill, 1869.
Irish Land Act, 1870.
Compensation for Disturbance Bill, 1880.
Irish Land Act, 1881.
Home Rule Bill, 1893.
Evicted Tenants Bill, 1894.
Town Tenants (Ireland) Act, 1906.
Irish Evicted Tenants Act, 1907.
Irish Land Act, 1909.

IV – LAND REFORM

Reduction or Repeal of the Corn Laws, 1830–1846.
Repeal of Game Laws (two Bills), 1827.
Ground Game Bill, 1880.
Settled Lands Bill, 1882.
Agricultural Holdings Bill, 1883.
Land Transfer Bill, 1887 and 1893.
Betterment Bill, 1893.
Agricultural Holdings Act, 1906.
Scotch Small Landholders Bill, 1907, 1908.
Scotch Land Values Bill, 1907, 1908.

V – RELIGIOUS LIBERTY AND EQUALITY

University Tests Abolition Bill, 1834, 1866, 1869, 1870.
Repeal of the Corporation and Test Acts, 1820–1828.
Jewish Disabilities Repeal Bill, 1833–1858.
Tithe Abatement Bill, 1834.
Bill for Legalising Marriages in Dissenting Chapels, 1834.
Bill to allow Nonconformist Ministers to Officiate in Workhouses, 1834.
Abolition of Church Rates, 1858–1869.
Burial Laws Amendment Bill, 1873–1880.
Education Bill, 1906.

VI – PATRONAGE AND PRIVILEGE

Bill for Abolition and Regulation of Sinecures, &c., 1812.
Bill to Establish County Courts, 1833–1848.
Bill to diminish Cost of Common Law Suits, 1833.
Court of Admiralty Jurisdiction Bill, 1839.
Real Property Conveyancing Bill, 1843.
Legalisation of Life Peerages, 1869.
Abolition of Army Purchase Bill, 1871.
County Courts Bill, 1909.

VII – CRIMINAL LAW

Abolition of Death Penalty for Theft of Goods worth 5s. from Shops, 1810.
Abolition of Death Penalty for Theft of Goods worth 40s. from Dwelling Houses
or Vessels in Rivers, 1811.
Abolition of Death Penalty for Shop-Lifting, 1813–1820.
Bill to Abolish Quartering and Disembowelling Traitors, 1814.
Abolition of Death Penalty for Men who Blackened their Faces in Night Robbery,
1820.
Abolition of Death Penalty for Forgery, 1830.
Abolition of Death Penalty for Sheep Stealing, 1839.
Abolition of Imprisonment for Debt, 1861.

VIII – SOCIAL REFORM

Bill for Promoting and Encouraging Industry amongst the Labouring Classes and
for the Relief and Regulation of the Necessitous Poor, 1807.
Bill for Establishing a System of National Education, 1807.
Bill to Increase Grant for Education, 1839.
Mines Regulation Bill, 1842.
Education of Miners' Children, 1860.
Artisans' Dwellings Bill, 1868.
Education Act, 1870.
Marriage with Deceased Wife's Sister Bill, 1879–1894.
Employers' Liability Bill, 1880.
Cornwall Sunday Closing Bill, 1883.
Bill to Prevent Pigeon Shooting, 1883.
Employers' Liability Bill, 1893.
Railway Servants' Hours of Labour Bill, 1893.
Welsh University Charter Bill, 1893.
Fishery Boats Bill, 1893.
Opening of Lincoln's Inn Fields Bill, 1893.
Tramways Over Bridges (London) Bill, 1905.
Aliens Bill, 1906.
Education (Provision of Meals) Act, 1906.
Licensing Bill, 1908.
Coal Miners (Eight Hours) Act, 1908.
Housing and Town Planning Act, 1909.

IX – FINANCE

Repeal of Paper Duty, 1860.
The Finance Bill, 1909.

(From Manchester Central Library, Election Ephemera, 1906–1910, Social Science
Reading Room.)

Notes

Introduction

1. E. Hughes (ed.), *Keir Hardie: His Writings and Speeches from 1888 to 1915* (Glasgow, 1924), p. 45.
2. R.G. White, *England Within and Without* (London, 1881), p. 393.
3. J. Clark, *English Society 1688–1832* (Oxford, 1986), and for analysis of his ideas, J. Innes, 'Jonathan Clark, Social History and England's "Ancien Regime"', *Past and Present*, CXV (1987), 165–200.
4. L.H. Grindon, *Lancashire: Brief Historical and Descriptive Notes* (London, 1882), pp. 65–76.
5. J.L. and Barbara Hammond, *The Village Labourer*, 5th edn (London, 1948), II, p. 134.
6. *The Times*, 17 December 1923.
7. See N. Gash, *Politics in the Age of Peel* (London, 1953); idem, *Reaction and Reconstruction in English Politics 1832–52* (London, 1965); and idem, *Sir Robert Peel* (London, 1972).
8. See A. Adonis, 'Aristocracy, Agriculture and Liberalism: The Politics, Finances and Estates of the Third Lord Carrington', *Historical Journal*, XXXI (1988), 871–97.
9. For the standard accounts of aristocratic connection in the eighteenth century, see J. Brewer, *Party Ideology and Popular Politics at the Accession of George III* (London, 1976), ch. 9; and W.A. Speck, *Stability and Strife: England 1714–1760* (London, 1977), ch. 6.
10. F.M.L. Thompson, *English Landed Society in the Nineteenth Century* (London, 1963), ch. 12.
11. Quoted in R. Samuel, *Island Stories: Unravelling Britain* (London, 1998), p. 224.
12. D. Cannadine, *The Decline and Fall of the British Aristocracy* (Yale, 1990); and idem, *Aspects of Aristocracy* (London, 1994), especially ch. 1. With its impish title 'The Making of the British Upper Classes' this chapter is a tribute to Thompson, whilst recognising the paucity of research into aristocratic life.
13. See A.J. Mayer, *The Persistence of the Old Regime: Europe to the Great War* (New York, 1981), pp. 26–8.
14. See David Cannadine, *The Decline and Fall of the British Aristocracy* (Yale, 1990); P. Harling, 'Rethinking "Old Corruption"', *Past and Present*, CXXXXXVII (1995), 127–58; P. Harling and P. Mandler, 'From Fiscal-Military State to Laissez-Faire State', *Journal of British Studies*, XXXII (1993), 44–70; and P. Mandler, *The Rise and Fall of the Stately Home* (New Haven, 1997), chs 6–7.
15. J. Bateman, *Acreocracy of England* (London, 1876); and R.S. Churchill, *Lord Derby: 'King of Lancashire'* (London, 1959).
16. R.R. James (ed.), *Chips: The Diaries of Sir Henry Channon* (London, 1967), p. 130.
17. *Manchester Examiner and Times*, 1 April 1876, p. 7.
18. See J. Harris, *Private Lives, Public Spirit: Britain 1870–1914* (Oxford, 1993), pp. 104–6, 184–7.

19. See B. Short, *Land and Society in Edwardian Britain* (Cambridge, 1997), ch. 1 and F.M.L. Thompson, *Gentrification and the Enterprise Culture: Britain 1780–1980* (Oxford, 2001), ch. 1.

20. See for the debate about the gentrification of British industry, M.J. Weiner, *English Culture and the Decline of the Industrial Spirit 1850–1980* (Cambridge, 1981), chs 7 and 9; L. Stone and J.C.F. Stone, *An Open Elite? England 1540–1880* (Oxford, 1984); W.D. Rubenstein, 'New Men of Wealth', *Past and Present*, LXXXXII (1981), 125–47; and Thompson, *Gentrification and the Enterprise Culture*, especially chs 2–3.

21. Rather curiously, discussion of this subject is omitted altogether from L. Colley, *Britons: Forging the Nation 1707–1837* (New Haven, 1992).

22. Cannadine, *Aspects of Aristocracy*, pp. 1–2.

23. O. Mosley, *My Life* (London, 1968), p. 19.

24. I.D. Whyte, *Landscape and History since 1500* (London, 2002), chs 3 and 4.

25. R. Colls, *Identity of England* (Oxford, 2003), ch. 4.

26. See D. Cannadine, *Ornamentalism: How the British Saw their Empire* (London, 2001), p. 34.

27. Ibid., chs 4, 5 and 7.

28. P. Lynch, *The Liberal Party in Rural England 1885–1910* (Oxford, 2002) and I. Packer, *Lloyd George, Liberalism and the Land: The Land Issue and Party Politics in England 1906–1914* (Royal Historical Society, 2001), chs 1–2.

29. Mandler, *The Rise and Fall of the Stately Home*, ch. 3.

30. The 'People's Canon' propounded by Rose shows a defiantly egalitarian and anti-aristocratic tendency in plebeian reading matter, see J. Rose, *The Intellectual History of the British Working Class* (New Haven, 2001), ch. 2.

31. See J.G.A. Pocock, *The Ancient Constitution and the Feudal Law* (Cambridge, 1957), ch. 6.

32. A. Trollope, *An Autobiography* (London, 1883), p. 265.

33. D. Wahrman, *Imagining the Middle Class: The Political Representation of Class in Britain c.1780–1840* (Cambridge, 1995), chs 9–10.

34. See on this issue of anti-aristocracy as an unrespectable faith, I. McCalman, *Radical Underworld: Prophets, Revolutionaries, and Pornographers in London, 1795–1840* (Oxford, 1988), especially chs 8 and 10.

35. J. Barker, *The Life of Joseph Barker, Written by Himself* (London, 1880), p. 287.

36. For an overview of the debate, see J. Belchem, *Popular Radicalism in Nineteenth Century Britain* (London, 1996), chs 6–7; E.F. Biagini and H.J. Reid (eds), 'Introduction' to *Currents of Radicalism: Popular Radicalism, Organised Labour and Party Politics in Britain 1850–1914* (Cambridge, 1991), pp. 1–19; E.F. Biagini, *Liberty, Retrenchment and Reform: Popular Liberalism in the Age of Gladstone 1860–1880* (Cambridge, 1992); M.C. Finn, *After Chartism: Class and Nation in English Radical Politics 1848–1874* (Cambridge, 1993); G.S. Jones, *Languages of Class: Studies in English Working Class History* (Cambridge, 1983), ch. 3; P. Joyce, *Visions of the People: Industrial England and the Question of Class 1848–1914* (Cambridge, 1991), chs 2–3; idem, *Democratic Subjects: The Self and the Social in Nineteenth Century England* (Cambridge, 1994), pp. 24–46; M. Taylor, *The Decline of British Radicalism 1847–1860* (Oxford, 1995); J. Vernon, *Politics and the People: A Study in English Political Culture c.1815–1867* (Cambridge, 1993), ch. 4; and

R. McWilliam, *Popular Politics in Nineteenth Century England* (London, 1998), chs 2 and 5.

37. J. Lawrence, 'Popular Radicalism and the Socialist Revival in Britain', *Journal of British Studies*, XXX1 (1992), 163–86.

38. See for the campaign against unjust landownership and aristocratic power, D.E. Martin, 'Land Reform' in P. Hollis (ed.), *Pressure from Without in Early Victorian England* (London, 1974), pp. 131–58; and R. Douglas, *Land, People and Politics: A History of the Land Question in the United Kingdom 1878–1952* (London, 1976), chs 3–4.

39. For James Mill's anti-aristocratic ideas, see J. Mill, 'Aristocracy', *London Review*, II (1836), 283–386 and J.S. Mill, *Autobiography of John Stuart Mill* (London, 1873), pp. 74–5.

40. The term is much quoted, but was first used by John Bright at a speech in Manchester in 1858; see J.E.T. Rogers (ed.), *Speeches on Questions of Public Policy by John Bright* (2 vols, London, 1868), I, pp. 373–99.

41. J. Keir Hardie, *From Serfdom to Slavery* (Edinburgh, 1907), p. 11.

42. See E.E. Barry, *Nationalisation in British Politics: The Historical Background* (London, 1965); and G.R. Searle, *The Liberal Party: Triumph and Disintegration 1886–1929* (London, 1992), ch. 2.

43. A.A. Walton, *History of the Landed Tenures of Great Britain and Ireland from the Norman Conquest to the Present Time* (London, 1865), p. 101. For Walton's anti-landlordism, see D. Mares, 'A Radical in Wales: Alfred A. Walton and Mid-Victorian Welsh Popular Radicalism', *The Welsh History Review*, XXI (2002), 271–91.

44. There is now a large literature on landownership and radicalism, but see for the origins of the radical position on the land, M. Chase, *The People's Farm: English Radical Agrarianism 1775–1840* (Oxford, 1988); and H. Perkin, 'Land Reform and Class Conflict in Victorian Britain' in his *The Structured Crowd: Essays in British Social History* (Brighton, 1981), pp. 100–35.

45. For a recent restatement of this position, see P. Worsthorne, *In Defence of Aristocracy* (London, 2004).

46. J. Morley, *The Life of Richard Cobden* (2 vols, 1896), II, pp. 455–7.

1   Aristocratic debauchery and working-class virtue: The case of Colonel Valentine Baker

1. 'John Hampden', *The Aristocracy of England: A History for the People* (London, 1856), p. 288.

2. G.K. Chesterton, *Come to Think of It: A Book of Essays* (London, 1930), p. 236.

3. Quoted in H.M. Hyde, *Mr and Mrs Beeton* (London, 1951), p. 157.

4. These themes are analysed in Belchem, *Popular Radicalism in Nineteenth Century Britain*, chs 6–7; and McWilliam, *Popular Politics in Nineteenth Century England*, ch. 5.

5. *People's Paper*, 8 December 1855, p. 1. The large number of aristocratic places and sinecures in the royal household that allowed the queen to be pampered and cosseted by courtly retainers are satirised in the *Northern Star*, 18 April 1840, p. 4.

6. See T.D. Murray and A.S. White, *Sir Samuel Baker: A Memoir* (London, 1895), pp. 1–6.

7. There are a number of popular studies of the Baker brothers. The most recent is B. Thompson, *Imperial Vanities: The Adventures of the Baker Brothers and Gordon of Khartoum* (London, 2002).
8. *People's Paper*, 17 March 1855.
9. *People's Advocate*, 17 July 1875, p. 6.
10. *Reynolds's Newspaper*, 11 July 1875, p. 1.
11. A. Humphreys, 'G.W.M. Reynolds, Popular Literature and Popular Politics', *Victorian Periodicals Review*, XVI (1983), 78–89; V. Berridge, 'Popular Sunday Newspapers and Mid-Victorian Society' in G. Boyce, P. Wingate and J. Curran (eds), *Newspaper History from the Seventeenth Century to the Present Day* (London, 1978), pp. 252–64; R. McWilliam, 'The Mysteries of G.W.M. Reynolds: Radicalism and Melodrama in Victorian Britain' in Malcolm Chase and Ian Dyck (eds), *Living and Learning: Essays in Honour of J.F.C. Harrison* (Aldershot, 1996), pp. 182–98; and I. Haywood, 'George W.M. Reynolds and the "Trafalgar Square Revolution": Radicalism, the Carnivalesque and Popular Culture in Mid-Victorian England', *Journal of Victorian Culture*, VII (2002), 23–59.
12. The phrase was used by Ernest Jones in the *People's Paper*, 8 December 1855, p. 1.
13. *The Times*, 12 July 1864, p. 11. Both cases were followed by attempts to produce safer travelling conditions for passengers. After the Briggs murder peep holes were drilled between carriages on some routes, but the practice was discontinued when there were complaints about invasion of privacy. Following the Baker case, female-only carriages were introduced, and remained in service in some areas until 1975.
14. Ibid., 3 August 1875, p. 9.
15. Ibid., pp. 10–11.
16. See V.A.C. Gatrell, *The Hanging Tree: Execution and the English People 1770–1868* (Cambridge, 1996), chs 2–3.
17. *The Weekly Dispatch*, 8 August 1875, pp. 9, 11.
18. *The Times*, 18 November 1887, p. 4.
19. *The Bee-Hive*, 14 August 1875, p. 3.
20. Ibid., 21 August 1875, p. 11. The penalties handed out in rape cases were traditionally harsh. See Gatrell, *The Hanging Tree*, ch. 17.
21. *The Weekly Dispatch*, 8 August 1875, p. 7.
22. G.J. Holyoake, *Sixty Years of An Agitator's Life* (London, 1906), p. 250.
23. *Reynolds's Newspaper*, 8 August 1875, p. 3.
24. Ibid., 3 July 1881, p. 5, and 10 July 1881, p. 3.
25. *Justice*, 29 April 1893, p. 2.
26. *De Morgan's Monthly*, 15 October 1876, pp. 4–5.
27. Reynolds was obsessed with the plight of impoverished and vulnerable needlewomen who became the playthings of their aristocratic customers and their flunkeys; see I. Haywood, 'Graphic Narratives and Discoveries of Horror: The Feminisation of Labour in Nineteenth Century Radical Fiction' in H.G. Klaus and S. Knight (eds), *British Industrial Fictions* (Cardiff, 2000), pp. 5–23.
28. *Reynolds's Newspaper*, 4 July 1875, p. 5.
29. A. Clark, 'The Politics of Seduction in English Popular Culture, 1748–1848' in J. Radford (ed.), *The Progress of Romance: The Politics of Popular Fiction*

(London, 1986), pp. 46–70; and S. Staves, 'British Seduced Maidens', *Eighteenth Century Studies*, XIV (1980/1), 42–55.

30. G.C. Brodrick, 'The Law and Custom of Primogeniture' in *Cobden Club Essays, Second Series, 1871–72* (London, 1872), p. 100.
31. J.E.T. Rogers, *Letters of J.E. Thorold Rogers and Mr. Henry Tupper on the History and Working of the Laws of Primogeniture and Entail* (Manchester, 1864), pp. 27–8.
32. M. Taylor, *Ernest Jones, Chartism and the Romance of Politics, 1819–1869* (Oxford, 2003), pp. 90–1.
33. See R. Blatchford, *Britain for the British* (London, 1902), pp. 51–62.
34. Hughes (ed.), *Keir Hardie: His Writings and Speeches*, p. 173.
35. See for the association between aristocracy and deviant and transgressive behaviour in London, J.R. Walkowitz, *City of Dreadful Delight: Narratives of Sexual Danger in Late Victorian London* (London, 1992), ch. 7, and for an examination of contemporary literature that celebrated the movement of libertines (often in disguise) between the classes and amongst the pleasure palaces of London, G. Dart, '"Flash Style": Pierce Egan and Literary London, 1820–28', *History Workshop Journal*, LI (2001), 180–205.
36. *Reynolds's Newspaper*, 3 February 1884, p. 4 and C. Tsuzuki (ed.), *Henry Hyndman, England for All: The Text Book of Democracy* (Brighton, 1973), p. 24.
37. Charles Bradlaugh, *John Churchill, Duke of Marlborough* (London, 1884), p. 1.
38. *Reynolds's Newspaper*, 26 June 1870, p. 2.
39. *The Alliance News*, 2 April 1870, p. 106. See for the publicity surrounding Randolph Churchill's drunken assault on a policeman, R.F. Foster, *Lord Randolph Churchill* (Oxford, 1981), pp. 13–15; and B. Harrison, *Drink and the Victorians: The Temperance Question in England* (new edition, Keele, 1994), pp. 204–5.
40. *People's Paper*, 23 September 1854, p. 4. The fate of the 1908 Licensing Bill which was thrown out by the Lords was determined at a meeting of peers at Lansdowne House in the West End, confirming for many Liberals the connection between drink and aristocracy; see Lord Willoughby de Broke, *The Passing Years* (London, 1924), pp. 246–7.
41. *Reynolds's Newspaper*, 20 June 1875, p. 2.
42. *Reynolds's Newspaper*, 28 January 1872, p. 3 and 27 January 1884, p. 3. Elsewhere they are described as 'public robbers'; see the *National Reformer*, 8 February 1874, pp. 91–2. Reformers often compared the history of landownership in Great Britain to an act of street mugging; see *The Single Tax*, 1 January 1901, p. 313.
43. D. Woodruff, *The Tichborne Claimant: A Victorian Mystery* (London, 1957), ch. 12; and M. Roe, *Kenealy and the Tichborne Cause: A Study in Mid-Victorian Populism* (Melbourne, 1974), pp. 163–97.
44. See for the Tichborne campaign, R. McWilliam, 'Radicalism and Popular Culture: The Tichborne Case and the Politics of "Fair Play"' in Biagini and Reid (eds), *Currents of Radicalism*, pp. 44–64.
45. *The Bee-Hive*, 14 August 1875, p. 10.
46. *Reynolds's Newspaper*, 14 January 1872, p. 4.
47. D.J. Kirwan, *Palace and Hovel or Phases of London Life: Being Personal Observations of an American in London* (London, 1870), p. 72.
48. *Weekly Dispatch*, 8 August 1875, p. 7.
49. *Reynolds's Newspaper*, 17 June 1866, p. 3.
50. *The Single Tax*, 1 February 1899, p. 2.

51. T.A. Devyr, *The Odd Book of the Nineteenth Century, or 'Chivalry' in Modern Days* (New York, 1882), p. 155.
52. *People's Paper*, 7 April 1855, p. 4.
53. Ibid., 30 September 1854, p. 4.
54. W. Benbow, *A Peep at the Peers: An Alphabetical List of All Peers who Sit in the House . . . Showing their Offices, Pensions, Grants, Church Preferment and Other Things Attached to the Peers and Their Families* (London, 1820), pp. 1–16; J. Mitford, *A Peep into W-r Castle* (London, 1820), pp. 2–17; and McCalman, *Radical Underworld*, pp. 166–73.
55. *Reynolds's Newspaper*, 6 July 1884, p. 1.
56. Ibid., 20 January 1884, p. 4.
57. Ibid., 28 March 1875, p. 2, and 3 April 1881, p. 3.
58. Loc. cit.
59. Ibid., 4 July 1875, p. 5.
60. Ibid., 17 March 1872, p. 4.
61. See A. Taylor, '*Reynolds's Newspaper*, Opposition to Monarchy and the Radical Anti-Jubilee: Britain's Anti-Monarchist Tradition Reconsidered', *Historical Research*, CVIII (1995), 318–37.
62. *Reynolds's Newspaper*, 10 March 1872, p. 2.
63. See J. Pearson, *Edward the Rake* (London, 1975), p. 61.
64. There is a curious slippage in anti-royal accounts during the period of the republican ferment of the 1870s between the careers of George IV and Albert Edward, Prince of Wales. Advertised to speak at Sowerby Bridge on 'George, Prince of Wales' in 1871, Charles Bradlaugh discovered that the town had been placarded with posters announcing a talk on 'Albert Edward, Prince of Wales', causing a large attendance and a visible police presence. See H. Bradlaugh Bonner, *Charles Bradlaugh: A Record of His Life and Work* (2 vols, London, 1894), I, p. 306.
65. *The Mysteries of the Court of London*, I–II (1850), p. 54. For the role of the Regency in setting the standard of royal misbehaviour see A. Taylor, '*Down with the Crown': British Anti-monarchism and Debates About Royalty Since 1790* (London, 1999), chs 1 and 3.
66. *The Bee-Hive*, 14 May 1870, p. 204.
67. T. Johnston, *Our Noble Families* (Glasgow, 1916), p. ix.
68. *Reynolds's Newspaper*, 28 March 1875, p. 2.
69. The term 'land pirates' often applied to the aristocracy in the radical press, cemented associations between usurped wealth and moral wrongdoing; see L.F. Post, *The Prophet of San Francisco* (New York, 1930), p. 12.
70. *Reynolds's Newspaper*, 6 March 1870, p. 2.
71. For comparisons between the British aristocracy and the Zulu tribes see the *National Reformer*, 30 November 1879, p. 781. For Donald Ross's pamphlet on land abuses in Ross-shire, see the *People's Paper*, 3 June 1854, p. 4.
72. O.D. Rudkin, *Thomas Spence and His Connections* (New York, 1927), p. 45.
73. *People's Paper*, 3 June 1854, p. 4.
74. *Reynolds's Newspaper*, 13 September 1868, p. 3.
75. 'Casey', *Who are the Bloodsuckers?* (ILP, 1905), pp. 2–3.
76. See a speech by Chamberlain at Birmingham alluded to in Willoughby de Broke, *The Passing Years*, p. 167.
77. *Reynolds's Newspaper*, 4 July 1875, p. 5.

78. Vitriolic images of 'stay-at-home' generals cohered around the Duke of Cambridge, the queen's cousin, during the Crimean campaign. Ernest Jones wrote: 'If we lose our army, we shan't lose our Duke after all. Our Grenadiers may never return, but His Royal Highness will come back. We will still have the joy of seeing him ride from Kew to Cambridge House and know that, at least, Russia left us this hope of our royalty untouched'; see the *People's Paper*, 16 September 1854, p. 4.

79. *The Weekly Dispatch*, 8 August 1875, p. 9.

80. See J. Parry, *The Rise and Fall of Liberal Government in Victorian Britain* (New Haven, 1993), pp. 269–70 and *Reynolds's Newspaper*, 25 October 1868, p. 3.

81. O. Anderson, *A Liberal State at War: English Politics and Economics during the Crimean War* (London, 1967), p. 107.

82. *People's Paper*, 13 January 1855, p. 1. For further accounts of Jones' 'Movement for the Army and Soldiers' Charter' see ibid., 6 January 1855, p. 1 and 10 February 1855, p. 1.

83. *Reynolds's Newspaper*, 3 April 1881, p. 3.

84. For the radical campaign against flogging in the armed services and the implications of the White Case, see S.S. Sprigge, *The Life and Times of Thomas Wakley* (London, 1897), *Punch*, 1 August 1846, and the *People's Paper*, 6 January 1855, p. 4, and 25 August 1855, p. 1.

85. *The Weekly Dispatch*, 8 August 1875, p. 9.

86. A.G. Srebnick, *The Mysterious Death of Mary Rogers: Sex and Culture in Nineteenth Century New York* (Oxford, 1995), ch. 6.

87. *The Single Tax*, 1 October 1899, p. 67.

88. Quoted in *Land Tax Cartoons from the Morning Leader Illustrating Mr Lloyd George's Great Speech at Limehouse* (London, 1909).

89. G.B. Shaw, 'Transition' in *Fabian Essays in Socialism* (London, 1889), pp. 188–9.

90. See C. Peters, *Thackeray: A Writer's Life* (Stroud, 1999), pp. 126–32; and D. Jerrold, *The History of St.Giles and St. James's* (London, 1851). A number of radicals and reformers had personal experience of this society. The Labour leader and Battersea MP, John Burns, was a former page-boy in a titled household in Hampstead. '"They also serve who only stand and wait" – but not upon the aristocracy', observed his biographer; see W. Kent, *John Burns: Labour's Lost Leader* (London, 1950), p. 7.

91. Devyr, *The Odd Book of the Nineteenth Century*, p. 155.

92. B. Harrison and P. Hollis (eds), *Robert Lowery: Radical and Chartist* (London, 1979), p. 10.

93. *Freedom*, 1 November 1897, pp. 68–9.

94. H. Evans, *Our Old Nobility*, 2nd edn (London, 1907), p. 29.

95. Charles Bradlaugh made this accusation about the opposition of the Duke of Buccleuch to the suburbanisation of Kettering; see the *National Reformer*, 6 March 1879, p. 169.

96. *United Irishman*, 24 March 1900, p. 5. Also see James Connolly's attack on the British Empire as a 'piratical enterprise' in the *Workers' Republic*, 20 November 1915.

97. 'Hampden', *The Aristocracy of England*, pp. 283, 287. 'John Hampden' was a pseudonym for William Howitt; see his obituary in the *National Reformer*, 9 March 1879, p. 152, which mentions 'his book on the aristocracy by "John Hampden" . . . known to many of our readers'.

98. *Reynolds's Newspaper*, 14 March 1880, p. 1.
99. Ibid., 23 April 1876, p. 3.
100. E.C. Booth, *Another England: Life, Living, Homes and Homemakers in Victoria* (London, 1869), p. 1.
101. Cannadine, *Ornamentalism*, chs 4–7.
102. C. Lansbury, *Arcady in Australia: The Evocation of Australia in Nineteenth Century English Literature* (Melbourne, 1970), pp. 43–4.
103. *The Republican*, 15 October 1887, p. 2.
104. For English echoes in the constitutional debates in Victoria and New South Wales in the 1850s see G. Martin, *Bunyip Aristocracy: The New South Wales Constitution Debate of 1853 and Hereditary Institutions in the British Colonies* (Dover, 1986), ch. 3; M. McKenna, *The Captive Republic: A History of Republicanism in Australia 1788–1996* (Cambridge, 1996), ch. 4, and A. Oldfield, *The Great Republic of the Southern Seas* (Melbourne, 1999), ch. 7. For a close study of the social and cultural life of the squatters see S.H. Roberts, *The Squatting Age in Australia, 1835–1847* (Melbourne, 1935), ch. 10.
105. Bright made the remark during a speech on British foreign policy in Birmingham in 1858; see A.J.P. Taylor, *The Trouble Makers: Dissent Over Foreign Policy 1792–1939* (London, 1957), p. 63.
106. *The People's Advocate*, 22 June 1850, p. 18.
107. *The Truth*, 3 October 1897, p. 1.
108. See for Norton's rambunctious populist style and its inspiration in *Reynolds's News*, A. Taylor and L. Trainor, 'Monarchism and Anti-monarchism: Anglo-Australian Comparisons *c.*1870–1901', *Social History*, XXIV (1999), 158–73 and M. Cannon, *John Norton, 1858–1916: An Australian Populist* (Melbourne, 1981), pp. 3–10; for Norton's offending articles against Victoria and the Prince of Wales see *The Truth*, 27 September 1896, p. 4 and 18 October 1896, p. 4.
109. See S. Lawson, *The Archibald Paradox: A Strange Case of Authorship* (Ringwood, 1983), pp. 104–11.
110. See for bohemian radicalism amongst Sydney's literary nationalists, N. Lindsay, *Bohemians at The Bulletin 1977* (Sydney, 1965), pp. 1–27.
111. See for the reworked version of the nineteenth century R. Price, *British Society 1680–1880: Dynamism, Containment and Change* (Cambridge, 2000).
112. See for a statement of G.W.M. Reynolds's principles, *Reynolds's Newspaper*, 11 July 1875, p. 1.

2 'The Apostle of Plunder': The influence of Henry George in England reconsidered

1. Freedom, 1 June 1887, p. 34.
2. Peter Alfred Taylor campaigning at Newcastle in 1859, quoted in J. Ramsay MacDonald, 'The Papers of Peter Alfred Taylor', *Socialist Review*, V (1910), 208.
3. A. Huxley, *Brave New World*, 2nd edn (London, 1946), p. 8.
4. S.B. Cord, *Henry George: Dreamer or Realist?* (Philadelphia, 1965), ch. 1.
5. See Besant's obituary of George in *The Times*, 6 November 1897.
6. H. Hyndman, *The Record of an Adventurous Life* (London, 1911), pp. 281–2, 291.

7. W. Wolff, *From Radicalism to Socialism: Men and Ideas in the Formation of Fabian Socialist Doctrine 1881–1889* (New Haven, 1975), p. 85; and E.P. Lawrence, *Henry George in the British Isles* (Michigan, 1957), pp. 48–9.

8. Victoria's interest in George is discussed in P. D'A. Jones, *Henry George and British Socialism* (New York, 1991), p. 206, and for the influence of Georgeism on Tolstoy, see D. Redfearn, *Tolstoy: Principles for a New World Order* (London, 1992), chs 11–12.

9. The tours produced a crop of 'little' Henry Georges, named after him and visible in reform politics into the middle twentieth century; see the biography of Henry George Mcghee, Labour MP for Penistone after 1935, in J.M. Bellamy and J. Saville (eds), *Dictionary of Labour Biography* (8 vols, London, 1972), I, pp. 229–30.

10. G.B. Shaw, *Sixteen Self-Sketches* (London, 1949), p. 38.

11. H. George, *Progress and Poverty: An Inquiry into the Causes of Industrial Depression* (London, 1884 edn), p. 6.

12. The best short summary of how the Single Tax might work and some of its drawbacks is Baron de Forest's memorandum in *The Land: The Report of the Land Inquiry Committee* (2 vols, London, 1913), I, pp. 449–57.

13. Martin, 'Land Reform', pp. 131–58.

14. The 'Free Breakfast Table' continued to provide the basis of proposed socialist budgets into the 1920s: see P. Snowden, *The Socialist's Budget* (London, 1907), p. 70.

15. Quoted in K. Cahill, *Who Owns Britain: The Hidden Facts Behind Landownership in the UK and Ireland* (Edinburgh, 2001), p. 31. Also see A. Arnold, 'The Abuses of a Landed Gentry', *The Nineteenth Century*, I (1877), 458–78; and Parry, *The Rise and Fall of Liberal Government in Victorian Britain*, pp. 243–5.

16. See the preface to Bateman, *The Great Landowners of Great Britain and Ireland*, and correspondence from J. Chapman to Henry George, 24 January 1884, Henry George Papers, New York Public Library.

17. A. Arnold, *Free Land* (London, 1880), p. 6.

18. T.T. Munger, *Land Tenure* (London, n.d.), p. 5. Henry Hyndman suggested that the figures in 'New Domesday' for land occupied by landowners like Buccleuch and the Duke of Devonshire might still be underestimated on the grounds that their multiplicity of titles disguised who owned what, where; see Tsuzuki (ed.), *H.M. Hyndman, England for All*, p. 22.

19. C.F.G. Masterman (ed.), *The Heart of the Empire: Discussion of Problems of Modern City Life* (London, 1901), pp. 5, 27–8.

20. See correspondence in the *Manchester City News*, 9 June 1912, p. 4, 15 June 1912, p. 6, and 22 June 1912, p. 9.

21. J. Cobden-Unwin, The Land Hunger: Life Under Monopoly (London, 1913), p. 54.

22. See W. Norton, 'Malcolm McNeill and the Emigrationist Alternative to Highland Land Reform 1886–1893', *The Scottish Historical Review*, LXX (1991), 16–30.

23. Packer, *Lloyd George, Liberalism and the Land*, pp. 28–32.

24. C.A. Barker, *Henry George* (Oxford, 1955), p. 621.

25. See D. Macfadyen, *Sir Ebenezer Howard and the Town Planning Movement* (Manchester, 1933), pp. 35–6; D. Crouch and C. Ward, *The Allotment: Its Language and Culture* (London, 1988), ch. 2; J.F. Wilkinson, 'Pages in the History

of Allotments', *Contemporary Review*, 65 (1894), 532–44; and D. Stemp, *Three Acres and a Cow: The Life and Work of Eli Hallamshire* (Cheam, 1995), pp. 66–75.

26. C. Gide, *Principles of Political Economy* (London, 1912), pp. 616–18.
27. *Land and Labour*, 1 November 1889, p. 1.
28. A.R. Wallace, *Land Nationalisation: Its Necessity and Its Aims* (London, 1896 edn), pp. 165–9, 184–5; P. Raby, *Alfred Russel Wallace: A Life* (London, 2001), pp. 229, 236; and J. Moore, 'Wallace's Malthusian Moment: The Common Context Revisited' in B. Lightman (ed.), *Victorian Science in Context* (Chicago, 1997), pp. 290–311.
29. For a speech by Helen Taylor on land nationalisation, see *Land and Labour*, 1 May 1891, p. 9. For J.S. Mill as land reformer, see D. Martin, *John Stuart Mill and the Land Question* (Hull, 1981), pp. 25–43; *The Bee-Hive*, 11 June 1870, p. 257; and the *National Reformer*, 21 September 1879, p. 621.
30. J. Marsh, *Back to the Land: The Pastoral Impulse in Victorian England 1880–1914* (London, 1982), ch. 1.
31. L.T. Hobhouse, *The Labour Movement* (London, 1908), ch. 4; A. Sykes, *The Rise and Fall of British Liberalism 1776–1988* (London, 1997), chs 4 and 5; and R. Douglas, *Land, People and Politics: A History of the Land Question in the United Kingdom 1878–1952* (London, 1976), ch. 4.
32. A. Offer, *Property and Politics 1870–1914: Landlordism, Law, Ideology and Urban Development in England* (Cambridge, 1981), ch. 22; and A.K. Russell, *Liberal Landslide: The General Election of 1906* (Newton Abbott, 1973).
33. C. Chesterton, *Gladstonian Ghosts* (London, 1905), p. 185, and for the blind alley of philanthropic land reform, *Justice*, 13 January 1912, p. 1.
34. Cobden-Unwin, *The Land Hunger*, p. 51. Radicals who opposed land reform as a doctrine pointed out that small rural proprietors had provided the bedrock of reactionary Bonapartist support in France; see C. Ellershaw, 'The Proletariat and the Land', *National Reformer*, 7 December 1879, pp. 785–6.
35. See J. Saville, 'Henry George and the British Labour Movement: A Select Bibliography with Commentary', *Bulletin of the Society for the Study of Labour History*, I (1960), 18–26.
36. G.B. Shaw, *The Intelligent Woman's Guide to Socialism and Capitalism* (London, 1929), p. 468.
37. For ruralism and the early Labour Party, see D. Matless, *Landscape and Englishness* (London, 1998), ch. 3; P. Ward, *Red Flag to Union Jack: Englishness, Patriotism and the British Left 1881–1924* (London, 1998); and C. Griffiths, 'Remembering Tolpuddle: Rural History and Commemoration in the Inter-War Labour Movement', *History Workshop Journal*, XXXXIV (1997), 145–69.
38. For the latest work on the culture of the autodidact, see Rose, *The Intellectual Life of the British Working-Classes*, ch. 2.
39. Georgeism generated an enormous quantity of printed material. See for a study of the Georgeite publisher William Reeves, M. Beaumont, 'William Reeves and Late Victorian Radical Publishing: Unpacking the Bellamy Library', *History Workshop Journal*, LV (2003), 91–110.
40. For George at the Oxford Union debate see the *Christian Socialist*, 1 June 1884, p. 1. Amongst his other English critics were the positivist intelligentsia. Frederic Harrison attacked him at a meeting in Newcastle, see the *Newcastle*

Weekly Chronicle, 9 February 1884, p. 5, and Henry Fawcett wrote anti-George polemics, see Cord, *Henry George*, pp. 47–8.

41. E.G. Fitzgibbon, *Essence of Progress and Poverty: Extracted from the American of Henry George and Done into and Dealt with in Plain English* (London, n.d.), p. 7.

42. D.C. Macdonald (ed.), *Birthright in Land by William Ogilvie* (London, 1891), p. xx.

43. J.H. Bengough, *The-Up-to-Date Primer: A First Book of Lessons for Little Political Economists* (New York, 1896), pp. 6, 74; and J.C. Wedgwood, *Memoirs of a Fighting Man* (London, 1941), pp. 67–8. Paradoxically, landlordism was also sometimes portrayed as a sly and avaricious cat; see a poem highlighting the threat posed by 'The Cat' in *The Single Tax*, 1 March 1898, p. 8.

44. See H. Pelling, *America and the British Left from Bright to Bevan* (London, 1956), pp. 1–48. George too liked to make this connection. See Henry George, 'The Reduction to Iniquity', *Nineteenth Century*, XVI (1884), 138–9.

45. *People's Paper*, 7 July 1855, p. 1.

46. H.A. Tulloch, 'Changing British Attitudes Towards the United States in the 1880s', *Historical Journal*, XX (1979), 824–40; G. Claeys, 'The Example of America a Warning to England?': The Transformation of America in British Radicalism and Socialism 1790–1850' in M. Chase and I. Dyck (eds), *Living and Learning: Essays in Honour of J.F.C. Harrison* (Aldershot, 1996), pp. 66–80; and J.L. Bronstein, 'From the Land of Liberty to Land Monopoly: The United States in a Chartist Context' in O. Ashton, R. Fyson and S. Roberts (eds), *The Chartist Legacy* (Woodbridge, 1999), pp. 147–70.

47. See the Duke of Argyll, 'The Prophet of San Francisco', *Nineteenth Century*, XV (1884), 537–58.

48. Post, *The Prophet of San Francisco*, p. 4. Critics of George also ridiculed his pretensions to frontier brigand status, portraying him as an untrustworthy drummer, peddling quack remedies. In this he followed in the steps of his father who was a door-to-door salesman of bibles. See J.E.T. Rogers, *Six Centuries of Work and Wages: The History of English Labour* (London, 1903 edn), p. 532.

49. The phrase is used in C.H. Harford, *Philip Henry Wicksteed: His Life and Work* (London, 1931), p. 197. Henry Hyndman recalled George's affable American persona which included the consumption of whelks in the street: see Hyndman, *Record of an Adventurous Life*, pp. 292–3.

50. Ibid., p. 7 and G.R. Geiger, *Henry George: A Biography* (London, 1939), p. 4.

51. Macdonald (ed.), *Birthright in Land*, p. xiii.

52. Memories of the support for the North during the American Civil War and the fight against slavery were very strong particularly in Lancashire, which suffered badly as a result of the Cotton Famine. Obituaries of working men often show an inherited pride in this achievement. A sketch of Councillor John Greenwood of Rossendale says of his father, a former Chartist: 'During the war for the liberation of slaves in America he nobly championed the cause of freedom, fearlessley expounding the principles which Lloyd Garrison so bravely lived and strove for. Though he has long ago answered the roll-call, his mantle has fallen upon his son who has upheld the tradition.' (*The Rossendale Worker*, 1 October 1909, p. 1.) On his tour of Britain in 1884, George visited the statue of William Wilberforce in Hull; see H. Rose, *Henry George: A Biographical, Anecdotal and Critical Sketch* (London, 1884), pp. 52–3.

53. Post, *The Prophet of San Francisco*, p. 27. Some opponents of George thought that he overstated the comparison between slaves and the landless poor in

Britain; see the 'Robin Goodfellow' column in the *Newcastle Weekly Chronicle*, 9 February 1884, p. 4.

54. The anti-slavery campaigner Wendel Phillips was fulsomely eulogised in an obituary in ibid., 9 February 1884, p. 4. There is also an obituary of the Union general Phil Sheridan 'who literally rode down the Confederacy and destroyed the last hopes of a cause that could only have been established amidst the blight of the principles on which human freedom reposes' in ibid., 11 August 1888, p. 4. The anti-Game Law campaigner H.J. Wilson liked nothing better than an edifying read from accounts of the Underground Railway smuggling slaves out of the American South; see M. Anderson, *Fighter for Freedom* (London, 1953), p. 71.
55. See a talk by William Clarke on Lowell at a meeting reported in *Seed-Time*, 1 April 1892, p. 15, and an article on 'Walt Whitman: The Man and His Message' in ibid., p. 1.
56. P. Snowden, *An Autobiography*, 1 (London, 1934), p. 73.
57. H. Burrows and J.A. Hobson (eds), *William Clarke: A Collection of His Writings* (London, 1908), p. xvi. The radicalism of the American poetic tradition of the 'mighty republic of the West' is also praised in the *Newcastle Weekly Chronicle*, 9 February 1884, p. 4.
58. *National Reformer*, 18 April 1875, pp. 242–3.
59. Loc. cit. Pro-Southern sympathy on the grounds that the Confederate armies were made up of gallant aristocratic cavaliers who are 'better gentlemen than their Northern brethren' was widespread in Britain. See Trollope, *Autobiography*, p. 153.
60. J. Symes, 'The Land Crisis – A Solution' in the *National Reformer*, 27 July 1879, 481–2.
61. Poultney Bigelow to George, 6 August 1890, Henry George Correspondence, NYPL.
62. Frederic Harrison first used this term about George's public meetings; see Lawrence, *Henry George in the British Isles*, p. 65.
63. J. Plowright describes George as 'not simply offering social salvation, but religious redemption'; see Plowright, 'Political Economy and Christian Polity: The Influence of Henry George in England Reassessed', *Victorian Studies*, XXX (1987), 235–52. Equally, landowners who failed to appreciate the selfishness of their actions and the degree to which they contravened God's word were portrayed as spiritually and morally stunted. See the ironic 'Society for the Propagation of the Gospel amongst Landlords' in *The Labour Annual for 1895* (London, 1895), p. 85.
64. Snowden, *An Autobiography*, pp. 48–9.
65. Wedgwood, *Memoirs of a Fighting Life*, pp. 60, 68.
66. G. Edwards, *From Crow-Scaring to Westminster: An Autobiography* (London, 1922), pp. 52–3.
67. B. Scates, *A New Australia: Citizenship, Radicalism and the First Republic* (Cambridge, 1997), p. 71. George was extremely popular in the Australian colonies. See idem, '"Wobblers": Single Taxers in the Labor Movement, 1889–1899', *Historical Studies* (Melbourne), XXI (1981), 174–96; and idem, '"Millennium or Pandemonium?": Radicalism in the Labour Movement, Sydney, 1889–1899', *Labour History*, L (1986), 72–92.
68. J. Coffey, 'Democracy and Popular Religion: Moody and Sankey's Mission to Britain, 1873–75' in E. Biagini (ed.), *Citizenship and Community: Liberals,*

Radicals and Collective Identities in the British Isles 1865–1931 (Cambridge, 1996), pp. 93–119, and for contemporary opinion that sees the famed evangelicals in the guise of radicals, *Reynolds's Newspaper*, 4 April 1875, p. 3, and 27 June 1875, p. 5.

69. R.L. Heilbroner, *The Worldly Philosophers* (New York, 1953), p. 180.

70. Quoted in W.H.G. Armytage, *Heavens Below: Utopian Experiments in England 1560–1960* (London, 1961), p. 316.

71. I. McLean, *Keir Hardie* (London, 1975), p. 164.

72. H. George, *Thy Kingdom Come: An Address by Henry George* (Land Values Publications, Glasgow, 1888), p. 10.

73. See Macdonald (ed.), *Birthright in Land*, p. x, and *Land and Labour*, 1 November 1890, p. 6.

74. Henry George, *Moses: An Address by Henry George* (United Committee for the Taxation of Land Values, n.d.), pp. 2, 6; and J. Arch, *From Ploughtail to Parliament: An Autobiography* (1890; re-printed, 1986), p. 73. Chartist preachers like J.R. Stephens and William Hill frequently employed this imagery; see E. Yeo, 'Chartist Religious Belief and the Theology of Liberation' in J. Obelkevich, L. Roper and R. Samuel (eds), *Disciplines of Faith: Studies in Religion, Politics and Patriarchy* (London, 1987), pp. 410–21.

75. *Christian Socialist*, 1 July 1884, p. 27. The issue of the portrayal of exiled Highlanders as the Children of Israel is discussed in D.E. Meek, 'The Land Question Answered from the Bible: The Land Issue and the Development of a Highland Theology of Liberation', *Scottish Geographical Magazine*, CIII (1987), 84–9. Comparisons of the Highlanders with the *Gracchi* (small landed proprietors) of ancient Rome occur amongst educated patrons of the Highland Land Leagues, but are not reflected at a more popular level; see J. Shaw, 'Land, People and Nation: Historicist Voices in the Highland land Campaign *c.*1850–1883' in Biagini (ed.), *Citizenship and Community*, pp. 305–24.

76. See the Henry George commemoration at Glasgow in *Land and Liberty*, 1 October 1920, pp. 501–2.

77. *The Labour Annual*, 1895, p. 85.

78. H. Lewis, *Free Trade in Land* (Bath, 1880), p. 7; and *Reynolds's Newspaper*, 3 February 1884, p. 1.

79. Quoted in A.B. Wakefield, *Ernest Jones, The People's Friend* (London, 1887), pp. 7–8.

80. R. Heath, *The English Peasant; Studies, Historical, Local and Biographic* (London, 1893), p. 4.

81. The phrase is Ernest Jones' used to describe the tradition of peasant revolt in the West Country; see the *People's Paper*, 14 January 1854, p. 1.

82. H. Cox, *Land Nationalisation* (London, 1892), p. 28. There is a marked Chartist tradition of interest in peasant revolt: see T. Cooper, *Captain Cobler or the Lincolnshire Rebellion: An Historical Romance of the Reign of Henry VIII* (London, 1850).

83. See *Reynolds's Newspaper*, 20 June 1875, p. 3, the *National Reformer*, 22 August 1875, p. 126; and G. Potter, 'The Labourers and the Vote', *The Nineteenth Century*, III (1878), 53–70.

84. A. Taylor, 'Shakespeare and Radicalism: The Uses and Abuses of Shakespeare in Nineteenth Century Popular Politics', *The Historical Journal*, XXXXV (2002), 357–79; and W. Stewart, *Robert Burns and the Common People* (London, 1925 edn),

especially p. 36. Stewart's *Robert Burns* is favourably reviewed in *Lansbury's Labour Weekly*, 27 February 1926, p. 8, under the title 'Our Robert Burns'. Such notions were staples of traditional radicalism. An orator at the South London Secular Society in 1876 declared that 'both Burns and his father were victims of the Land Laws', see the *National Reformer*, 6 February 1876, p. 93. Georgeites saw him as a premature Single Taxer; see *The Single Tax*, 1 April 1899, p. 8.

85. C. Bradlaugh, *The Coming Struggle: The Land, the People and the Coming Struggle* (Freethought Publishing, 1880 edn), p. 4.

86. Quoted in Stemp, *Three Acres and a Cow*, p. 193, and 'Hampden', *The Aristocracy of England*, p. 305. The 'legal trickery' of Scottish land appropriations was also condemned in T. Johnston, *Our Noble Families* (Glasgow, 1916 edn), p. 12. The traditional popular dislike of lawyers is described in C. Hill, *Liberty Against the Law: Some Seventeenth Century Controversies* (London, 1996), pp. 265–9 and reiterated in *Reynolds's Newspaper*, 6 March 1898, p. 2.

87. Wallace, *Land Nationalisation*, pp. 126–30.

88. *Bolton Guardian*, 29 January 1884, p. 8. Also see for Henry George in Bolton, *Justice*, 9 February 1884, p. 7.

89. Speech by Patrick Barry at St James's Hall in the *National Reformer*, 15 February 1880, p. 98. For a further account of this meeting see *Reynolds's Newspaper*, 15 February 1880, p. 3.

90. McCalman, *Radical Underworld*, ch. 2. Benbow's account of corrupt and debauched aristocrats, *A Peep at the Peers*, provided the model for Johnston, *Our Noble Families*. See p. 139 for his debt to Benbow.

91. H.R. Fox Bourne, *The House of Lords* (London, 1881), p. 20.

92. Johnston, *Our Noble Families*, pp. 42–3.

93. W.T. Stead, *Peers or People: The House of Lords Weighed in the Balance and Found Wanting* (London, 1907 edn), p. 38.

94. Fox Bourne, *The House of Lords*, p. 19.

95. Blatchford, *Britain for the British*, p. 53. Blatchford remained a committed land reformer throughout his life; see *Merrie England*, 1908, pp. 60–81. There was considerable interest in tramps at the end of the nineteenth century, perhaps fuelled by concerns about the rootless urban proletariat; see M.A. Crowther, 'The Tramp' in R. Porter (ed.), *Myths of the English* (London, 1992), pp. 91–113. As part of this sentiment, the reminiscences of tramps achieved a wide readership amongst bohemian reformers and radicals; see W.H. Davies, *The Autobiography of a Super-Tramp* (London, 1908), chs 1–2. George Bernard Shaw ridiculed this tendency which he saw as derived from a sentimental reading of George Borrow, and Christian Socialist interest in St Francis of Assisi; see Shaw, *The Intelligent Woman's Guide to Socialism and Capitalism*, p. 219.

96. See, for example, comments in the *Manchester Guardian*, 11 January 1884, p. 5; J. Morrison Davidson, *Concerning Some Precursors of Henry George* (Labour Leader Publishing Department, Glasgow, 1899), pp. 57–75; M. Beer, *The Pioneers of Land Reform: Thomas Spence, William Ogilvie, Thomas Paine* (London, 1920), pp. v–viii; J.R. Lancashire, 'A Forerunner of Henry George', *Manchester City News*, 6 November 1920, p. 4; and A. George de Mille, *Henry George: Citizen of the World* (Chapel Hill, 1950), p. 172.

97. 'Georgeite' in the *Dublin Independent*, 30 July 1912.

98. The pamphlet was probably by William Ogilvie; see Snowden, *An Autobiography*, I, p. 48.

99. See the Henry George memorial meeting held in Glasgow in *The Single Tax*, 1 October 1901, p. 77.
100. C. Wicksteed, *The Land for the People: How to Obtain it and How to Manage it* (London, 1894), p. 5.
101. This tradition is explored in J.L. Bronstein, *Land Reform and Working-Class Experience in Britain and the United States* (Stanford, 1999), pp. 24–6.
102. George was a great admirer of Joseph Chamberlain describing him as the 'coming man'; see George to Thomas Walker, 30 January 1884, George Collection, NYPL.
103. *Newcastle Weekly Chronicle*, 9 February 1884, p. 4.
104. Elsewhere in the country, the ex-Owenite Dr F.R. Lees was one of those who endorsed Georgeism in the early 1880s; see F. Lees, *Dr F. R. Lees: A Biography* (London, 1904), pp. 189–90.
105. *Newcastle Weekly Chronicle*, 16 February 1884, p. 4.
106. Burrows and Hobson (eds), *William Clarke*, p. xvi and for the Puritan tradition more generally Samuel, *Island Stories: Unravelling Britain*, pp. 276–322.
107. *Seed-Time*, 1 April 1891, pp. 8–13.
108. C.V. Wedgwood, *The Last of the Radicals: The Life of Josiah Wedgwood MP* (London, 1951), p. 70 and the *Christian Socialist*, 1 July 1884, p. 29.
109. Harrington's ideas were analysed in the *Newcastle Weekly Chronicle*, 2 February 1884, p. 4. For Chartist interest in him see Harrison and Hollis (eds), *Robert Lowery*, p. 68.
110. George to McGhee, 15 August 1884, Henry George Correspondence, NYPL.
111. See the account of George's arrest by J.L. Joynes in *The Freeman's Journal*, 8 September 1882, p. 3.
112. George to Mrs Annie George, 12 January 1884, Henry George Correspondence, NYPL.
113. George to Thomas Walker, 14 February 1884, Henry George Correspondence, NYPL.
114. Extract from letter by Miss Clarke enclosed in correspondence from Herbert Burrows to George, 1 March 1884, Henry George Correspondence, NYPL.
115. See the obituary of George by George Julian Harney in the *Newcastle Weekly Chronicle*, 6 November 1897, and the obituary in the *Labour Leader*, 27 November 1897.
116. H. Hutchinson to George, 3 July 1884, Henry George Correspondence, NYPL.
117. The phrase is S. Kudak's in 'A Sword of a Song: Swinburne's Republican Aesthetics in Songs before Sunrise', *Victorian Studies*, XXXXIII (2001), 253–78.
118. Wedgwood, *Memoirs of a Fighting Life*, p. 68.
119. Sketch of Wedgwood in *The Standard: A Journal to Advocate the Rights of the People in the Land*, 15 January 1914, p. 1 (copy in Josiah Wedgwood papers, Hanley Public Library, Stoke).
120. *Land and Liberty*, 1 August 1920, pp. 454–5.
121. For Massey's poem see *Land and Labour*, 1 March 1891, p. 5. For memories of George Dawson preserved by the Georgeite movement, see William Cope to George, 19 March 1884, Henry George Correspondence, NYPL. Ernest Jones was recalled in the *Single Tax*, 1 July 1897, p. 2, and 1 February 1900, pp. 130–1. Bronterre O'Brien was quoted in the issue for 1 April 1902, p. 174, and both Jones and O'Brien featured in a commemoration to George reported in the issue for 1 October 1901, p. 59.

122. For the Chartist land resolution at the convention of 1848 see *Land and Labour*, 1 April 1891, p. 2 and for the presence of Chartist veterans during the Red Van tour of Derbyshire see ibid., 1 October 1891, p. 7.

123. Ibid., 1 June 1900, p. 189.

124. That these were amongst Cobden's last coherent words is attested to by witnesses quoted in D. Read, *Cobden and Bright: A Victorian Political Partnership* (London, 1967), p. 189. For a discussion of the significance of this rhyme see Wicksteed, *The Land for the People*, p. 55, and for Cobden's speech on land reform, A. Arnold, 'Free Trade in Land', *Contemporary Review*, XX (1872), 880–1; and J.E.T. Rogers, *Cobden and Modern Political Opinion: Essays on Certain Political Topics* (London, 1873), ch. 3.

125. See for a sketch of Matthew Gass, *The Single Tax*, 1 February 1900, pp. 130–1.

126. *Justice*, 28 June 1884, p. 1. Also see *Land and Labour*, 1 November 1890, pp. 5–6 and 1 January 1891, p. 4 for the pioneering work of the London County Council (LCC) in preserving public spaces in London.

127. There are descriptions of Georgeite demonstration under the 'Reformer's Tree' in Hyde Park in the *Christian Socialist*, 1 August 1884, p. 5.

128. See George's speech at the Town Hall, Newcastle in the *Newcastle Weekly Chronicle*, 2 February 1884, p. 5.

129. George, *Progress and Poverty*, p. 39.

130. See Rose, *The Intellectual Life of the British Working-Class*, p. 108. Karl Marx was highly critical of economic arguments about 'natural man'. He wrote 'political economists are fond of Robinson Crusoe'; see A.M. McBriar, *Fabian Socialism and English Politics 1884–1918* (Cambridge, 1962), p. 30.

131. *The Single Tax*, 1 February 1925, p. 30, and for George's parable of the brickworks see George, *Thy Kingdom Come*, p. 6.

132. A. White, *The Problems of a Great City* (London, 1886), p. 179. This is similar to the description of his ideas as 'a feverish fantasy of illiterate thousands' in J.L. Thomas, *Alternative America: Henry George, Edward Bellamy, Henry Demarest Lloyd and the Adversary Tradition* (Harvard, 1983), p. 357.

133. For the Welsh revival of 1905 see R. Hayward, 'From the Millennial Future to the Unconscious Past: The Transformation of Prophecy in Early Twentieth Century Britain' in B. Taithe and T. Thornton (eds), *Prophecy: The Power of Inspired Language in History 1300–2000* (Stroud, 1997), pp. 161–80.

134. J.W. Burrow, *The Crisis of Reason: European Thought 1848–1914* (New Haven, 2000), pp. 113–17. During these years there was fierce debate about whether or not the institutions of village community life came from a pan-European tradition of tribal liberty, dispersed from the forests of Germany to the margins of Europe by successive waves of invaders. In Britain the tendency within the academy was to dispute the similarities between the German 'mark' and the English village, and to suggest that 'more things went to the making of England than were imported in the keels of the English invader'; see F. Seebohm, *The English Village Community* (London, 1883), p. xv; and G.L. Gomme, *The Village Community with Special Reference to the Origin and Form of its Survival in Britain* (London, 1890), ch. 9.

135. See H. Allingham and S. Dick, *Cottage Homes of England* (London, 1909), ch. 13; and K. Sayer, *Country Cottages: A Cultural History* (Manchester, 2000), chs 3 and 4.

136. G. Darley, *Villages of Vision* (London, 1975), p. 114; and P.C. Gould, *Early Green Politics: Back to Nature, Back to the Land, and Socialism in Britain 1880–1900* (Brighton, 1988), ch. 6.

137. For the broader tradition of land militancy within popular politics see A. Howkins, 'From Diggers to Dongas: The Land in English Radicalism', *History Workshop Journal*, LIV (2002), 1–23.

138. See Cannadine, *The Decline and Fall of the British Aristocracy*, ch. 3; and idem, *Aspects of Aristocracy*.

139. Miners often wrote to George in person. One claimed that 'even you, sir, with your large, sympathetic heart, cannot realize the terrible state we are in'. See a fragment of correspondence from a Hamilton miner to George, dated 10 February 1884, George Correspondence, NYPL. The Yellow Vans movement of 1897 was made possible by contributions from the Cleveland Miners' Association and the Northumberland miners. See D'A Jones, *Henry George and British Socialism*, p. 226. For the militancy of miners in land reform campaigns see E. Davies and D. Evans, *Land Nationalisation: The Key to Social Reform* (London, 1921), pp. 114–26; and F. Reid, *Keir Hardie, The Making of a Socialist* (London, 1978), chs 2–3.

140. I. Mclean has made a convincing case for Hardie's Georgeism, see his *Keir Hardie*, chs 1–2. Hardie's obsessive land reform interests feature in Hughes (ed.), *Keir Hardie's Speeches and Writings*, pp. 45–6.

141. The phrase is Tom Nairn's in his discussion of the House of Lords in *After Britain: New Labour and the Return of Scotland* (London, 2000), pp. 45–6.

142. See the Duke of Argyll, 'The Prophet of San Francisco', pp. 537–58; and George, 'The Reduction to Iniquity', pp. 134–55.

143. See for the career of Argyll, Barker, *Henry George*, p. 408; and C. Rumsey, *The Rise and Fall of British Republican Clubs 1871–1874* (Oswestry, 2000), p. 200.

144. Offer, *Property and Politics*, p. 200.

145. Georgeites realised that the Single Tax meant the break-up of the royal landed fortune; see *The Single Tax*, 1 January 1897, p. 1.

146. *Bolton Guardian*, 12 January 1884, p. 5. Other newspaper reports showed the speech as less subversive. Nevertheless, John Ruskin, who was scheduled to chair the meeting and could have restrained some of the wilder excesses, was unable to be present; see the *Weekly Dispatch*, 13 January 1884, p. 4. In his writings George complained about the financial burden of royalty and speculated about the consequences of setting them adrift 'to make a living for themselves'; see George, *Progress and Poverty*, p. 214.

147. Quoted in letter from William Cope to George, 21 March 1884, George Collection, NYPL.

148. See A. Taylor, 'Republicanism Reappraised: Anti-monarchism and the English Radical Tradition 1850–1872' in J. Vernon (ed.), *Re-reading the Constitution: New Narratives in the Political History of England's Long Nineteenth Century* (Cambridge, 1996), pp. 154–78.

149. *The Single Tax*, 1 May 1898, p. 12.

150. See M.K. Ashby, *Joseph Ashby of Tysoe 1859–1919* (Cambridge, 1961), pp. 156–7. From the 1870s contemporaries were alarmed by urban militants who canvassed and campaigned in the villages in an apparent bid to introduce subversive doctrines of land reform into the countryside. See J.A. Bridges, *Reminiscences of a Country Politician* (London, 1906), pp. 127–8 and for a

hostile view of Georgeite subversion, Lord Bramwell, *Nationalisation of Land: A Review of Mr Henry George's Progress and Poverty* (Liberty and Property Defence League, 1884), p. 11.

151. George was refused access to Exeter Hall in 1884. See George to Thomas Walker, 5 March 1884, George Collection, NYPL; Rose, *Henry George*, pp. 50, 53, and *The Tribune*, 22 April 1907 (cutting in the Wedgwood Papers, Hanley Library, Stoke).
152. J.A. Hobson, 'The Influence of Henry George in England', *Fortnightly Review*, LXII (1897), 835–44.
153. A. Howe, 'Towards the "Hungry Forties": Free Trade in Britain c.1880–1906' in Biagini (ed.), *Citizenship and Community*, pp. 193–218.
154. *Justice*, 24 January 1884, p. 6.
155. The term 'National Inheritance' was much used as a title for pamphlets and lectures, see the *National Reformer*, 21 December 1873, p. 397.
156. J.C. Wedgwood, *Henry George for Socialists* (ILP, 1908), pp. 6–7.
157. Cobden-Unwin, *The Land Hunger*, p. 54.
158. Martin, *John Stuart Mill and the Land Question*, pp. 24–38.
159. *Manchester Examiner and Times*, 1 March 1882, p. 5.
160. Rose, *Henry George*, p. 90.
161. See L. Goodwyn, *Democratic Promise: The Populist Movement in America* (New York, 1976), ch. 1; and Thomas, *Alternative America*, chs 3 and 5.
162. See S. Yeo, 'A New Life: The Religion of Socialism in Britain, 1883–1896', *History Workshop Journal*, IV (1977), 5–56.
163. Hobson, 'The Influence of Henry George in England', p. 841.
164. Packer, *Lloyd George, Liberalism and the Land*, ch. 1.
165. M. Fels, *Joseph Fels* (London, 1920), especially ch. 5.
166. H. Tracey (ed.), *The Book of the Labour Party: Its History, Growth, Policy and Leaders* (London, 1925), pp. 312–28; and *Fifty Points for Labour and a Hundred Against the Tories and Liberals* (Labour Party, 1929), point 16.

3 Hunting, moral outrage, and radical opposition to animal abuse in nineteenth- and early twentieth-century Britain

1. 'Samaritan' in the *Manchester City News*, 10 May 1924, p. 4.
2. A. Ponsonby, *The Decline of Aristocracy* (London, 1912), p. 143.
3. 'A Ballad made for the Delectation of all True Sportsmen', *Punch*, VIII (1845), 58.
4. *Reynolds's Newspaper*, 28 January 1872, p. 3.
5. *The Bee-Hive*, 1 April 1871, p. 13. For an overview of radicalism in the 1870s see Belchem, *Popular Radicalism in Nineteenth-Century Britain*, ch. 6; and Howkins, 'From Diggers to Dongas', 1–23.
6. Stead, *Peers or People?*, p. 173.
7. The episode became known as the affair of the 'Old Brown Dog' after the construction of a statue commemorating the dog in Battersea and riots arising out of attempts by anti-vivisectors to tear it down. See Coral Lansbury, *The Old Brown Dog: Women, Workers and Vivisection in Edwardian England* (Madison, Wisconsin, 1985), chs 1 and 4.
8. H. Kean, *Animal Rights: Political and Social Change in Britain since 1800* (London, 1998), ch. 8; idem, 'The Feminist and Socialist Response to Vivisection', *History*

Workshop Journal, IXXXX (1995), 6–32; and D. Weinbren, 'Against all Cruelty: The Humanitarian League 1891–1919' in ibid., XXXVIII (1994), 86–105.

9. *Reynolds's Newspaper*, 4 July 1875, p. 3.
10. See a campaign led by the trade unionist Henry Broadhurst in the *Manchester City News*, 31 March 1888, p. 4. For Byron's criticism of fishing in his poem 'Don Juan', see F.D. Smith and B. Wilcox, *Sold for Two Farthings: Being the Views of Countryfolk on Cruelty to Animals* (London, 1950), p. 135.
11. D. Donald, '"Beastly Sights": The Treatment of Animals as a Moral Theme in Representations of London c.1820–1850' in Donald (ed.), *The Metropolis and its Image: Constructing Identities for London c.1750–1950* (London, 1999), pp. 48–78.
12. For the radical notion of the 'Norman Yoke' see C. Hill, 'The Norman Yoke' in his *Puritanism and Revolution* (1955), pp. 50–122; and J. Belchem, 'Republicanism, Popular Constitutionalism and the Radical Platform in Early Nineteenth Century England', *Social History*, VI (1981), 1–35.
13. For Paine's political ideas see J. Keane, *Tom Paine: A Political Life* (1995), chs 9 and 10.
14. J. Ridley, *Fox Hunting* (1990), pp. 78–80; D. Landry, *The Invention of the Countryside: Hunting, Walking and Ecology in English Literature 1671–1831* (2001); and K. Thomas, *Man and the Natural World: Changing Attitudes in England 1500–1800* (London, 1983), pp. 60–165.
15. P.D.G. Thomas, *John Wilkes: A Friend to Liberty* (Oxford, 1996), p. 276.
16. Ridley, *Fox Hunting*, p. 79. Guy Paget's history of the Althorp and Pytchley Hunt is emblematic of this trend. Written in the 1930s, it features anti-Semitic and anti-Bolshevik digressions. See G. Paget, *The History of the Althorp and Pytchley Hunt 1634–1920* (London, 1937), pp. 62, 210. When in 1949 huntsmen opposed proposals by the post-war Labour government to end hunting, the campaign was embraced by Conservatives as a symbol of individualism against the soulless bureaucracy of the socialist state. See Smith and Wilcox, *Sold for Two Farthings*, pp. 40–1, 174–7.
17. Short, *Land and Society in Victorian Britain*, p. 25.
18. D.C. Itzkowitz, *Peculiar Privilege: A Social History of English Foxhunting 1753–1885* (London, 1977), chs 4 and 10.
19. D.E. Allen, *The Naturalist in Britain: A Social History* (London, 1976), pp. 141–2.
20. William Maccall in the *National Reformer*, 27 February 1876, pp. 132–3.
21. T.E. Kebbel, *The Battle of Life: A Retrospect of Sixty Years* (London, 1912), p. 253.
22. Anti-hunting militants sometimes overlooked the advantages conferred on rural communities by the patrons of the wealthier hunts. They included 'cast-off clothing, and well paid odd jobs . . . and the gifts of hares and rabbits'. See L.M. Springall, *Labouring Life in Norfolk Villages 1834–1914* (London, 1936), pp. 72–3.
23. H. Ritvo, *The Animal Estate: The English and Other Creatures in the Victorian Age* (London, 1987), chs 1–2.
24. G. Hendrick and W. Hendrick (eds), *The Savour of Salt: A Henry Salt Anthology* (Fontwell, 1989), p. 91.
25. Fox-Bourne, *The House of Lords*, pp. 6–8; C. Dilke, *On The Cost of the Crown* (London, 1871), p. 9; and R. Williams, *The Contentious Crown: Public Discussion of the British Monarchy in the Reign of Queen Victoria* (Aldershot, 1997), pp. 65–6.
26. A.L. Thorold, *The Life of Henry Labouchere* (London, 1913), p. 212.
27. Dilke, *On the Cost of the Crown*, p. 9.

28. White, *England Within and Without*, pp. 337–8.
29. 'Jif', *Bumbles, Drones, and Working Bees: A Lecture* (London, 1881), p. 12.
30. The term is used in the memoirs of H.J. Massingham, *Remembrance: An Autobiography* (London, 1942), p. 144.
31. *Reynolds's Newspaper*, 22 August 1875, p. 3.
32. The radical journalist Samuel Beeton used this term to mercilessly satirise the court's predilection for hunting in 'The Coming K...' in *Beeton's Christmas Annual* (1872), p. 20. See on Beeton, H.M. Hyde, *Mr and Mrs Beeton* (London, 1951), p. 148.
33. J. Gore, *King George V: A Personal Memoir* (London, 1941), pp. 229–33.
34. *Speeches of Mr P.A. Taylor in the House of Commons on the Game Laws* (London, 1869), p. 12; and C.E.M. Joad, *The Untutored Townsman's Invasion of the Country* (London, 1945), p. 121. By the 1890s even the journal of sporting landowners, *The Field*, was urging restraint. See *The Field*, 23 September 1899, p. 513.
35. See the guidebook of the *Sheffield Clarion Ramblers, 1937–38* (Sheffield, 1938), pp. 31–2.
36. H. Alken, *The National Sports of Great Britain* (London, 1903), p. 35.
37. Critics of the deer-reserves believed that they were eroding the traditional Highland way of life. See a speech by Sir George Trevelyan at Stornaway reported in *Land and Labour*, 1 November 1890, p. 6.
38. See Lord Ribblesdale, *The Queen's Hounds and Stag-Hunting: Recollections* (1897).
39. S. Weintraub, *The Importance of Being Edward: King in Waiting 1841–1901* (London, 2000), pp. 151–2.
40. *The Bee-Hive*, 11 June 1870, pp. 265–6.
41. *National Reformer*, 16 November 1879, pp. 714–15.
42. Colley, *Britons: Forging the Nation 1707–1830*, pp. 170–3.
43. Hammonds, *Village Labourer*, p. 132.
44. James Wentworth Day, *King George V as a Sportsman* (London, 1935), p. 278.
45. *Truth*, 14 January 1892, p. 55.
46. *The Field*, 10 November 1900, p. 703, and 1 December 1900, p. 857. There is an examination of the connections between hunting and warfare in J. Bourke, *An Intimate History of Killing* (London, 1999), pp. 139–40.
47. *The Field*, 23 December 1899, p. 973.
48. M. Adams, 'The Blessings of Sport', *The Humane Review*, X (1909), 49–57.
49. Trollope, *An Autobiography*, pp. 176–7. Distance from the land, and unfamiliarity with rural ways, became a common slur directed against all land and blood-sports reformers. Opponents of Lloyd George's 1909 budget accused him of an 'abysmal lack of knowledge' of rural affairs; see G.E. Raine, *Lloyd George and the Land: An Exposure and an Appeal* (London, 1914), p. 15.
50. S. Sassoon, *Memoirs of a Fox-Hunting Man*, 2nd edn (London, 1940), p. 35.
51. Wentworth Day, *King George V as a Sportsman*, p. 52.
52. *The Field*, 21 April 1900, p. 513.
53. *Warwick and Warwickshire Advertiser*, 3 January 1874, p. 2. My thanks to Detlev Mares for this reference.
54. Republican MPs like Auberon Herbert, a keen huntsman in his youth, but revolted by the pastime in later life, and Henry Fawcett, who was blinded in a hunting accident, demonstrate a conflation between the dislike of hunting, and hostility to the aristocratic hunting cadres that surrounded the throne.

Both MPs supported Sir Charles Dilke's campaign to curb Civil List payments to the court and royal offspring in 1871. See S. Gwynn and G.M. Tuckwell, *The Life of the Rt. Hon. Sir Charles W. Dilke* (2 vols, 1917), I, ch. 10.

55. *The Field*, 21 April 1900, p. 513. Figures like Rosalie Chichester represent the sentimental side of aristocratic attitudes towards animals. In a pen portrait of her in old age she is described as living and sleeping 'in her drawing-room which is made into an aviary. Birds fly over her bed and perch on a clutter of bric-a-brac and masses of flowers'. See J. Lees-Milne, *Caves of Ice: Diaries 1946 and 1947* (London, 1983), p. 51, and for a pen portrait of her, J. Gaze, *Figures in a Landscape: A History of the National Trust* (London, 1988), pp. 107–10.

56. See a meeting in opposition to hunting at the Tower Hamlets Radical Club, Mile End in the *National Reformer*, 6 February 1876, p. 93.

57. Lady Florence Dixie, 'The Horrors of Sport', *Humane Review*, VI (1906), 36–64.

58. *National Reformer*, 18 July 1875, p. 43.

59. *Reynolds's Newspaper*, 3 February 1872, p. 3.

60. *Lansbury's Labour Weekly*, 8 August 1925, p. 1.

61. See *The Field*, 23 December 1899, p. 973.

62. A. Maitland, *Speke and the Discovery of the Source of the Nile* (London, 1971), pp. 209–19. Speke subsequently became an icon for hunters who portrayed him 'dying peacefully at home' whilst engaged in a sport he loved; see The *Field*, 1 December 1900, p. 857.

63. *The Clarion*, 2 January 1892, pp. 1, 5. This accident is also recalled in Wentworth Day, *King George V as a Sportsman*, p. 55.

64. See Thompson, *Gentrification and the Enterprise Culture*, pp. 104–8; and G.C. Brodrick, *English Land and English Landlords* (London, 1881), p. 183.

65. *The Bee-Hive*, 18 June 1870, p. 274.

66. *Warwick and Warwickshire Advertiser*, 11 April 1868, p. 3. Also see for Anti-Game Law sentiment, 'The Evils of the Game Laws', *Howitt's Journal*, III (1848), 226–31.

67. C. Kirby, 'The Attack on the English Game Laws in the Forties', *Journal of Modern History*, IV (1932), 18–37. The Anti-Game Law Movement also had an incarnation for the early Labour Party which was still viscerally attached to the memory of ancestral wrongs like the Game Laws which had helped clear the people off the land. *Reynolds's Newspaper* continued the campaign against the Game Laws into the 1890s. James Connell argued that the regular exposures of the unjust nature of the laws by the paper was chiefly responsible for moderating their effects in the counties bordering London; see J. Connell, 'The Game Laws', *The Humane Review*, II (1901), 58.

68. A. Besant, 'The English Land System' in the *National Reformer*, 11 January 1880, p. 17.

69. J. Stratton, 'Cruel Sports', *The Humane Review*, IX (1908), 39.

70. H. Salt, 'The Sportsman at Bay', ibid., VII (1907), 183. Alternatively, some contemporaries portrayed pheasant-rearing as a way of earning rich recompense for very little effort. At the turn of the twentieth century the following saying was current: 'Up gets seven and six (the cost of rearing the bird). Bang goes two pence (the cost of the cartridge). And down comes half a crown (the value of the pheasant).' See F. Archer, *Poacher's Pie* (London, 1976), p. 44.

71. See for biological notions of parasitism at the service of politics in the 1890s, P. Cain, *Hobson and Imperialism: Radicalism, New Liberalism and Finance*

1887–1938 (Oxford, 2002), ch. 5, and for its role in explaining the relationship between genders, O. Schreiner, *Woman and Labour* (London, 1911), ch. 1.

72. *Land and Labour*, 1 February 1891, p. 6.

73. See *The Call*, 24 July 1919, p. 6.

74. J. Stratton, 'Sports, Legitimate and Illegitimate', *The Humane Review*, IV (1904), 324.

75. H. Salt, *Seventy Years Among Savages* (1921), pp. 152–3.

76. In the 1840s Albert's enthusiasm for the *battue* was satirized in *Punch* which showed him enthusiastically shooting game inside Windsor Castle; see *Punch*, VIII (1845), 56.

77. Rev. H.A. Macpherson, *The Pheasant: Its Natural History* (1895; reprinted, 1986), pp. 105–6. For Prince Albert's love of the *battue* see Harry Hopkins, *The Long Affray: The Poaching Wars 1760–1914* (1985), pp. 213–14.

78. Anti-Normanism was a staple of the republican and land-reform movements of the 1870s; see Martin, 'Land Reform', pp. 131–58.

79. E.A. Freeman, *The Morality of Field Sports*, 2nd edn (Animal Friends Society, 1914), p. 18.

80. *Speeches of Mr P.A. Taylor*, p. 9, and the 'Estates of the Aristocracy' in *Reynolds's Newspaper*, 4 April 1875, p. 3.

81. *Liberty*, 12 May 1883, p. 4.

82. J. Connell, *The Truth about the Game Laws* (Humanitarian League, 1898), pp. 37–45.

83. Kebbel, *The Battle of Life*, p. 229. For urban and rural attitudes towards poaching, see D.J.V. Jones, 'The Poacher: A Study in Victorian Crime and Protest', *The Historical Journal*, XXII (1979), 825–60. Charles Kingsley's 'The Poacher's Widow', sometimes known as 'The Bad Squire', became an anthem for the Anti-Game Law League, often given away with League publications. For its full text see John Mulgan (ed.), *Songs of Freedom* (London, 1938), pp. 123–5, and *The Labourers' Herald*, 4 December 1874, p. 7. For its performance in metropolitan clubland in the 1870s, see the *National Reformer*, 5 March 1876, p. 157. Other poaching songs sung by radicals included 'The Poacher' by Cairn Tiera (see ibid., 3 February 1878, p. 951) and 'Leawood Hall' by Ernest Jones: see M. Creuss (ed.), *In Memorium, Ernest Jones* (Manchester, 1879), pp. 40–5. The radical MPs, P.A. Taylor and H.J. Wilson, were accused of being 'poachers' friends' on the basis of their support for the abolition of the Game Laws; see *The Game Laws: Speech of Mr P.A. Taylor in the House of Commons, March 2 1880* (Anti-Game Law League, 1880), p. 37; and W.S. Fowler, *A Study in Radicalism and Dissent: The Life and Times of H.J. Wilson, 1833–1914* (London, 1961), p. 15.

84. G.J. Holyoake in the *National Reformer*, 9 April 1876, pp. 225–6. For contemporary criticism of imported French styles of imperial display, see A. Taylor, *'Down with the Crown': British Anti-Monarchism and Debates about Royalty since 1790* (London, 1999), ch. 3. As late as 1879 the radical press was highly critical of the royal family's public mourning for Bonaparte's son, killed in the Zulu War; see *The Labourer*, 2 August 1879, p. 2.

85. Rev. J. Stratton, *The Decline and Fall of the Royal Buckhounds* (Humanitarian League, 1901), p. 18.

86. See on this point, *Speeches of Mr P.A. Taylor*, p. 35.

87. M.S. Gretton, *A Corner of the Cotswolds through the Nineteenth Century* (London, 1914), p. 170.

88. *National Reformer*, 18 July 1875, p. 43. The diarist Richard Lowry recalled that on a visit to Chillingham Park in 1872, Albert Edward, the Prince of Wales, shot and killed one of the last elderly bulls from the endangered wild Chillingham Cattle; see N. McCord, 'Victorian Newcastle Observed: The Diary of Richard Lowry', *Northern History*, XXXVII (2000), 237–59 and the 'gallant adventures' described in *Reynolds's Newspaper*, 25 July 1875, p. 1.

89. J.M. Mackenzie, *The Empire of Nature: Hunting, Conservation and British Imperialism* (Manchester, 1988), chs 1–2.

90. H.J. Massingham, *The English Countryman: A Study of the English Tradition* (London, 1942), p. 102.

91. Quoted in A.H. Higginson, *Foxhunting: Theory and Practice* (London, 1948), pp. 210–11. The morality of intrusion on tenants' land by the hunt was much debated in hunting circles. See *The Field*, 14 January 1899, p. 61, 28 January 1899, p. 103, and 18 February 1899, p. 217.

92. H. Salt, 'Access to Mountains', *The Humane Review*, IX (1908), 247–52.

93. *Speeches of Mr P.A. Taylor*, p. 17.

94. Joad, *The Untutored Townsman's Invasion of the Country*, pp. 123–4.

95. H. George, *Thy Kingdom Come*, p. 9.

96. Adams, 'The Blessings of Sport', p. 57.

97. Such notions harmonised with the popular vision of English history as a national epic of liberty against imported despotism. See A. Briggs, *The Collected Essays of Asa Briggs* (2 vols, Brighton, 1985), ii, pp. 215–35.

98. C. Knight, *Passages in a Working Life During Half a Century with a Prelude to Early Reminiscences* (3 vols, London, 1864), III, p. 52.

99. Ridley, *Fox-Hunting*, p. 88; Paget, *History of the Althorp and Pytchley Hunt*, pp. 204–6; and A. Sinclair, *Death by Fame: A Life of Elisabeth, Empress of Austria* (New York, 1998), pp. 102–8.

100. *Reynolds's Newspaper*, 5 March 1882, p. 5.

101. I.F. Grigor, *Highland Resistance: The Radical Tradition in the Scottish North* (Edinburgh, 2000), pp. 140–1.

102. Cobden-Unwin, *The Land Hunger*, p. 54.

103. A. Stansfield, *Essays and Sketches: Being a Few Selections from the Prose Writings of Twenty Years* (Manchester, 1897), p. 66.

104. A. Clarke, *Moorlands and Memories: Rambles and Rides in the Fair Places of Steam Engine Land* (Bolton, 1920), p. 121.

105. S. Partington, *Truth Further Vindicated. Winter Hill Right of Way Dispute: New Light on Bolton History* (Bolton, 1899), p. 26. Tresspass issues on moorlands and mountains remained an issue among urban radicals until the 1930s. See E.A. Barker, *The Forbidden Land: A Plea for Public Access to Mountains, Moors and Other Waste Lands in Great Britain* (London, 1924), pp. 8–22; and H. Taylor, *A Claim on the Countryside* (Edinburgh, 1997), pp. 45–50.

106. *The Labourer*, 31 January 1880, p. 2.

107. H. Salt, 'Robert Buchanan as Humanitarian', *Humane Review*, VI (1906), 58.

108. Samuel Baker was the author of a number of tracts extolling the virtues of hunting in a colonial setting; see, for example, Sir Samuel W. Baker, *The Rifle and Hound in Ceylon* (London, 1890), chs 1–2.

109. See Mackenzie, *The Empire of Nature*, chs 3, 4 and 5.

110. J.A. Froude, *Oceana or England and Her Colonies* (London, 1886), pp. 105–7.

111. R. Stanley (ed.), *W. Archer, Tourist to the Antipodes: William Archer's Australian Journey 1876–77* (St Lucia, Queensland, 1977), p. 48; and F. Eldershaw, *Australia as it Really is, in its Life, Scenery and Adventure* (London, 1854), p. 113.
112. S. Winsten, *Henry Salt and His Circle* (London, 1951), chs 7 and 10.
113. Mackenzie, *The Empire of Nature*, ch. 7.
114. H. Russell, *With the Prince in the East: A Record of the Royal Visit to India and Japan* (London, 1922), pp. 69–70.
115. See D. Nash, 'Charles Bradlaugh, India and the Many Chameleon Destinations of Republicanism' in D. Nash and A. Taylor (eds), *Republicanism In Victorian Society* (Stroud, 2000), pp. 106–24.
116. M. Cartmill, *A View to a Death in the Morning: Hunting and Nature Through History* (New York, 1993), ch. 8; and Ritvo, *The Animal Estate*, ch. 6.
117. *Reynolds's Newspaper*, 25 July 1875, p. 1.
118. *People's Advocate*, 15 April 1876, p. 5.
119. *Reynolds's Newspaper*, 5 March 1876, p. 5.
120. William Maccall in the *National Reformer*, 27 February 1876, pp. 132–3.
121. *The Weekly Dispatch*, 28 November 1875, p. 1.
122. G. Brooke-Shepherd, *The Uncle of Europe: The Social and Diplomatic Life of Edward VII* (London, 1975), p. 46. Despite the claims of courtiers about the prowess of royal marksmen the radical press asserted that it was common practice at pheasant shoots to mix dead pheasants up with the actual kill in order to flatter the shooting party; see *The Labourers' Herald*, 4 December 1874, p. 4.
123. G.F. Morant, *Game Preservers and Bird Preservers: Which are Our Friends?* (1875), p. 169.
124. J. Passmore, 'The Treatment of Animals', *Journal of the History of Ideas*, XXXVI (1975), 195–218.
125. *The Times*, 28 December 1897, p. 8. For the wider role of women in agitations against the use of bird feathers in fashion, see Allen, *The Naturalist in Britain*, pp. 198–9.
126. *Newcastle Weekly Chronicle*, 3 April 1875, p. 4. For an extended treatment of bull-fighting and its relationship to royal ritual in Spain see A. Schubert, *Death and Money in the Afternoon: A History of the Spanish Bullfight* (Oxford, 1999), chs 2 and 6.
127. For Shelley, see Henry Salt, 'Shelley as a Pioneer', *The Humane Review*, II (1902), 54–66; Salt, *Seventy Years Amongst Savages*, p. 90 and for Burns, A.H. Japp, 'Robert Burns as Humanitarian Poet', *The Humane Review*, VI (1906).
128. V. Sheppard, *My Head Against the Wall: A Decade in the Fight Against Blood Sports* (1979), p. viii, and for a contemporary view of More as a social reformer critical of established patterns of land-holding, *The Commonweal*, 1 January 1886, pp. 5–6.
129. For disruption of the hunts during the land war in Ireland see Ridley, *Fox Hunting*, pp. 123–4; L.P. Curtis, 'Stopping the Hunt 1881–1882: An Aspect of the Irish Land War' in C.H.E. Philpin (ed.), *Nationalism and Popular Protest in Ireland* (Cambridge, 1987), pp. 349–402; and P. Bull, *Land, Politics and Nationalism: A Study of the Irish Land Question* (Dublin, 1996), pp. 123–5.
130. Winsten, *Salt and His Circle*, chs 11–12.
131. Paget, *Althorp and Pytchley Hunt*, p. 62.

132. See G. Jaeger, *Health Culture* (London, 1902), p. 59.
133. Ramblers were seen by landowners and gamekeepers as the subversive, spiritual heirs of poaching, particularly where their activities, like that of poachers, interfered with hunting and undermined the great estate system. See T. Stephenson, *Forbidden Land: The Struggle for Access to Mountain and Moorland* (Manchester, 1989), p. 89. For the example of George Herbert Bridges Ward of Sheffield, the 'Prince of the Ramblers', who researched manorial records to locate ancient rights of way, see the *Transactions of the Hunter Archeological Society*, VIII (1957), pp. 30–1.
134. G. Christian (ed.), *A Victorian Poacher: James Hawker's Journal* (Oxford, 1978), p. 23.
135. J. Connell, *Confessions of a Poacher* (London, 1901), p. 268.
136. The Irish radical and Chartist, Thomas Ainge Devyr was a former poacher, see his *The Odd Book of the Nineteenth Century*, p. 55; Philip Snowden was an ex-gamekeeper, see P. Snowden, *An Autobiography* (2 vols, 1934), I, pp. 49–50; and Hugh Dalton was an inveterate rambler who left red flags on the moorlands and fells to mark his passing, see B. Pimlott, *Hugh Dalton* (London, 1985), pp. 455–6.
137. Cobden-Unwin, *The Land Hunger*, pp. 202–4.
138. *The Commonweal*, 14 February 1920, p. 3.
139. P. Kropotkin, *Fields, Factories and Workshops* (1901), p. 47.
140. See E. Carpenter, *Towards Industrial Freedom* (London, 1917), pp. 123–4 and for the 'vicious example' set by the Sandringham shooting estates in Norfolk, *Reynolds's Newspaper*, 11 February 1872, p. 2.
141. H. Rider Haggard, *Rural England: Being an Account of Agricultural and Social Researches Carried Out In the Years 1901 and 1902* (2 vols, London, 1902), I, pp. 522–43; and Anthony Allfrey, *Edward VII and His Jewish Court* (London, 1991), pp. 1–15.
142. L.E.O. Charlton, *This Cruelty Called Sport* (League Against Cruel Sports, 1939), pp. 44–5.
143. *Justice*, 9 February 1884, p. 4.
144. Lord Willoughby de Broke, *The Passing Years*, p. 167.
145. R. Blatchford, *Stunts* (1921), p. 193.

4 'Lords of Misrule': Liberalism, the House of Lords and the campaign against privilege 1870–1911

1. *The Political Magazine*, 1 July 1832, p. 413.
2. H. Brookes, *The Peers and the People, and the Coming Reform* (London, 1857), p. 3.
3. J. Clayton, *The Truth About the Lords: Fifty Years of the New Nobility 1857–1907* (London, 1907), p. 17.
4. *The Poems of Algernon Charles Swinburne in Six Volumes* (London, 1904), VI, pp. 96–9.
5. *National Reformer*, 22 August 1875, p. 116.
6. Ibid., 1 June 1873, pp. 345–6.
7. Cutting from the *Staffordshire Sentinel*, 9 October 1908 in the Josiah Wedgwood Papers, Hanley Public Library, Stoke-on-Trent.
8. Stead, *Peers or People?*, p. 79.

9. A. Ponsonby, *Queen Victoria* (London, 1933), p. 113.
10. For a complete list of these measures see Evans, *Our Old Nobility*, pp. 14–16.
11. George to McGhee, 15 August 1884, and George to Thomas Walker, 9 September 1884, Henry George Correspondence, NYPL.
12. Stead, *Peers or People?*, p. 89.
13. D. Spring, 'Land and Politics in Edwardian England', *Agricultural History*, LVIII (1984), 17–42; and Sykes, *Rise and Fall of British Liberalism*, p. 159.
14. 'The Peers and the Land', election ephemera 1906–1910 (308 N6 V.108) MCRL. For the original speech see the *People's Paper*, 8 November 1856, pp. 1, 4.
15. See, for example, E. Allyn, *Lords versus Commons: A Century of Conflict and Compromise 1830–1930* (New York, 1931), pp. 116–21; E.A. Smith, *The House of Lords in British Politics and Society 1815–1911* (London, 1992), ch. 9; and A. Adonis, *Making Aristocracy Work: The Peerage and the Political System in Britain 1884–1914* (Oxford, 1992), chs 7–9.
16. *Justice*, 6 July 1895, p. 4.
17. *Christian Socialist*, 1 September 1884, pp. 56–7.
18. See S. Reynolds and B. and T. Woolley, *Seems So! A Working-Class View of Politics* (London, 1911), pp. 132–3.
19. Chesterton, *Gladstonian Ghosts*, p. 173.
20. Biagini, *Liberty, Retrenchment and Reform*, ch. 5. Biagini's work draws on the observations of H. Jephson, *The Platform: Its Rise and Progress* (2 vols, London, 1892), II, pp. 608–9.
21. *Freethinker's Magazine*, 1 October 1850, p. 129 and 1 July 1850, p. 42.
22. *Radical*, 1 September 1888, pp. 6–7.
23. *Poor Man's Guardian*, 9 May 1835, pp. 523–4. Richard Carlile preached a holistic view of society that saw monarchy, aristocracy, and the Anglican Church's prescriptive advice on sex and procreation as part of the same sanctimonious totality; see M.L. Bush, *What is Love: Richard Carlile's Philosophy of Sex* (London, 1998), pp. 1–51; and for the aristocratic system as 'a huge octopus', 'Civis Mundi', *The Land Question and How to Solve it* (Glasgow, n.d.), p. 8.
24. *People's Paper*, 10 July 1858, p. 1.
25. *Howitt's Journal*, 15 April 1848, p. 255.
26. Stead, *Peers or People?*, p. 231. Gladstone came close to endorsing this view. He commented at a speech at Newcastle: 'There was a power not upon the throne, or behind the throne, but between the throne and the people'; quoted in the *Manchester Guardian*, 13 September 1893, p. 5.
27. Anon, *The Peers' Plunder and the People's Poverty* (Liverpool Financial Reform Association, 1884), pp. 1–2.
28. J. Clayton, *Leaders of the People: Studies in Democratic History* (London, 1910), p. 335.
29. *Birmingham Daily Post*, 7 December 1871, p. 5. Also see C.C. Cattell, *Abolition of the House of Lords* (Birmingham, 1872).
30. *Reynolds's Newspaper*, 27 June 1897, p. 6. See for Bute ibid., 6 June 1897, p. 5. In the 1870s the *National Reformer* ran a similar column entitled 'Our Aristocracy'; see the *National Reformer*, 3 December 1871, p. 355; 25 February 1872, pp. 114–15; and 17 March 1872, p. 163. Also see *The Republican*, 1 September 1882, pp. 425–6; 1 October 1882, p. 439; and 1 September 1883, p. 521. For secularist hostility to the aristocracy see G. Standring, *The People's History of the Aristocracy* (London, 1891).

31. *English Labourers' Chronicle*, 1 October 1881, p. 4.
32. J. Hodge, *Workman's Cottage to Windsor Castle* (London, 1931), p. 6; and Snowden, *An Autobiography*, I, p. 41.
33. A. Taylor, '"The Best Way to Get What he Wanted": Ernest Jones and the Boundaries of Liberalism in the Manchester Election of 1868', *Parliamentary History* XVI (1997), 185–204.
34. Idem, '"Commons-Stealers", "Land-Grabbers" and "Jerry-Builders": Space, Popular Radicalism and the Politics of Public Access in London, 1848–1880', *International Review of Social History*, XXXX (1995), 383–407.
35. The case for Gladstone's later radicalism has been re-examined in M. Barker, *Gladstone and Radicalism: The Reconstruction of Liberal Policy in Britain 1885–1894* (Brighton, 1975), pp. 171–3; and D.M. Schreuder, 'The Making of Mr Gladstone's Posthumous Career: The Role of Morley and Knaplund as "Monument Masons" 1903–1927' in B. Kinzer (ed.), *The Gladstonian Turn of Mind: Essays Presented to J. B. Comacher* (Toronto, 1985), pp. 197–237.
36. *The Single Tax*, 1 June 1898, p. 4. Similar sentiments were expressed by Keir Hardie in an obituary of Gladstone in the *Labour Leader*, 28 May 1898, pp. 178–9.
37. Quoted in R. Jenkins, *Gladstone* (London, 1995), pp. 495–6; and Matthew, *Gladstone 1875–1898*, p. 177.
38. *Anecdotes of the Rt. Hon. W. E. Gladstone by an Oxford Man* (London, n.d.), p. 32.
39. H.C.G. Matthew (ed.), *Gladstone Diaries* (13 vols, Oxford, 1986), XIII, appendix 1, p. 431.
40. H.C.G. Matthew, *Gladstone 1875–1898* (Oxford, 1995), p. 355.
41. R. Jenkins, *Asquith* (London, 1964), pp. 227–8. Tory fears of imminent royal disintegration were apparently confirmed when a pamphlet *Bigamy Sanctified* by E.R. Mylius appeared in 1911 disputing the succession and suggesting that George V already had a wife before his marriage to Mary; see D. Dutton, *Simon: A Political Biography of Sir John Simon* (London, 1992), p. 16.
42. R.R. James, *Rosebery* (London, 1963), ch. 10. For his objections to the Lords see Lord Rosebery, *The Reform of the House of Lords* (Edinburgh, 1884), pp. 3–31.
43. *The Premier's Battle Cry: Mr Asquith's Speech at the National Liberal Club* (*Yorkshire Observer*, 1910), p. 4.
44. D. Lloyd George, *Better Times: Speeches by the Rt. Hon. David Lloyd George* (London, 1910), pp. 221–2.
45. E.R. Pearce-Edgcombe, *The Last Function of the House of Lords* (Manchester, 1884), p. 38.
46. J.E. Woolacott, *The House of Lords: A Lecture* (National Secular Society, 1884), p. 3.
47. A. Mackenzie, *The Peers and the Franchise: The House of Lords* (London, 1884), p. 10.
48. *The Republican*, 1 September 1884, pp. 41–2.
49. See 'Publius', *The House of Lords: What shall We Do with it?* (Manchester, 1884); and *The Peers and the People: What shall We Do with the House of Lords?* (London, 1884).
50. Lord Carrington, 'Recollections of my Life from Public School to Privy Seal', Autobiographical Fragment, Rosebery Papers, National Library of Scotland (MSS 10229).
51. For example the lines 'The House of Peers, Throughout the War / Did Nothing in Particular / And Did it Very Well' in W.S. Gilbert's *Iolanthe*, II (1882). Disraeli famously quipped on the occasion of his elevation to the Lords

'I am dead; dead but in the Elysium Fields'; see Smith, *The House of Lords*, pp. 142–3. Lord Hartington claimed to have dreamed that he was addressing the House of Lords, and then woke up to find that he was. There are numerous versions of this story, but it is related best in Snowden, *Autobiography*, I, p. 41.

52. G.A. Denison, *Why Should the Bishops Continue to Sit in the House of Lords?* (Pamphlet, London, 1850), pp. 36–7.
53. Stephens and the Woolleys, *Seems So!*, p. 304.
54. Quoted in a sketch of Wilfred Lawson in the *Liberal Almanak* (Halifax, 1887), p. 10. For Lawson and his vendetta against the House of Lords see G.W.E. Russell (ed.), *Sir Wilfred Lawson, A Memoir* (London, 1909), pp. 216–17.
55. K.O. Morgan, *David Lloyd George: Welsh Radical and World Statesman* (Cardiff, 1963), p. 44; and M. Pugh, *Lloyd George* (London, 1988), pp. 49–50.
56. *Peers v. the People: What's the Use of the House of Lords?* (Manchester, 1884), pp. 17–18.
57. Pugh, *Lloyd George*, p. 54.
58. Lord Willoughby de Broke mentioned the 'fun' involved in comparing 'notes from the last season' at meetings of die-hards called to subvert Liberal legislation. See Willoughby de Broke, *The Passing Years*, p. 247.
59. 'Publius', *The House of Lords?*, p. 3.
60. *Wigan Observer*, 25 August 1871, p. 5.
61. *People's Paper*, 8 November 1857, p. 1. Also see for associations between aristocracy and pauperdom, S. Hughan, *Hereditary Peers and Hereditary Paupers* (London, 1885), especially pp. 63–70.
62. *The Single Tax*, 1 June 1898.
63. Pugh, *Lloyd George*, chs 1–3.
64. See the *Birmingham Daily Post*, 14 October 1884, pp. 4–5; the *Newcastle Weekly Chronicle*, 18 October 1884, p. 3; and *Reynolds's Newspaper*, 19 October 1884, pp. 2, 4. The events surrounding this episode are described in Foster, *Lord Randolph Churchill*, pp. 162–3.
65. *Newcastle Weekly Chronicle*, 5 July 1884, p. 4.
66. David Lloyd George referred specifically to the 1832 House of Lords crisis in a speech at Walworth in 1909; see *Better Times*, p. 221.
67. *English Labourers' Chronicle*, 2 August 1884, pp. 2–4.
68. *Newcastle Weekly Chronicle*, 26 July 1884, p. 3.
69. *Manchester Guardian*, 18 August 1884, p. 6.
70. P. Percival, *Failsworth Folk and Failsworth Memories* (Manchester, 1901), pp. 5–6, Joan Smith, 'Labour Traditions in Glasgow and Liverpool', *History Workshop*, XVII (1984), 32–56; and G. Walker, *Thomas Johnston* (Manchester, 1988), pp. 9–12.
71. H.C.G. Matthew, 'Disraeli, Gladstone and the Politics of Mid-Victorian Budgets', *Historical Journal*, XXII (1979), 615–43.
72. B.K. Murray, *The People's Budget 1909–1910* (Oxford, 1980).
73. Election Leaflets, 1906–1910 (308 N6 V.108), MCRL.
74. H. Storey, *The House of Lords: History of the Fight between the People and the Peers, Statement of Liberal Policy, Examination of the Government's Proposals* (Liberal Party, 1927), pp. 8–9.
75. 'A Peer', 'The Peers and the Situation', *National Review*, LIV (1909), 241–2. The intemperate language of some radicals who fantasised about Committees of

Public Safety fuelled the sense of crisis on the part of the aristocracy. See the *County Forum Gazette*, 18 August 1883, p. 1.

76. The best guide to the historical principles of Liberalism is Sykes, *The Rise and Fall of British Liberalism*, ch. 1.

77. Hughan, *Hereditary Peers and Hereditary Paupers*, p. 123.

78. Willoughby de Broke, *The Passing Years*, p. 175. Also see Brodrick, *English Land and English Landlords*, p. 418; J.M. Davidson, *The Old Order and the New: From Individualism to Collectivism* (London, 1904), pp. 146–7; and *Land and Liberty*, 1 May 1894, p. 9.

79. A.G. Symonds, 'The House of Lords: Not a Second Chamber or Senate', Election Ephemera 1906–1910 (308 N6 V.108), MCRL (see appendix 2).

80. Stead, *Peers or People?*, p. 38 and ch. 9. The standard account of the corruption charges surrounding the Irish peerage is J.G.S. MacNeill, *Titled Corruption: The Sordid Origin of Some Irish Peerages* (Dublin, 1894).

81. See T.W. Moody, *Davitt and Irish Revolution 1846–1882* (Oxford, 1981), p. 3. There was outrage from both English and Irish radicals that the Anglo-Irish aristocracy sought to retain their power and position in a post-Home Rule state. For a defence of the aristocratic Ascendancy see comments by Lady Florence Dixie in *The Freeman's Journal*, 23 August 1882, p. 2.

82. 'Civis Mundi', *The Land Question*, pp. 11–12.

83. *Barnsley Chronicle*, 15 August 1885.

84. See *Reynolds's Newspaper*, 15 August 1875, p. 1.

85. Stead, *Peers or People?*, p. 172.

86. *Manchester Guardian*, 18 August 1884, p. 6.

87. Evans, *Our Old Nobility*, p. 160.

88. Thorold, *The Life of Henry Labouchere*, p. 217.

89. Ibid., pp. 208–26.

90. Ibid., p. 220.

91. *Justice*, 12 November 1887 and 14 July 1888.

92. For the outline of the Newcastle proposals, see S. Maccoby, *The English Radical Tradition 1763–1914* (London, 1952), pp. 207–8, and for later National Liberal Federation manifestos on the Lords, the *Manchester Guardian*, 13 September 1893, p. 5.

93. Gwynne and Tuckwell, *The Life of the Rt. Hon. Sir Charles W. Dilke*, I, p. 145.

94. C. O'Leary, *The Elimination of Corrupt Practices in British Elections* (Oxford, 1962), p. 214.

95. Willoughby de Broke, *The Passing Years*, p. 252.

96. W.T. Stead, 'The General Election, 1895: The Poster in Politics', *Review of Reviews*, XII (1895), 168–76.

97. Willoughby de Broke, *The Passing Years*, p. 256.

98. 'Jif', *Bumbles, Drones, and Working Bees: A Lecture* (London, 1881), p. 9.

99. J.S. Ellis, 'Reconciling the Celt: British National Identity, Empire and the 1911 Investiture of the Prince of Wales', *Journal of British Studies*, XXXVII (1988), 391–418.

100. Evans, *Our Old Nobility*, p. 1.

101. F. Owen, *Lloyd George: His Life and Times* (London, 1954), p. 195.

102. See especially L. Barrow and I. Bullock, *Democratic Ideas and the British Labour Movement 1880–1914* (Cambridge, 1997), chs 1–3.

103. The standard account is R. McKibben, *The Evolution of the Labour Party 1910–1924* (London, 1974), chs 1, 6 and the conclusion.
104. P. Clarke, 'The Social Democratic Theory of the Class Struggle' in J. Winter (ed.), *The Working Class in Modern British History* (Cambridge, 1983), pp. 3–18; and S. Fielding, P. Thompson and N. Tiratsoo, *'England Arise': The Labour Party and Popular Politics in 1940s Britain* (Manchester, 1995), ch. 4.
105. See D. Butler, 'By-elections and Their Interpretation' in C. Cook and J. Ramsden (eds), *By-elections in British Politics* (London, 1997), pp. 1–12.
106. *Republican*, 1 August 1884, p. 39.
107. W.T. Stead, *Fifty Years of the House of Lords* (London, 1880), p. 63.
108. J.R. MacDonald, *Tories and the House of Lords: An Exposure of Their Trickery* (London, 1910), pp. 16–17.
109. C.C. Weston, 'Salisbury and the Lords 1868–1895', *Historical Journal*, XXV (1982), 103–29; and idem, *The House of Lords and Ideological Politics: Lord Salisbury's Referendal Theory and the Conservative Party 1846–1922* (American Philosophical Society, 1991).
110. I. Bullock and S. Reynolds, 'Direct Legislation and Socialism: How British and French Socialists Viewed the Referendum in the 1890s', *History Workshop*, XXIV (1987), 62–81; J. Sketchley, *Shall the People Govern Themselves?* (Pamphlet, London, 1896), pp. 10–11; and the *Labour Echo*, 13 April 1895, p. 4.
111. *New Age*, 19 September 1895, p. 396.
112. *Labour Leader*, 6 May 1910, p. 280.
113. Evans, *Our Old Nobility*, pp. 6–7. Some Labour pamphleteers alleged that peers acted as 'decoy-ducks' conferring a veneer of respectability on their firms in company board-rooms; see H.R. Stockman, *Labour and the Lords: An Indictment* (Labour Party, 1909), pp. 10–11.
114. W.C. Macpherson, *The Baronage and the Senate or the House of Lords in the Past, the Present and the Future* (London, 1893), p. 74.
115. *New Age*, 10 October 1895, p. 17. In 1911 Cecil Chesterton suggested that new peers should be made up of dockers and workers, rather than employers or wealthy contributors to Liberal Party funds; see ibid., 30 March 1911, p. 512.
116. *Labour Echo*, 13 April 1895, p. 4. Also see the *Republican*, 1 September 1883, pp. 521–2 on the question of 'capitalists' in the House of Lords.
117. *Bradford Observer*, 30 October 1894, p. 6.
118. Ibid., 29 October 1894, p. 4.
119. *Labour Leader*, 28 May 1898, pp. 178–9.
120. Pugh, *Lloyd George*, pp. 51, 185.
121. Ramsay MacDonald invoked Shakespeare as an opponent of the Lords. See the cover of his pamphlet, *Tories and the House of Lords*.
122. J. Vernon, 'Narrating the Constitution: The Discourse of "The Real" and the Fantasies of Nineteenth Century Constitutional History' in Vernon (ed.), *Re-reading the Constitution*, pp. 204–29. Supporters of the Lords also made play with Cromwell's remark that the House of Lords was necessary to protect the people against 'an omnipotent House of Commons – the horridest arbitrariness that ever existed in the world'; see Willoughby de Broke, *The Passing Years*, p. 259.
123. *Poems of Algernon Swinburne*, VI, p. 340. For the debates surrounding the construction of statues commemorating Cromwell, and his place in radical culture more generally, see P. Karsten, *Patriot-Heroes in England and America:*

Political Symbolism and Changing Values over Three Centuries (Madison, 1978), chs 6 and 7.

124. J. Arch, 'The Labourers and the Vote', *The Nineteenth Century*, III (1878), 48–52.
125. Labouchere Thorold, *Life of Henry Labouchere*, chs 7 and 8.
126. *Leeds Mercury*, 13 November 1885.
127. *Reynolds's Newspaper*, 27 July 1884, p. 1.
128. The phrase is used in *Our Land*, 1 December 1909, p. 300.
129. J. Ramsay MacDonald, 'A Plea for Puritanism', *The Socialist Review*, 1 February 1912, pp. 422–30. There is an extended treatment of the rediscovery of Puritanism in popular politics in Samuel, *Island Stories*, pp. 276–322.
130. See B. Worden, *Roundhead Reputations: The English Civil War and the Passions of Posterity* (London, 2001), p. 247; and R. Howell, 'Who Needs Another Cromwell? The Nineteenth Century Image of Oliver Cromwell' in R.C. Richardson (ed.), *Images of Cromwell: Essays by and for Roger Howell, Jr* (Manchester, 1993), p. 97.
131. *Our Land*, 1 December 1909, p. 301.
132. *Labour Leader*, 24 September 1909.
133. *The Single Tax*, 1 January 1898, p. 3.

5 Plutocracy

1. W.M. Thackeray, *The Book of Snobs by One of Themselves*, 1989 edn (London, 1848), p. 40.
2. S. and B. Webb, 'What is Socialism? The Development of Science, Art and Religion Untrammelled by Plutocracy', *New Statesman*, 19 July 1913, pp. 461–3.
3. 'An Old Radical', ibid., 24 May 1913, pp. 216–17.
4. E. Waugh, *Work Suspended and Other Stories*, 2001 edn (London, 1943), p. 111.
5. Evans, *Our Old Nobility*, p. 7.
6. Ponsonby, *The Decline of Aristocracy*, pp. 313–14. For Ponsonby's role at court and his subsequent conversion to socialism, see Mosley, *My Life*, p. 217.
7. Quoted in Harris, *Private Lives, Public Spirit*, p. 256.
8. A. Allfrey, *Edward VII and His Jewish Court* (London, 1991); and J. Camplin, *The Rise of the Plutocrats: Wealth and Power in Edwardian England* (London, 1978), pp. 132, 156.
9. J. Buchan, *The King's Grace 1910–1935* (London, 1935), p. 28.
10. See discussion of Buchan's novel *The Half-Hearted* and kindred works in A. Lownie, *John Buchan: The Presbyterian Cavalier* (London, 2002), pp. 66, 138.
11. P. Mairet, *Aristocracy and the Meaning of Class Rule: An Essay Upon Aristocracy Past and Future* (London, 1931), pp. 7–9.
12. G. Potter, 'The Labourers and the Vote', *Nineteenth Century*, III (1878), 53–70.
13. One exception to this tendency is Walter Bagehot, who saw the worship of new money for old money as 'politically useful ... if it be skilfully used'. See W. Bagehot, *The English Constitution*, 2nd edn (London, 1872), p. 30.
14. Day, *King George V as a Sportsman*, pp. 276–7.
15. See K. Lunn, 'Political Anti-semitism before 1914: Fascism's Heritage' in Lunn and R.C. Thurlow (eds), *British Fascism* (London, 1980), pp. 20–40.

16. Lees-Milne, *Caves of Ice*, p. 92.
17. Quoted in M. Chase, 'This is no Claptrap: This is our Heritage' in C. Shaw and M. Chase (eds), *The Imagined Past: History as Nostalgia* (Manchester, 1989), pp. 141–2.
18. D. Jerrold, 'On the Influence of Hilaire Belloc' in D. Woodruff (ed.), *For Hilaire Belloc: Essays in Honour of his Seventy-Second Birthday* (London, 1942), p. 12.
19. R. Perrott, *The Aristocrats: A Portrait of Britain's Nobility and their Way of Life Today* (London, 1968), p. 76; and J. Baxendale, '"I had seen a lot of Englands": J.B. Priestly, Englishness and the People', *History Workshop Journal*, LI (2001), 87–111.
20. E.A. Barker, *The Forbidden Land: A Plea for Public Access to Mountains, Moors and Other Waste Lands in Great Britain* (London, 1924), p. 29.
21. R. Mckibben, *Classes and Culture in England 1918–1951* (Oxford, 1998), p. 17.
22. James (ed.), *Chips*, p. 177.
23. Mckibben, *Classes and Culture in England*, ch. 1; and G.J. De Groot, *The First World War* (London, 1999), ch. 1.
24. *Cant and Humbug* (ILP, 1936), p. 8. Recently the charge that the Establishment was keen to collude in the overthrow of a monarch who failed to play the role of king has been reappraised; see S. Williams, *The People's King: The True Story of the Abdication* (London, 2003), ch. 1.
25. H.R.H. The Duke of Windsor, *The Crown and the People 1902–1953* (London, 1953), p. 7.
26. Ibid., pp. 9–10.
27. M. Collins, 'The Fall of the English Gentleman: The National Character in Decline *c*.1918–1970', *Historical Research*, LXXV (2002), 90–111.
28. H. Belloc, *The House of Commons and Monarchy* (London, 1920), p. 177; and *The New Age*, 13 May 1920, p. 22.
29. M. Ward, *Gilbert Keith Chesterton* (London, 1944), p. 268.
30. *Lansbury's Labour Weekly*, 30 January 1926, p. 1.
31. See *The Daily Herald*, 3 July 1925, p. 7; and 2 October 1925, p. 1.
32. *Lansbury's Labour Weekly*, 28 March 1925, p. 2.
33. Confounding Channon's expectations, de Clifford was cleared of the charge. See James (ed.), *Chips*, p. 47.
34. See R. Dallek, *John F. Kennedy, An Unfinished Life 1917–1963* (London, 2003), pp. 48–54.
35. E. Waugh, *Decline and Fall*, 1928 (London, 2001), p. 8.
36. J. Johnson, *The Men Behind the War: A Startling Exposure of the Financial Interests Who are Exploiting the War* (Communist Party of Great Britain, 1940), pp. 13–14. George Orwell famously judged the aristocracy as wanting during wartime, with the result that the situation was usually saved 'by people comparatively low on the social scale'; see the essays in G. Orwell, *The Lion and the Unicorn* (London, 1962), p. 32.
37. S. Haxey, *Tory MP* (London, 1939), ch. 6.
38. Ibid., p. 128.
39. Ibid., p. 157.
40. Ibid., pp. 170–1.
41. Belloc, *The House of Commons and Monarchy*, pp. 97–8.
42. See M. Fordham, *The Rebuilding of Rural England* (London, 1924), p. 9.

43. C. Hollis, *Quality or Equality?* (London, 1944), p. 17.
44. *The Commonweal*, 20 March 1920, p. 3.
45. *Lansbury's Labour Weekly*, 2 January 1926, p. 11. Also see for attacks on the Duke of Northumberland's wealth as an example of the continuing injustices in landownership, ibid., 30 January 1926, p. 1, and 27 February 1926, p. 15; and *The Daily Herald*, 17 August 1925, p. 6.
46. *The Workers' Weekly*, 23 June 1923, p. 1.
47. For the decline of the aristocratic families of the Irish Ascendency, see M. Bence-Jones, *Twilight of the Ascendancy* (London, 1987); and for W.B. Yeats, R.F. Foster, *Paddy and Mr Punch: Connections in Irish and English History* (London, 1993), ch. 11.
48. Cannadine, *The Decline and Fall of the British Aristocracy*, ch. 11.
49. Mosley, *My Life*, pp. 217–18. For the political career of Charles Trevelyan see D. Cannadine, *G.M. Trevelyan: A Life in History* (London, 1992), chs 2, 3 and 4.
50. The Marquess of Normanby who sat as a Labour Peer in Attlee's government was popularly known as the 'Red Marquess'; see his obituary in *The Guardian*, 3 February 1994, p. 17.
51. M.I. Cole (ed.), *Beatrice Webb's Diaries 1912–1924* (London, 1954), pp. 236–7.
52. *Lansbury's Labour Weekly*, 31 October 1925, p. 17.
53. E. Estorick, *The Biography of Sir Stafford Cripps* (London, 1949), p. 2.
54. Cole (ed.), *Beatrice Webb's Diaries 1912–1924*, pp. 242–3.
55. Hollis, *Quality or Equality?*, p. 10.
56. James, *Chips*, p. 140.
57. Mosley, *My Life*, pp. 17, 191.
58. G. Aldred, *Socialism and Parliament Part 1: Socialism or Parliament, the Burning Issue of Today* (Glasgow, 1942), pp. 18–19.
59. A. Huxley, *Antic Hay*, 1977 edn (London, 1923), p. 62.
60. Fascist aristocrats are a recurrent feature of inter-war writing. The pro-Fascist rural writer, Henry Williamson, recalled that he was recruited into the BUF by a fictionalised Norfolk aristocrat, Lady Sunne (actually Dorothy, Viscountess Downe) in 1937; see H. Williamson, *The Story of a Norfolk Farm* (London, 1942), pp. 186–7.
61. *Who Backs Mosley? Fascist Promise and Fascist Performance* (Labour Research Department, 1934), pp. 2–3. These criticisms of the Mosley family were in a long tradition in Manchester; in 1901 the *Manchester Guardian* remarked: 'it must be confessed that it was principally by the irritation they caused that Manchester people knew their lords'. See the *Manchester Guardian*, 13 July 1901, p. 6.
62. Mosley was sensitive on the subject of his ancestor's misdeeds. He commented 'I was never able to understand why I should be held responsible for events so many years before I was born.' See Mosley, *My Life*, p. 3.
63. R. Griffiths, *Fellow Travellers of the Right: British Enthusiasts for Nazi Germany 1933–39* (London, 1980), pp. 168–71.
64. Ibid., p. 11.
65. R. Thurlow, *Fascism in Britain: From Oswald Mosley's Blackshirts to the National Front* (London, 1998 edn), p. 5; and R. Skidelsky, *Oswald Mosley* (London, 1975), ch. 1.
66. See N. Rose, *The Cliveden Set: Portrait of an Exclusive Fraternity* (London, 2001), ch. 8.

67. H. Thorsten, 'Who's Who in the Cliveden Baronage', *Tribune*, 25 March 1938, p. 5.
68. *Sidelights on the Cliveden Set: Hitler's Friends in Britain* (CPGB, 1938), p. 10.
69. Thorsten, 'Who's Who in the Cliveden Baronage', p. 5.
70. W.H. Williams, 'Londonderry Traditions', in ibid., 8 April 1938, p. 5; and for the Londonderry ancestry, Evans, *Our Old Nobility*, pp. 142–6.
71. A. Calder, *The Myth of the Blitz* (London, 1991), pp. 259–60.
72. J.B. Priestley, *Blackout in Gretley* 1987 (London, 1942), pp. 176–7.
73. See Mandler, *The Rise and Fall of the Stately Home*, p. 36.
74. Skidelsky, *Oswald Mosley*, p. 301, W.E.D. Allen, *Fascism in Relation to British History and Character* (BUF, 1935), pp. 5–8; and O. Mosley, *The Alternative* (London, 1947), pp. 27–8.
75. A.L. Glasfurd, 'Fascism and the English Tradition', *Fascist Quarterly*, I (1935), 360–4.
76. A.K. Chesterton, *Oswald Mosley: Portrait of a Leader* (London, 1936), p. 10; and Mosley, *My Life*, ch. 1.
77. Ibid., p. 11.
78. For Bryant's dubious and quasi-Fascist politics, see A. Roberts, *Eminent Churchillians* (London, 1994), ch. 6.
79. A. Bryant, *English Saga 1840–1940* (London, 1940), pp. 45–6.
80. Chesterton, *Oswald Mosley*, p. 9.
81. Mandler, *The Fall and Rise of the Stately Home*, chs 6 and 7.
82. J.W. Day, 'The Coast of Enchanted Wings' in R. Harman (ed.), *Countryside Character* (London, 1946), p. 116.
83. R. Gardiner, 'Rural Reconstruction' in H.J. Massingham (ed.), *England and the Small Farmer: A Symposium* (London, 1940), p. 92.
84. Joad, *The Untutored Townsman's Invasion of the the Country*, p. 199. Many of the great aristocratic houses were shut up during the Second World War, and never really recovered their status and social function; see a lament for 'the end of a chapter' in James (ed.), *Chips*, p. 224.
85. Chase, 'This is no claptrap: this is our heritage', pp. 128–46.
86. Massingham, *Remembrance*, p. 32
87. Gardiner, 'Rural Reconstruction', p. 92.
88. Massingham, *The English Countryman*, pp. 86–7.
89. Idem, *Chiltern Country* (London, 1940), p. 96 and for the influences of H.W. Massingham's radical journalistic Liberalism on his son's ideas, A.F. Havighurst, *Radical Journalist: H.W. Massingham* (Cambridge, 1974), p. 21.
90. See P. Fussell, *The Great War and Modern Memory* (London, 1975), chs 4–5.
91. For this term see Gardiner, 'Rural Reconstruction', p. 104.
92. There is now an extensive literature on Gardiner and Lymington. See in particular, G. Boyes, *The Imagined Village: Culture, Ideology and the English Folk Revival* (Manchester, 1993), ch. 7; M. Chase, 'Rolf Gardiner: An Inter-war Cross-Cultural Case Study' in B. Hake and S. Marriott (eds), *Adult Education Between Cultures* (Leeds, 1994), pp. 225–41; Griffiths, *Fellow Travellers of the Right*, pp. 319–23; and idem, *Patriotism Perverted* (London, 1998); and P. Wright, *The Village that Died for England: The Strange Story of Tyneham* (London, 1995), chs 12 and 13.
93. Massingham, *The Englishman Countryman*, pp. 100–5, 140; Mairet, *Aristocracy and the Meaning of Class Rule*, p. 95; D. Matless, *Landscape and Englishness*

(London, 1998), ch. 4, W.J. Keith, *The Rural Tradition* (Toronto, 1975), ch. 12; and C. Palmer, 'Christianity, Englishness and the Southern English Countryside: A Study of the Work of H.J. Massingham', *Social and Cultural Geography*, III (2002), 25–38.

94. See P. Conford, *The Origins of the Organic Movement* (Edinburgh, 2001), chs 7 and 9.

95. See for the roots of the Social Credit movement in particular, J. Hargrave, *Social Credit Clearly Explained: 101 Questions Answered* (London, 1945), especially pp. 15–20.

96. W. Stafford, '"This Once Happy Country": Nostalgia for Pre-modern Society' in Chase (ed.), *The Imagined Past*, pp. 33–41; and G.K. Chesterton, *William Cobbett* (London, 1925), pp. 176–7.

97. Such ideas derived from R.H. Tawney, *The Agrarian Problem in the Sixteenth Century* (London, 1912), pp. 131–9.

98. D. Hyde, *I Believed: The Autobiography of a Former British Communist* (London, 1950), p. 212.

99. H. Read, *Poetry and Anarchism* (London, 1947), p. 9. For the outlook of a British aristocratic anarchist, see J.M. Kenworthy, *Sailors, Statesmen and Others* (London, 1933).

100. Massingham, *Remembrance*, pp. 83–4.

101. See C.S. Orwin, *Speed the Plough* (London, 1942), especially ch. 7.

102. Day, *King George V as a Sportsman*, pp. 290–1.

103. Massingham, *Chiltern Country*, pp. 70, 80.

104. P. Howard, 'Back to Earth' in R. Harman (ed.), *Countryside Mood* (London, 1946), p. 62.

105. Lees-Milne, *Caves of Ice*, p. 249.

106. The term is used in Perrott, *The Aristocrats*, p. 4.

107. See the obituary of Lord Sackville, Vita Sackville-West's cousin, in *The Guardian*, 29 March 2004, p. 34.

108. The full history of the National Trust remains to be written, but see Gaze, *Figures in a Landscape*, chs 8–9; and D. Cannadine, *In Churchill's Shadow* (London, 2003), ch. 10.

109. '"Wooden Liars" because trespass is a civil mater, not a criminal offence, so a trespasser cannot be prosecuted, only sued'. See Stephenson, *Forbidden Land*, p. 88.

110. Ibid., pp. 205–6.

111. R. Hewison, *The Heritage Industry: Britain in a Climate of Decline* (London, 1987), ch. 3.

112. See H. Newby, *Green and Pleasant Land: Social Change in Rural Britain* (London, 1979), ch. 2.

Conclusions

1. *The Observer*, 12 December 1993, p. 10.

2. Obituary of Andrew Cavendish, Eleventh Duke of Devonshire, in *The Guardian*, 5 May 2004, p. 25; also see *The Independent*, 6 May 2004, pp. 40–1.

3. G.R. Searle, *A New England: Peace and War 1886–1918* (Oxford, 2004).

4. *The Guardian*, 1 June 2000, p. 23; and 27 November 2001, p. 18.

5. Ibid., 13 August 1994, p. 19.
6. Ibid., 22 January 2004, p. 3.
7. See *The Independent*, 20 December 1996, p. 21
8. Ibid., 21 January 2000, pp. 3, 7; and *The Guardian*, 20 January 2000, p. 22, and 21 January 2000, p. 21.
9. Ibid., 6 February 2004, p. 18.
10. For the Blandford and Bristol cases see *The Independent*, 12 June 1993, p. 17; and *The Guardian*, 23 July 1994, p. 2.
11. *The Observer*, 30 April 1995, p. 23.
12. See the obituary of Lady Diana Mosley in ibid., 14 August 2003, p. 27.
13. *The Observer*, 12 December 1993, p. 10.
14. *The Guardian*, 23 January 2003, p. 14.
15. Ibid., 17 April 2002, pp. 2–3 and 29 April 2002, p. 7. For a recent treatment of public access issues that emphasises the continuities with older styles of radicalism, see M. Shoard, *A Right to Roam* (Oxford, 1999), chs 3–4.
16. D. Cox, 'Whose Liberty, whose Livelihood?', *New Statesman*, 16 September 2002, p. 24.
17. *The Guardian*, 20 September 2002, p. 17.
18. Emrys (ed.), *Keir Hardie: His Writings and Speeches*, p. 46.

Bibliography

Manuscript sources

Election Ephemera and Leaflets, 1906–1910, Manchester Central Library, Social Science Reading Room.
Henry George Papers, New York Public Library.
Josiah Wedgwood, MP, Collected Newspaper Cuttings, Hanley Record Office, Stoke on Trent.

Newspapers and periodicals

Alliance News, 1870.
Barnsley Chronicle, 1885.
Bee-Hive, 1869–1875.
Birmingham Daily Post, 1871–1884.
Bolton Guardian, 1884.
Bradford Observer, 1894.
Christian Socialist, 1884.
Clarion, 1892.
Commonweal, 1920.
Daily Herald, 1925.
De Morgan's Monthly, 1876–1877.
Dublin Independent, 1912.
English Labourers' Chronicle, 1881–1884.
Freedom, 1887–1897.
Freeman's Journal, 1882.
Freethinker's Magazine, 1850.
Guardian, 1994–2004.
Howitt's Journal, 1848.
Humane Review, 1904–1909.
Independent, 1994–2004.
Justice, 1889–1912.
Labour Annual, 1895.
Labour Echo, 1895.
Labour Leader, 1897–1910.
Labourers' Herald, 1874.
Land and Labour, 1889–1891.
Lansbury's Labour Weekly, 1925–1926.
Leeds Mercury, 1885.
Liberal Almanac (Halifax, 1887).
Liberty, 1883.
Manchester City News, 1912–1920.
Manchester Examiner and Times, 1882.

Manchester Guardian, 1884–1893.
National Reformer, 1871–1881.
New Age, 1895.
Newcastle Weekly Chronicle, 1884–1888.
New Statesman, 1913 and 2002.
Northern Star, 1842–1848.
Observer, 1993–1995.
Our Land, 1909–1910.
People's Advocate (Australia), 1850.
People's Advocate, 1875–1876.
People's Paper, 1853–1858.
Political Magazine, 1832.
Prestwich Division Liberal Almanac, 1908–1910.
Punch, 1845.
Radical, 1888.
Republican, 1887–1889.
Reynolds's Newspaper, 1872–1880.
Rossendale Worker, 1909.
Seed-Time, 1891.
Single Tax, 1897–1925.
The Call, 1919.
The Field, 1899–1900.
The Labourer, 1879–1880.
The Times, 1875.
Tribune, 1938.
Truth (Australia), 1896–1897.
United Irishman, 1900.
Weekly Dispatch, 1875–1884.
Wigan Observer, 1871.
Workers' Republic, 1915.
Workers' Weekly, 1923.

Primary printed sources

Aldred, G. *Socialism and Parliament Part I: Socialism or Parliament, the Burning Issue of Today* (Glasgow, 1942).
Alken, H. *The National Sports of Great Britain* (London, 1903).
Allen, W.E.D. *Fascism in Relation to British History and Character* (BUF, 1935).
Allingham, H. and Dick, S. *Cottage Homes of England* (London, 1909).
Allyn, E. *Lords versus Commons: A Century of Conflict and Compromise 1830–1930* (New York, 1931).
Arch, J. 'The Labourers and the Vote', *The Nineteenth Century*, III (1878), 48–52.
Argyll, Duke of 'The Prophet of San Francisco', *Nineteenth Century*, XV (1884), 537–58.
Arnold, A. 'Free Trade in Land', *Contemporary Review*, XX (1872), 880–96.
——. 'The Abuses of a Landed Gentry', *The Nineteenth Century*, I (1877), 458–78.
——. *Free Land* (London, 1880).
Bagehot, W. *The English Constitution* (2nd edn, London, 1872).

Baker, S.W. *The Rifle and Hound in Ceylon* (London, 1890).

Barker, E. *The Forbidden Land: A Plea for Public Access to Mountains, Moors and Other Waste Lands in Great Britain* (London, 1924).

Barker, J. *The Life of Joseph Barker, Written by Himself* (London, 1880).

Baron de Forest, 'Memorandum' in *The Land: The Report of the Land Enquiry Committee* (2 vols, London, 1913), I, pp. 445–70.

Bateman, J. *Acreocracy of England* (London, 1876).

——. *The Great Landowners of Britain and Ireland* (London, 1879).

Beer, M. *The Pioneers of Land Reform: Thomas Spence, William Ogilvie, Thomas Paine* (London, 1920).

Belloc, H. *The House of Commons and Monarchy* (London, 1920).

Benbow, W. *A Peep at the Peers: An Alphabetical List of all Peers who Sit in the House . . . Showing their Offices, Pensions, Grants, Church Preferment and Other Things Attached to the Peers and their Families* (London, 1820).

Bengough, J.H. *The-Up-To-Date-Primer: A First Book of Lessons for Little Political Economists* (New York, 1896).

Blatchford, R. *Britain for the British* (London, 1902).

——. *Stunts* (London, 1921).

Booth, E.C. *Another England: Life, Living, Homes and Homemakers in Victoria* (London, 1869).

Bradlaugh, C. *The Coming Struggle: The Land, the People and the Coming Struggle* (London, 1880).

——. *John Churchill, Duke of Marlborough* (London, 1884).

Bradlaugh Bonner, H. *Charles Bradlaugh: A Record of His Life and Work* (2 vols, London, 1894).

Bridges, J.A. *Reminiscences of a Country Politician* (London, 1906).

Brodrick, G.C. 'The Law of Custom and Primogeniture', *Cobden Club Essays Second Series, 1871–2* (London, 1872).

——. *English Land and English Landlords* (London, 1881).

Brookes, H. *The Peers and the People, and the Coming Reform* (London, 1857).

Bryant, A. *English Saga 1840–1940* (London, 1940).

Buchan, J. *The King's Grace 1910–1935* (London, 1935).

Burrows, H. and Hobson, J.A. (eds), *William Clarke: A Collection of His Writings* (London, 1908).

Cant and Humbug (Independent Labour Party, 1936).

Carpenter, E. *Towards Industrial Freedom* (London, 1917).

'Casey', *Who are the Bloodsuckers?* (ILP, 1905).

Cattell, C.C. *Abolition of the House of Lords* (Birmingham, 1872).

Charlton, L.E.O. *This Cruelty Called Sport* (League Against Cruel Sports, 1939).

Chesterton, A.K. *Oswald Mosley: Portrait of a Leader* (London, 1936).

Chesterton, C. *Gladstonian Ghosts* (London, 1905).

Chesterton, G.K. *William Cobbett* (London, 1925).

——. *Come to Think of it: A Book of Essays* (London, 1930).

Christian, G. (ed.), *A Victorian Poacher: James Hawker's Journal* (London, 1978).

'Civis Mundi' *The Land Question and How to Solve it* (Glasgow, n. d.).

Clarke, A. *Moorlands and Memories: Rambles and Rides in the Fair Places of Steam Engine Land* (Bolton, 1920).

Clayton, J. *The Truth about the Lords: Fifty Years of the New Nobility 1857–1907* (London, 1907).

——. *Leaders of the People: Studies in Democratic History* (London, 1910).

Cobden-Unwin, J. *The Land Hunger: Life Under Monopoly* (London, 1913).

Cole, M.I. (ed.), *Beatrice Webb's Diaries 1912–1924* (London, 1954).

Connell, J. *The Truth about the Game Laws* (Humanitarian League, 1898).

——. *Confessions of a Poacher* (London, 1901).

Cooper, T. *Captain Cobler or the Lincolnshire Rebellion: An Historical Romance of the Reign of Henry VIII* (London, 1850).

Cox, H. *Land Nationalisation* (London, 1892).

Creuss, M. (ed.), *In Memoriam, Ernest Jones* (Manchester, 1879).

Davidson, J.M. *Eminent Radicals In and Out of Parliament* (London, 1880).

——. *The Old Order and the New: From Individualism to Collectivism* (London, 1904).

Davies, E. and Evans, D: *Land Nationalisation: The Key to Social Reform* (London, 1921).

Davies, W.H. *Autobiography of a Super-Tramp* (London, 1908).

Day, J.W. *King George V as a Sportsman* (London, 1935).

——. 'The Coast of Enchanted Wings' in Harman, R. (ed.), *Countryside Character* (London, 1946), pp. 105–20.

De Broke, Lord Willoughby, *The Passing Years* (London, 1924).

De Mille, A.G. *Henry George: Citizen of the World* (Chapel Hill, 1950).

Denison, G.A. *Why Should the Bishops Continue to Sit in the House of Lords?* (London, 1850).

Devyr, T.A. *The Odd Book of the Nineteenth Century, or 'Chivalry' in Modern Days* (New York, 1882).

Dilke, C. *On the Cost of the Crown* (London, 1871).

Dixie, F. 'The Horrors of Sport'; *Humane Review*, VI (1906), 36–64.

Edwards, G. *From Crow-Scaring to Westminster: An Autobiography* (London, 1922).

Eldershaw, F. *Australia as it Really is, in its Life, Scenery and Adventures* (London, 1850).

Escott, T.H. *Society in London* (London, 1885).

Estorick, E. *The Biography of Sir Stafford Cripps* (London, 1949).

Evans, H. *Our Old Nobility* (London, 1907).

Fels, M. *Joseph Fels* (London, 1920).

Fifty Points for Labour and a Hundred Against the Tories and Liberals (Labour Party, 1929).

Fitzgibbon, E.G. *Essence of Progress and Poverty: Extracted from the American of Henry George and Done into and Dealt with in Plain English* (London, 1891).

Fordham, M. *The Rebuilding of Rural England* (London, 1924).

Fox-Bourne, H.R. *The House of Lords* (London, 1881).

Freeman, E.A. *The Morality of Field Sports* (London, 1914 edn).

Froude, J.A. *Oceana or England and Her Colonies* (London, 1886).

Gardiner, R. 'Rural Reconstruction' in Massingham, H.J. (ed.), *England and the Small Farmer: A Symposium* (London, 1940), pp. 91–107.

Geiger, G.R. *Henry George: A Biography* (London, 1939).

George, H. *Progress and Poverty: An Inquiry into the Causes of Industrial Depression* (London, 1884 edn).

——. 'The Reduction to Iniquity', *Nineteenth Century*, XVI (1884), 138–9.

——. *Thy Kingdom Come: An Address by Henry George* (Glasgow, 1888).

——. *Moses: An Address by Henry George* (United Committee for the Taxation of Land Values, n.d.).

Gide, C. *Principles of Political Economy* (London, 1912).

Glasfurd, A.L. 'Fascism and the English Tradition', *Fascist Quarterly*, I (1935), 360–4.

Gomme, G.L. *The Village Community with Special Reference to the Origin and Form of its Survival in Britain* (London, 1890).

Gore, J. *King George V: A Personal Memoir* (London, 1941).

Grindon, L.H. *Lancashire: Brief Historical and Descriptive Notes* (London, 1882).

Gwynn, S. and Tuckwell, G.M. *The Life of the Rt. Hon. Sir Charles Dilke* (2 vols, London, 1917).

Hammond, J.L. and B. *The Village Labourer* (London, 1911).

Harford, C.H. *Philip Henry Wicksteed: His Life and Works* (London, 1931).

Hargrave, J. *Social Credit Clearly Explained: 101 Questions Answered* (London, 1945).

Haxey, S. *Tory MP* (London, 1939).

Heath, R. *The English Peasant: Studies Historical, Local and Biographical* (London, 1893).

Higginson, A.H. *Foxhunting: Theory and Practice* (London, 1948).

H.R.H. The Duke of Windsor, *The Crown and the People 1902–1953* (London, 1953).

Hobhouse, L.T. *The Labour Movement* (London, 1908), ch. 4.

Hobson, J.A. 'The Influence of Henry George in England', *Fortnightly Review*, LXII (1897), 835–44.

Hodge, J. *Workman's Cottage to Windsor Castle* (London, 1931).

Hollis, C. *Quality or Equality?* (London, 1944).

Holyoake, G.J. *Sixty Years of an Agitator's Life* (London, 1906).

Howard, P. 'Back to Earth' in Harman, R. (ed.), *Countryside Mood* (London, 1943), pp. 45–64.

Howitt, W. *The Aristocracy of England: A History for the People* (London, 1856).

Hudson, R. *George V: Our Sailor King* (London, 1910).

Hughan, S. *Hereditary Peers and Hereditary Paupers* (London, 1885).

Hughes, E. (ed.), *Keir Hardie: His Writings and Speeches from 1888 to 1915* (Glasgow, 1924).

Hyde, D. *I Believed: The Autobiography of a Former British Communist* (London, 1950).

Hyndman, H. *The Record of an Adventurous Life* (London, 1911).

Jaeger, G. *Health Culture* (London, 1902).

Jephson, H. *The Platform: Its Rise and Progress* (2 vols, 1892).

Jerrold, D. *The History of St. Giles and St. James's* (London, 1851).

——. 'On the Influence of Hilaire Belloc' in Woodruff, D. (ed.), *For Hilaire Belloc: Essays in Honour of his Seventy-Second Birthday* (London, 1942), pp. 9–17.

'Jif', *Bumbles, Drones and Working Bees: A Lecture* (London, 1881).

Johnson, J. *The Men Behind the War: A Startling Exposure of the Financial Interests who are Exploiting the War* (Communist Party of Great Britain, 1940).

Johnston, T. *Our Noble Families* (Glasgow, 1916 edn).

Kebbel, T.E. The *Battle of Life: A Retrospect of Sixty Years* (London, 1912).

Kenworthy, J.C. *Sailors, Statesmen and Others* (London, 1933).

Kirby, C. 'The Attack on the English Game Laws in the Forties', *Journal of Modern History*, IV (1932), 18–37.

Kirwan, D.J. *Palace and Hovel or Phases of London Life: Being Personal Observations of an American in London* (London, 1870).

Knight, C. *Passages in a Working Life during Half a Century with a Prelude to Early Reminiscences* (2 vols, London, 1864).

Kropotkin, P. *Fields, Factories and Workshops* (London, 1901).

Land Tax Cartoons from the Morning Leader Illustrating Mr. Lloyd George's Great Speech at Limehouse (London, 1909).

Lees, F. *Dr F.R. Lees: A Biography* (London, 1904).

Lees-Milne, J. *Caves of Ice: Diaries, 1946 and 47* (London, 1983).

Lewis, H. *Free Trade in Land* (Bath, 1880).

Lloyd George, D. *Better Times: Speeches by the Rt. Hon. David Lloyd George* (London, 1910).

Lord Bramwell, *Nationalisation of Land: A Review of Mr Henry George's Progress and Poverty* (Liberty and Property Defence League, 1884).

Lord Rosebery, *The Reform of the House of Lords* (Edinburgh, 1884).

Lord Ribblesdale, *The Queen's Hounds and Stag-Hunting: Some Recollections* (London, 1897).

MacDonald, D.C. (ed.), *Birthright in Land by William Ogilvie* (London, 1891).

MacDonald, J.R. *Tories and the House of Lords: An Exposure of Their Trickery* (London, 1910).

——. 'The Papers of Peter Alfred Taylor', *Socialist Review*, V (1910), 208.

——. 'A Plea for Puritanism', *The Socialist Review*, 1 February 1912, pp. 422–30.

Macfadyen, D. *Sir Ebenezer Howard and the Town Planning Movement* (Manchester, 1933).

Mackenzie, A. *The Peers and the Franchise: The House of Lords* (London, 1884).

MacNeill, J.G.S. *Titled Corruption: The Sordid Origins of Some Irish Peerages* (Dublin, 1894).

Macpherson, H.A. *The Pheasant: Its Natural History* (London, 1895).

Macpherson, W.C. *The Baronage and the Senate or the House of Lords in the Past, the Present and the Future* (London, 1893).

Mairet, P. *Aristocracy and the Meaning of Class Rule: An Essay Upon Aristocracy Past and Future* (London, 1931).

Massingham, H.J. *Chiltern Country* (London, 1940).

——. *Remembrance* (London, 1941).

——. *The English Countryman: A Study of the English Tradition* (London, 1942).

Masterman, C.F.C. (ed.), *The Heart of the Empire: Discussion of Problems of Modern City Life* (London, 1901).

Matthew, H.C.G (ed.), *The Gladstone Diaries*, XII (Oxford, 1986).

McKenna, M. *The Captive Republic: A History of Republicanism in Australia 1788–1996* (Cambridge, 1996).

Mill, J. 'Aristocracy', *The London Review*, II (1836), 283–306.

Mill, J.S. *Autobiography of John Stuart Mill* (London, 1873).

Mitford, J. *A Peep into W-r Castle* (London, 1820).

Morant, G.F. *Game Preservers and Bird Preservers: Which are our Friends?* (London, 1875).

Morley, J. *The Life of Richard Cobden* (2 vols, London, 1896).

Mosley, O. *The Alternative* (London, 1947).

——. *My Life* (London, 1968).

Mulgan, J. (ed.), *Poems of Freedom* (London, 1938).

Munger, T.T. *Land Tenure* (n.d., London).

Murray, T.D. and White, A.S. *Sir Samuel Baker: A Memoir* (London, 1895).

Orwell, G. *The Lion and the Unicorn* (London, 1962).

Orwin, C.S. *Speed the Plough* (London, 1942).

Paget, G. *The History of the Althorp and Pytchley Hunt 1634–1920* (London, 1937).

Partington, S. *Truth Further Vindicated. Winter Hill Right of Way Dispute: New Light on Bolton History* (Bolton, 1899).

Pearce-Edgcombe, *The Last Function of the House of Lords* (Manchester, 1884).

Peers and the Budget: Why Some of them Voted against it (Birmingham, 1910).

Peers and the People: What shall We Do with the House of Lords? (London, 1884).

Peers' Plunder and the People's Poverty (Liverpool, 1884).

Peers v. the People: What's the Use of the House of Lords? Manchester, 1884).

Percival, P. *Failsworth Folk and Failsworth Memories* (Manchester, 1901).

Poems of Algernon Charles Swinburne in Six Volumes (London, 1904).

Ponsonby, A. *The Decline of Aristocracy* (London, 1912).

——. *Queen Victoria* (London, 1933).

Post, L.F. *The Prophet of San Francisco: Personal Memoirs and Interpretations of Henry George* (New York, 1930).

Potter, G. 'The Labourers and the Vote', *The Nineteenth Century*, III (1878), 53–70.

'Publius', *The House of Lords: What shall We Do with it?* (Manchester, 1884).

Raine, G.E. *Lloyd George and the Land: An Exposure and an Appeal* (London, 1914).

Read, H. *Poetry and Anarchism* (London, 1947).

Reynolds, G.W.M. *The Mysteries of the Court of London* (2 vols, London, 1850).

Reynolds, S. and Woolley, B. and T. *Seems So! A Working-Class View of Politics* (London, 1911).

Rider Haggard, H. *Rural England: Being an Account of Agricultural and Social Researches Carried Out in the Years 1901 and 1902* (2 vols, London, 1902).

Roberts, S. *The Squatting Age in Australia, 1835–1847* (Melbourne, 1935).

Rogers, J.E.T. *Letters of J.E. Thorold Rogers and Mr Henry Tupper on the History and Working of the Laws of Promogeniture and Entail* (Manchester, 1864).

——. *Cobden and Modern Political Opinion: Essays on Certain Political Topics* (London, 1873).

——. *Six Centuries of Work and Wages: The History of English Labour* (London, 1903 edn).

Rose, H. *Henry George: A Biographical, Anecdotal and Critical Sketch* (London, 1884).

Rudkin, O.D. *Thomas Spence and His Connections* (New York, 1927).

Russell, G.W.E. (ed.), *Sir Wilfred Lawson: A Memoir* (London, 1909).

Russell, H. *With the Prince in the East: A Record of the Royal Visit to India and Japan* (London, 1922).

Salt, H. 'Shelley as a Pioneer', *Humane Review*, II (1902), 54–66.

Salt, H. *Seventy Years among Savages* (London, 1921).

Schreiner, O. *Woman and Labour* (London, 1911).

Seebohm, F. *The English Village Community* (London, 1883).

Sewell, J.P.C. (ed.), *Personal Letters of King Edward VII* (London, 1930).

Shaw, G.B. 'Transition', *Fabian Essays in Socialism* (London, 1889), pp. 173–201.

——. *Sixteen Self-Sketches* (London, 1949).

——. *The Intelligent Woman's Guide to Socialism and Capitalism* (London, 1928).

Sheffield Clarion Ramblers Guidebooks (Sheffield, 1936–1948).

Sidelights on the Cliveden Set: Hitler's Friends in Britain (Communist Party of Great Britain, 1938).

Sketchley, J. *Shall the People Govern Themselves?* (London, 1896).

Smith, F.D. and Wilcox, B. *Sold for Two Farthings: Being the Views of Countryfolk on Cruelty to Animals* (London, 1950).

Snowden, P. *The Socialist's Budget* (London, 1907).

——. *An Autobiography* (2 vols, London, 1934).

Sprigge, S.S. *The Life and Times of Thomas Wakley* (London, 1897).

Springhall, L.M. *Labouring Life in Norfolk Villages 1834–1914* (London, 1936).

Standring, G. *The People's History of the Aristocracy* (London, 1891).

Stanley, R. (ed.), *W. Archer, Tourist to the Antipodes: William Archer's Australian Journal* (St Lucia, Queensland, 1977).

Stansfield, A. *Essays and Sketches: Being a Few Selections from the Prose Works of Twenty Years* (Manchester, 1897).

Stead, W.T. *Fifty Years of the House of Lords* (London, 1880).

——. 'The General Election, 1895: The Poster in Politics', *Review of Reviews*, XII (1895), 168–76.

——. *Peers or People? The House of Lords Weighed in the Balance and Found Wanting* (London, 1907).

Stewart, W. *Robert Burns and the Common People* (London, 1925).

Stockman, H.R. *Labour and the Lords: An Indictment* (Labour Party, 1909).

Storey, H. *The House of Lords: History of the Fight between the People and the Peers, Statement of Liberal Policy, Examination of the Government's Proposals* (Liberal Party, 1927).

Stratton, J. *The Decline and Fall of the Royal Buckhounds* (Humanitarian League, 1901).

Tawney, R.H. *The Agrarian Problem in the Sixteenth Century* (London, 1912).

Taylor, P.A. *The Game Laws: Speech by Mr P.A. Taylor in the House of Commons, March 2 1880* (Anti-Game Law League, 1880).

Thorold, A.L. *The Life of Henry Labouchere* (London, 1913).

Tracey, H. (ed), *The Book of the Labour Party: Its History, Growth, Policy and Leaders* (London, 1925).

Trollope, A. *An Autobiography* (London, 1883).

Wakefield, A.B. *Ernest Jones, the People's Friend* (London, 1887).

Wallace, A.R. *Land Nationalisation, its Necessity and its Aims* (London, 1896 edn).

Walton, A.A. *History of the Landed Tenures of Great Britain and Ireland from the Norman Conquest to the Present Time* (London, 1865).

Ward, M. *Gilbert Keith Chesterton* (London, 1944).

Webb, S. and B. 'What is Socialism? The Development of Science, Art and Religion Untrammelled by Plutocracy', *New Statesman*, 19 July 1913, pp. 461–3.

Wedgwood, J.C. *Henry George for Socialists* (ILP, 1908).

——. *Memoirs of a Fighting Man* (London, 1941).

White, A. *The Problems of a Great City* (London, 1886).

White, R.G. *England Within and Without* (London, 1881).

Who Backs Mosley? Fascist Promise and Fascist Performance (Labour Research Department, 1934).

Wicksteed, C. *The Land for the People: How to Obtain it, and How to Manage it* (London, 1894).

Wilkinson, J.F. 'Pages in the History of Allotments', *Contemporary Review*, LXV (1894), 532–44.

Williamson, H. *The Story of a Norfolk Farm* (London, 1942).

Woolacott, J.E. *The House of Lords: A Lecture* (National Secular Society, 1884).

Secondary sources

Adonis, A. 'Aristocracy, Agriculture and Liberalism: The Politics, Finance and Estates of the Third Lord Carrington', *Historical Journal*, XXXI (1988), 871–97.
——. *Making Aristocracy Work: The Peerage and the Political System in Britain 1884–1914* (Oxford, 1992).
Allen, D.E. *The Naturalist in Britain: A Social History* (London, 1976).
Allfrey, A. *Edward VII and His Jewish Court* (London, 1991).
Anderson, M. *Fighter for Freedom* (London, 1953).
Anderson, O. *A Liberal State at War: English Politics and Economics during the Crimean War* (London, 1967).
Archer, F. *Poacher's Pie* (London, 1976).
Armytage, W.H.G. *Heavens Below: Utopian Experiments in England 1560–1960* (London, 1961).
Ashby, M.K. *Joseph Ashby of Tysoe 1859–1919* (Cambridge, 1961).
Barker, C.A. *Henry George* (Oxford, 1955).
Barker, E.A. *The Forbidden Land: A Plea for Public Access to Mountains, Moors and Other Waste Lands in Great Britain* (London, 1924).
Barker, M. *Gladstone and Radicalism: The Reconstruction of Liberal Policy in Britain 1885–1894* (Brighton, 1975).
Barrow, L. and Bullock, I. *Democratic Ideas and the British Labour Movement 1880–1914* (Cambridge, 1997).
Barry, E.D. *Nationalisation in British Politics: The Historical Background* (London, 1965).
Baxendale, J. '"I had seen a lot of Englands": J.B. Priestly, Englishness and the People', *History Workshop Journal*, LI (2001), 87–111.
Beaumont, M. 'William Reeves and Late Victorian Radical Publishing: Unpacking the Bellamy Library', *History Workshop Journal*, LV (2003), 91–110.
Belchem, J. 'Republicanism, Popular Constitutionalism and the Radical Platform in Early Nineteenth Century England', *Social History*, VI (1981), 1–35.
——. *Popular Radicalism in Nineteenth Century Britain* (London, 1996).
Bence-Jones, M. *Twilight of the Ascendancy* (London, 1987).
Berridge, V. 'Popular Sunday Newspapers and Mid-Victorian Society' in Boyce, G., Wingate, P. and Curran, J. (eds), *Newspaper History from the Seventeenth Century to the Present Day* (London, 1978), pp. 252–64.
Biagini, E.F. *Liberty, Retrenchment and Reform: Popular Liberalism in the Age of Gladstone 1860–1880* (Cambridge, 1992).
Biagini, E.F. and Reid, H.J. 'Introduction' in Biagini and Reid (eds), *Currents of Radicalism: Popular Radicalism, Organised Labour and Party Politics in Britain 1850–1914* (Cambridge, 1991), pp. 1–19.
Bourke, J. *An Intimate History of Killing: Face-to-Face Killing in Twentieth Century Warfare* (London, 1999).
Boyes, G. *The Imagined Village: Culture, Ideology and the English Folk Revival* (Manchester, 1993).
Brewer, J. *Party Ideology and Popular Politics at the Accession of George III* (London, 1976).
Bronstein, J.L. *Land Reform and Working-Class Experience in Britain and the United States* (Stanford, 1999).

Bronstein, J.L. 'From the Land of Liberty to Land Monopoly: The United States in a Chartist Context' in Ashton, O., Fyson, R. and Roberts, S. (eds), *The Chartist Legacy* (Woodbridge, 1999), pp. 147–70.
Brooke-Shepherd, G. *The Uncle of Europe: The Social and Diplomatic Life of Edward VII* (London, 1975).
Bull, P. *Land, Politics and Nationalism: A Study of the Irish Land Question* (Dublin, 1996).
Bullock, I. and Reynolds, S. 'Direct Legislation and Socialism: How British and French Socialists Viewed the Referendum in 1890', *History Workshop Journal*, XXIV (1987), 62–81.
Burrow, J.W. *The Crisis of Reason: European Thought 1848–1914* (New Haven, 2000).
Bush, M.L. *What is Love: Richard Carlile's Philosophy of Sex* (London, 1998).
Butler, D. 'By-elections and their Interpretation' in Cook, C. and Ramsden, J. (eds), *By-elections in British Politics* (London, 1997), pp. 1–12.
Cahill, K. *Who Owns Britain: The Hidden Facts Behind Landownership in the U.K. and Ireland* (Edinburgh, 2001).
Cain, P. *Hobson and Imperialism: Radicalism, New Liberalism and Finance 1887–1938* (Oxford, 2002).
Calder, A. *The Myth of the Blitz* (London, 1991).
Camplin, J. *The Rise of the Plutocrats: Wealth and Power in Edwardian England* (London, 1978).
Cannadine, D. *The Decline and Fall of the British Aristocracy* (London, 1990).
——. *G. M. Trevelyan: A Life in History* (London, 1992).
——. *Aspects of Aristocracy: Grandeur and Decline in Modern Britain* (London, 1994).
——. *Ornamentalism: How the British Saw their Empire* (London, 2001).
——. *In Churchill's Shadow* (London, 2003).
Cannon, M. *John Norton, 1858–1916: An Australian Populist* (Melbourne, 1981).
Cartmill, M. *A View to a Death in the Morning: Hunting and Nature Through History* (New York, 1993).
Chase, M. *The People's Farm: English Radical Agrarianism 1775–1840* (Oxford, 1988).
——. 'This is no Claptrap: This is our Heritage' in Shaw, C. and Chase, M. (eds), *The Imagined Past: History as Nostalgia* (Manchester, 1989), pp. 128–46.
——. 'Rolf Gardiner: An Inter-War Cross-Cultural Case Study' in Hake, B. and Marriott, S. (eds), *Adult Education Between Cultures* (Leeds, 1994), pp. 225–41.
Churchill, R.S. *Lord Derby: 'King of Lancashire'* (London, 1959).
Claeys, G. 'The Example of America a Warning to England? The Transformation of America in British Radicalism and Socialism 1790–1850' in Chase, M. and Dyck, I. (eds), *Living and Learning: Essays in Honour of J.F.C. Harrison* (Aldershot, 1996), pp. 66–80.
Clark, A. 'The Politics of Seduction in English Popular Culture, 1748–1848' in Jean Radford (ed.), *The Progress of Romance: The Politics of Popular Fiction* (London, 1986), pp. 46–70.
Clark, J. *English Society 1688–1832* (Oxford, 1986).
Clarke, P. 'The Social Democratic Theory of the Class Struggle' in Winter, J. (ed.), *The Working Class in Modern British History* (1983), pp. 3–18.
Coffey, J. 'Democracy and Popular Religion: Moody and Sankey's Mission to Britain 1873–75' in Biagini, E. (ed.), *Citizenship and Community: Liberals,*

Radicals and Collective Identities in the British Isles 1865–1931 (Cambridge, 1996), pp. 93–119.

Colley, L. *Britons: Forging the Nation 1707–1830* (New Haven, 1992).

Collins, M. 'The Fall of the English Gentleman: The National Character in Decline *c*.1918–1970', *Historical Research*, LXXV (2002), 90–111.

Colls, R. *Identity of England* (Oxford, 2003).

Conford, P. *The Origins of the Organic Movement* (Edinburgh, 2001).

Cord, S.B. *Henry George: Dreamer or Realist?* (Philadelphia, 1965).

Crouch, D. and Ward, C. *The Allotment: Its Language and Culture* (London, 1988).

Crowther, M.A. 'The Tramp' in Porter, R. (ed.), *Myths of the English* (London, 1992), pp. 91–113.

Curtis, L.P. 'Stopping the Hunt 1881–1882: An Aspect of the Irish Land War' in Philpin, C.H.E. (ed.), *Nationalism and Popular Protest in Ireland* (Cambridge, 1987), pp. 349–402.

Dallek, R. *John F. Kennedy, An Unfinished Life 1917–1963* (London, 2003).

Darley, G. *Villages of Vision* (London, 1975).

Dart, G. '"Flash Style": Pierce Egan and Literary London, 1820–28', *History Workshop Journal* no. LI (2001), 180–205.

D'A. Jones, P. *Henry George and British Socialism* (New York, 1991).

De Groot, G.J. *The First World War* (London, 1999).

Donald, D. '"Beastly Sights": The Treatment of Animals as a Moral Theme in Representations of London *c*.1820–1850' in Donald, D. (ed.), *The Metropolis and its Image: Constructing Identities for London c.1750–1950* (London, 1999), pp. 48–78.

Douglas, R. *Land, People and Politics: A History of the Land Question in the United Kingdom 1878–1952* (London, 1976).

Dutton, D. *Simon: A Political Biography of Sir John Simon* (London, 1992).

Ellis, J.S. 'Reconciling the Celt: British National Identity and the 1911 Investiture of the Prince of Wales', *Journal of British Studies*, XXXVII (1988), 391–418.

Fielding, S., Thompson, P. and Tiratsoo, N. *'England Arise': The Labour Party and Popular Politics in 1940s Britain* (Manchester, 1995).

Finn, M.C. *After Chartism: Class and Nation in English Radical Politics 1848–1874* (Cambridge, 1993).

Foster, R.F. *Lord Randolph Churchill* (Oxford, 1981).

——. *Paddy and Mr Punch: Connections in English and Irish History* (London, 1993).

Fowler, W.S. *A Study in Radicalism and Dissent: The Life and Times of H.J. Wilson 1833–1914* (London, 1961).

Fussell, P. *The Great War and Modern Memory* (London, 1975).

Gash, N. *Politics in the Age of Peel* (London, 1953).

——. *Reaction and Reconstruction in English Politics 1832–1852* (London, 1965).

——. *Sir Robert Peel* (London, 1972).

Gatrell, V.A.C. *The Hanging Tree: Execution and the English People 1770–1868* (Cambridge, 1996).

Gaze, J. *Figures in a Landscape: A History of the National Trust* (Frome, 1988).

Goodwyn, L. *Democratic Promise: The Populist Movement in America* (New York, 1976).

Gould, P.C. *Early Green Politics: Back to Nature, Back to the Land, and Socialism in Britain 1880–1900* (Brighton, 1988).

Griffiths, C. 'Remembering Tolpuddle: Rural History and Commemoration in the Inter-War Labour Movement', *History Workshop Journal*, XXXXIV (1997), 145–69.

Griffiths, R. *Fellow Travellers of the Right: British Enthusiasts for Nazi Germany 1933–39* (London, 1980).
——. *Patriotism Perverted* (London, 1998).
Grigor, I.F. *Highland Resistance: The Radical Tradition in the Scottish North* (Edinburgh, 2000).
Harling, P. 'Rethinking "Old Corruption"', *Past and Present*, CXXXXVII (1995), 127–58.
Harling, P. and Mandler, P. 'From Fiscal-Military State to *Laissez-Faire* State, *Journal of British Studies*, XXXII (1993), 44–70.
Harris, J. *Private Lives, Public Spirit: Britain 1870–1914* (Oxford, 1993).
Harrison, B. *Drink and the Victorians: The Temperance Question in England* (new edn, Keele, 1994).
Harrison, B. and Hollis, P. (eds), *Robert Lowery: Radical and Chartist* (London, 1979).
Havighurst, A.F. *Radical Journalist: H.W. Massingham* (Cambridge, 1974).
Hayward, R. 'From the Millennial Future to the Unconscious Past: The Transformation of Prophecy in Early Twentieth Century Britain' in Taithe, B. and Thornton, T. (eds), *Prophecy: The Power of Inspired Language in History, 1300–2000* (Stroud, 1997), pp. 161–80.
Haywood, I. 'George W.M. Reynolds, and the "Trafalgar Square Revolution": Radicalism, the Carnivalesque and Popular Culture in Mid-Victorian England', *Journal of Victorian Culture*, VII (2002), 23–59.
——. 'Graphic Narratives and Discoveries of Horror: The Feminisation of Labour in Nineteenth Century Radical Fiction' in Klaus, H. Gustav and Knight, S. (eds), *British Industrial Fictions* (Cardiff, 2002), pp. 5–23.
Heilbroner, R.L. *The Wordly Philosophers* (New York, 1953).
Hendrick, G. and Hendrick, W. (eds), *The Savour of Salt: A Henry Salt Anthology* (Fontwell, 1989).
Hewison, R. *The Heritage Industry: Britain in a Climate of Decline* (London, 1987).
Hill, C. (ed.), 'The Norman Yoke', *Puritanism and Revolution* (London, 1955).
——. *Liberty Against the Law: Some Seventeenth Century Controversies* (London, 1996).
Hopkins, H. *The Long Affray: The Poaching Wars 1760–1914* (London, 1985).
Howe, A. 'Towards the "Hungry Forties": Free Trade in Britain *c.*1880–1906' in Biagini, E.F. *Citizenship and Community: Liberals, Radicals and Collective Identities in the British Isles 1865–1931* (Cambridge, 1996), pp. 193–218.
Howell, R. 'Who Needs Another Cromwell? The Nineteenth Century Image of Oliver Cromwell' in Richardson, R.C. (ed.), *Images of Oliver Cromwell: Essays by and for Roger Howell Jr* (Manchester, 1993), pp. 90–8.
Howkins, A. 'From Diggers to Dongas: The Land in English Radicalism', *History Workshop Journal*, LIV (2002), 1–23.
Humphreys, A. 'G.W.M. Reynolds, Popular Literature and Popular Politics', *Victorian Periodicals Review*, XVI (1983), 78–89.
Hyde, H.M. *Mr and Mrs Beeton* (London, 1951).
Innes, J. 'Jonathan Clark, Social History and England's "Ancien Regime"', *Past and Present*, CXV (1987), 165–200.
Itzkowitz, D.C. *Peculiar Privilege: A Social History of English Foxhunting 1753–1885* (Cambridge, 1977).
James, R.R. *Rosebery* (London, 1963).

——. (ed.), *Chips: The Diaries of Sir Henry Channon* (London, 1967).

Jenkins, R. *Asquith* (London, 1964).

——. *Gladstone* (London, 1995).

Jerrold, D. 'On the Influence of Hilaire Belloc' in Woodruff, D. (ed.), *For Hilaire Belloc: Essays in Honour of his Seventy-Second Birthday* (London, 1942), pp. 9–17.

Joad, C.E.M. *The Untutored Townsman's Invasion of the Country* (London, 1945).

Jones, D.J.V. 'The Poacher: A Study in Victorian Crime and Protest', *Historical Journal*, XXII (1979), 825–60.

Jones, G.S. *Languages of Class: Studies in English Working Class History* (Cambridge, 1983).

Joyce, P. *Visions of the People: Industrial England and the Question of Class, 1848–1914* (Cambridge, 1991).

——. *Democratic Subjects: The Self and the Social in Nineteenth Century England* (Cambridge, 1994).

Karsten, P. *Patriot-Heroes in England and America: Political Symbolism and Changing Values Over Three Centuries* (Madison, 1978).

Kean, H. 'The Feminist and Socialist Response to Vivisection', *History Workshop Journal*, IXXXX (1995), 6–32.

Keane, J. *Tom Paine: A Political Life* (London, 1995).

Keith, W.J. *The Rural Tradition* (Toronto, 1975).

Kent, W. *John Burns, Labour's Lost Leader* (London, 1950).

Kudak, S. '"A Sword of a Song": Swinburne's Republican Aesthetics in Songs Before Sunrise', *Victorian Studies*, XXXXIII (2001), 253–78.

Landry, D. *The Invention of the Countryside: Hunting, Walking and Ecology in English Literature 1671–1831* (London, 2001).

Lansbury, C. *Arcady in Australia: The Evocation of Australia in Nineteenth Century English Literature* (Melbourne, 1970).

——. *The Old Brown Dog: Women, Workers and Vivisection in Edwardian England* (Madison, 1985).

Lawrence, E.P. *Henry George in the British Isles* (Michigan, 1957).

Lawrence, J. 'Popular Radicalism and the Socialist Revival in Britain', *Journal of British Studies*, XXXI (1992), 163–86.

Lawson, S. *The Archibald Paradox: A Strange Case of Authorship* (Ringwood, 1983).

Lownie, A.L. *John Buchan: The Presbyterian Cavalier* (London, 2002).

Lunn, K. 'Political Anti-semitism before 1914: Fascism's Heritage' in Lunn, K. and Thurlow, R.C. (eds), *British Fascism* (London, 1980), pp. 20–40.

Lynch, P. *The Liberal Party in Rural England 1885–1910* (Oxford, 2002).

Maccoby, S. *The English Radical Tradition 1763–1914* (London, 1952).

Mackenzie, J.M. *The Empire of Nature: Hunting and Conservation* (Manchester, 1987).

Mairet, P. *Aristocracy and the Meaning of Class Rule: An Essay Upon Aristocracy Past and Future* (London, 1931).

Maitland, A. *Speke and the Discovery of the Nile* (London, 1971).

Mandler, P. *The Rise and Fall of the Stately Home* (New Haven, 1997).

Mares, D. 'A Radical in Wales: Alfred A. Walton and Mid-Victorian Welsh Popular Radicalism', *The Welsh History Review*, XXI (2002), 271–91.

Marsh, J. *Back to the Land: The Pastoral Impulse in Victorian England 1880–1914* (London, 1982).

Martin, D. 'Land Reform' in Hollis, P. (ed.), *Pressure from Without in Early Victorian England* (London, 1974), pp. 131–58.

——. *John Stuart Mill and the Land Question* (Hull, 1981).

Martin, G. *Bunyip Aristocracy: The New South Wales Constitution Debate of 1853 and Hereditary Institutions in the British Colonies* (Dover, 1986).

Matless, D. *Landscape and Englishness* (London, 1998).

Matthew, H.C.G. 'Disraeli, Gladstone and the Politics of Mid-Victorian Budgets', *Historical Journal*, XXII (1979), 615–43.

——. *Gladstone 1875–1898* (Oxford, 1995).

McBriar, A.M. *Fabian Socialism and English Politics 1884–1918* (Cambridge, 1962).

McCalman, I. *Radical Underworld: Prophets, Revolutionaries and Pornographers in London, 1795–1840* (Oxford, 1988).

McCord, N. 'Victorian Newcastle Observed: The Diary of Richard Lowry', *Northern History*, XXXVII (2000), 237–59.

Mckibben, R. *The Evolution of the Labour Party 1910–1914* (London, 1974).

——. *Classes and Culture in England 1918–1951* (London, 1998).

McLean, I. *Keir Hardie* (London, 1975).

McWilliam, R. 'Radicalism and Popular Culture: The Tichborne Case and the Politics of "Fair Play"' in Biagini, E.F. and Reid, A. (eds), *Currents of Radicalism: Popular Radicalism, Organised Labour and Party Politics in Britain, 1850–1914* (Cambridge, 1991), pp. 44–64.

——. 'The Mysteries of G.W.M. Reynolds: Radicalism and Melodrama in Victorian Britain' in Chase, M. and Dyck, I. (eds), *Living and Learning: Essays in Honour of J.F.C. Harrison* (Aldershot, 1996), pp. 182–98.

——. *Popular Politics in Nineteenth Century England* (London, 1998).

Meek, D.E. 'The Land Question Answered from the Bible: The Land Issue and the Development of a Highland Theory of Liberation', *Scottish Geographical Magazine*, CIII (1987), 84–9.

Moody, T.W. *Davitt and Irish Revolution 1846–1882* (Oxford, 1981).

More, J. 'Wallace's Malthusian Moment: The Common Context Revisited' in Lightman, B. (ed.), *Victorian Science in Context* (Chicago, 1997), pp. 290–311.

Morgan, K.O. *David Lloyd George: Welsh Radical and World Statesman* (Cardiff, 1963).

Murray, B.K. *The People's Budget 1909–1910* (Oxford, 1980).

Nairn, T. *After Britain: New Labour and the Return of Scotland* (London, 2000).

Nash, D. 'Charles Bradlaugh, India and the many Chameleon Destinations of Republicanism' in Nash, D. and Taylor, A. (eds), *Republicanism in Victorian Society* (Stroud, 2000), pp. 106–24.

Newby, H. *Green and Pleasant Land: Social Change in Rural Britain* (London, 1979).

Norton, W. 'Malcolm McNeill and the Emigrationist Alternative to Highland Land Reform 1886–1893', *The Scottish Historical Review*, LXX (1991), 16–30.

Offer, A. *Property and Politics 1870–1914: Landlordism, Law, Ideology and Urban Development in England* (Cambridge, 1981).

Oldfield, A. *The Great Republic of the Southern Seas* (Melbourne, 1999).

O'Leary, C. *The Elimination of Corrupt Practises in British Elections* (Oxford, 1962).

Owen, F. *Lloyd George: His Life and Times* (London, 1954).

Packer, I. *Lloyd George, Liberalism and the Land* (Woodbridge, 2001).

Palmer, C. 'Christianity, Englishness and the Southern English Countryside: A Study of the Work of H.J. Massingham', *Social and Cultural Geography*, III (2002), 25–38.

Parry, J. *The Rise and Fall of Liberal Government in Victorian England* (New Haven, 1993).

Passmore, J. 'The Treatment of Animals', *Journal of the History of Ideas*, XXXVI (1975), 195–218.

Pearson, J. *Edward the Rake* (London, 1975).

Pelling, H. *America and the British Left from Bright to Bevan* (London, 1956).

Perkin, H. (ed.), 'Land Reform and Class Conflict in Victorian Britain', *The Structured Crowd: Essays in British Social History* (Brighton, 1981), pp. 100–35.

Perrott, R. *The Aristocrats: A Portrait of Britain's Nobility and Their Way of Life Today* (London, 1968).

Peters, C. *Thackeray: A Writer's Life* (Stroud, 1999).

Pimlott, B. *Hugh Dalton* (London, 1985).

Plowright, J. 'Political Economy and Christian Polity: The Influence of Henry George in England Reassessed', *Victorian Studies*, XXX (1987), 235–52.

Pocock, J.G. *The Ancient Constitution and the Feudal Law* (Cambridge, 1957).

Price, R. *British Society 1680–1880: Dynamism, Containment, Change* (Cambridge, 2000).

Prochaska, F. *Royal Bounty: The Making of a Welfare Monarchy* (London, 1995).

Pugh, M. *Lloyd George* (London, 1988).

Raby, P. *Alfred Russel Wallace: A Life* (London, 2001).

Read, D. *Cobden and Bright: A Victorian Political Partnership* (London, 1967).

Redfearn, D. *Tolstoy: Principles for a New World Order* (London, 1992).

Reid, F. *Keir Hardie: The Making of a Socialist* (London, 1978).

Ridley, J. *Fox Hunting* (London, 1990).

Ritvo, H. *The Animal Estate: The English and Other Creatures in the Victorian Age* (New Haven, 1987).

Roberts, A. *Eminent Churchillians* (London, 1994).

Roe, M. *Kenealy and the Tichborne Claimant: A Study in Mid-Victorian Populism* (Melbourne, 1974).

Rose, N. *The Cliveden Set: Portrait of an Exclusive Fraternity* (London, 2001).

Rubenstein, W.D. 'New Men of Wealth', *Past and Present*, LXXXXII (1981), 125–47.

Rumsey, C. *The Rise and Fall of British Republican Clubs 1871–1874* (Oswestry, 2000).

Rose, J. *The Intellectual Life of the British Working Classes* (New Haven, 2001).

Russell, A.K. *Liberal Landslide: The General Election of 1906* (Newton Abbott, 1973).

Samuel, R. *Island Stories: Unravelling Britain* (London, 1998).

Sayer, K. *Country Cottages: A Cultural History* (Manchester, 2000).

Searle, G.R. *A New England? Peace and War 1886–1918* (Oxford, 2004).

Scates, B. '"Wobblers": Single Taxers in the Labour Movement 1889–1899', *Historical Studies*, XXI (1981), 174–96.

Scates, B. '"Millennium or Pandemonium?": Radicalism in the Labour Movement, Sydney, 1889–1899', *Labour History*, L (1986), 72–92.

——. *A New Australia: Citizenship, Radicalism and the First Republic* (Cambridge, 1997).

Schreuder, D.M. 'The Making of Mr Gladstone's Posthumous Career: The Role of Morley and Knaplund as "Monument Masons" 1903–1927' in Kinzer, B. (ed.), *The Gladstonian Turn of Mind: Essays presented to J. B. Comacher* (Toronto, 1985), pp. 197–237.

Schubert, A. *Death and Money in the Afternoon: A History of the Spanish Bullfight* (Oxford, 1999).

Searle, G.R. *The Liberal Party: Triumph and Disintegration 1886–1929* (London, 1992).

——. *A New England? Peace and War 1886–1914* (Oxford, 2004).

Shaw, J. 'Land, People and Nation: Historicist Voices in the Highland Land Campaign *c.*1850–1883' in Biagini, E.F. (ed.), *Citizenship and Community: Liberals, Radicals and Collective Identities in the British Isles, 1865–1931* (Cambridge, 1996), pp. 305–24.

Sheppard, V. *My Head Against the Wall: A Decade in the Fight Against Blood Sports* (London, 1979).

Shoard, M. *A Right to Roam* (Oxford, 1999).

Short, B. *Land and Society in Edwardian Britain* (Cambridge, 1997).

Sinclair, A. *Death by Fame: A Life of Elizabeth, Empress of Austria* (New York, 1998).

Skidelsky, R. *Oswald Mosley* (London, 1975).

Smith, E.A. *The House of Lords in British Politics and Society 1815–1911* (London, 1992).

Smith, J. 'Labour Traditions in Glasgow and Liverpool', *History Workshop Journal*, XVII (1984), 32–56.

Speck, W.A. *Stability and Strife: England 1714–1760* (London, 1977).

Spring, D. 'Land and Politics in Edwardian England', *Agricultural History*, LVIII (1984), 17–42.

Srebnick, A.G. *The Mysterious Death of Mary Rogers: Sex and Culture in Nineteenth Century New York* (Oxford, 1995).

Stafford, W. '"This Once Happy Country": Nostalgia for Pre-Modern Society' in Shaw, C. and Chase, M. (eds), *The Imagined Past: History as Nostalgia* (Manchester, 1989), pp. 33–42.

Staves, S. 'British Seduced Maidens', *Eighteenth Century Studies*, XIV (1980/81), 42–55.

Stemp, D. *Three Acres and a Cow: The Life and Work of Eli Hallamshire* (Cheam, 1995).

Stephenson, T. *Forbidden Land: The Struggle for Access to Mountain and Moorland* (Manchester, 1989).

Stone, L. and Stone, J.F.C. *An Open Elite? England 1540–1880* (Oxford, 1984).

Sykes, A. *The Rise and Fall of British Liberalism 1776–1988* (London, 1997).

Taylor, A. '*Reynolds's Newspaper*, Opposition to Monarchy and the Radical Anti-Jubilee: Britain's Anti-monarchist Tradition Reconsidered', *Historical Research*, 108 (1995), 318–37.

——. '"Commons-Stealers", "Land-Grabbers" and "Jerry-Builders": Space, Popular Radicalism and the Politics of Public Access in London 1848–1880', *International Review of Social History*, XXXX (1995), 383–407.

——. 'Republicanism Reappraised: Anti-monarchism and the English Radical Tradition 1850–1872' in Vernon, J. (ed.), *Re-reading the Constitution: New Narratives in the Political History of England's Long Nineteenth Century* (Cambridge, 1996), pp. 154–78.

——. '"The Best Way to Get What He Wanted": Ernest Jones and the Boundaries of Liberalism in the Manchester Election of 1868', *Parliamentary History*, XVI (1997), 185–204.

——. '*Down with the Crown*': British 'Anti-monarchism and Debates about Royalty since 1790* (London, 1999).

——. 'Shakespeare and Radicalism: The Uses and Abuses of Shakespeare in Nineteenth Century Popular Politics', *The Historical Journal*, XXXXV (2002), 357–79.

Taylor, A. and Trainor, L. 'Monarchism and Anti-monarchism: Anglo-Australian Comparisons *c.*1870–1901', *Social History*, XXIV (1999), 158–73.

Taylor, A.J.P. *The Trouble Makers: Dissent over Foreign Policy 1792–1939* (London, 1957).

Taylor, H. *A Claim on the Countryside* (Edinburgh, 1997).
Taylor, M. *The Decline of British Radicalism 1847–1860* (Oxford, 1995).
——. *Ernest Jones, Chartism and the Romance of Politics, 1819–1869* (Oxford, 2003).
Thomas, J.L. *Alternative America: Henry George, Edward Bellamy, Henry Demarest Lloyd and the Adversary Tradition* (Harvard, 1983).
Thomas, K. *Man and the Natural World: Changing Attitudes in England 1500–1800* (London, 1983).
Thomas, P.D.G. *John Wilkes: A Friend to Liberty* (Oxford, 1996).
Thompson, B. *Imperial Vanities: The Adventures of the Baker Brothers and Gordon of Khartoum* (London, 2002).
Thompson, F.M.L. *English Landed Society in the Nineteenth Century* (London, 1963).
——. *Gentrification and the Enterprise Culture in Britain 1780–1980* (Oxford, 2001).
Thurlow, R. *Fascism in Britain: From Oswald Mosley's Blackshirts to the National Front* (London, 1998 edn).
Tsuzuki, C. (ed.), *Henry Hyndman, England for All: The Text Book of Democracy* (Brighton, 1973).
Tulloch, H.A. 'Changing British Attitudes Towards the United States in the 1880s', *Historical Journal*, XX (1979), 824–40.
Vernon, J. *Politics and the People: A Study in English Political Culture c.1815–1867* (Cambridge, 1993).
——. 'Narrating the Constitution: The Discourse of "the real" and the Fantasies of Nineteenth Century Constitutional History' in Vernon (ed.), *Re-reading the Constitution: New Narratives in the Political History of England's Long Nineteenth Century* (Cambridge, 1996), pp. 204–29.
Wahrman, D. *Imagining the Middle Class: The Political Representation of Class in Britain c.1780–1840* (Cambridge, 1995).
Walker, G. *Thomas Johnston* (Manchester, 1988).
Walkowitz, J. *City of Dreadful Delight: Narratives of Sexual Danger in Late Victorian London* (London, 1992).
Ward, P. *Red Flag to Union Jack: Englishness, Patriotism and the British Left 1881–1924* (London, 1998).
Wedgwood, C.V. *The Last of the Radicals: The Life of Josiah Wedgwood M.P.* (London, 1951).
Weinbren, D. 'Against all Cruelty: The Humanitarian League 1891–1919', *History Workshop Journal*, XXXVIII (1994), 86–105.
Weiner, M.J. *English Culture and the Decline of the Industrial Spirit 1850–1980* (Cambridge, 1981).
Weintraub, S. *The Importance of Being Edward: King in Waiting 1841–1901* (London, 2000).
Weston, C.C. 'Salisbury and the Lords 1868–1895', *Historical Journal*, XXV (1982), 103–29.
——. *The House of Lords and Ideological Politics: Lord Salisbury's Referendal Theory and the Conservative Party 1846–1922* (American Philosophical Society, 1991).
Whyte, I.D. *Landscape and History since 1500* (London, 2002).
Williams, R. *The Contentious Crown: Public Discussion of the British Monarchy in the Reign of Queen Victoria* (Aldershot, 1997).
Williams, S. *The People's King: The True Story of the Abdication* (London, 2003).
Winsten, S. *Henry Salt and His Circle* (London, 1951).

Wolff, W. *From Radicalism to Socialism: Men and Ideas in the Formation of Fabian Socialist Doctrine 1881–1889* (New Haven, 1975).

Woodruff, D. *The Tichborne Claimant: A Victorian Mystery* (London, 1957).

Worboys, M. 'British Medicine and its Past at Queen Victoria's Jubilees and the 1900 Centennial', *Medical History*, XLV (2001), 461–82.

Worden, B. *Roundhead Reputations: The English Civil War and the Passions of Posterity* (London, 2001).

Worsthorne, P. *In Defence of Aristocracy* (London, 2004).

Wright, P. *The Village that Died for England: The Strange Story of Tyneham* (London, 1995).

Yeo, E. 'Chartist Religious Belief and the Theology of Liberation' in Obelkevich, J., Roper, L. and Samuel, R. (eds), *Disciplines of Faith: Studies in Religion, Politics and Patriarchy* (London, 1987), pp. 410–21.

Yeo, S. 'A New Life: The Religion of Socialism in Britain 1883–1896', *History Workshop Journal*, IV (1977), 5–56.

Works of literature

Huxley, A. *Brave New World*, 2nd edn (London, 1978).

Priestley, J.B. *Blackout at Gretley*, 3rd edn (London, *1987*).

Sassoon, S. *Memoirs of a Fox Hunting Man*, 2nd edn (1940).

Waugh, E. *Decline and Fall*, 4th edn (London, 2001).

——. *Work Suspended and Other Stories*, 6th edn (London, 2001).

Works of reference

Bellamy, J. and Saville, J. (eds), *Dictionary of Labour Biography* (8 vols, 1972–1987).

Saville, J. 'Henry George and the British Labour Movement: A Select Bibliography with Commentary', *Bulletin of the Society for the Study of Labour History*, I (1960), 18–26.

Index